GREENHOUSES:
FROM DESIGN
TO HARVEST

TO D.A.S.
"The greatest adventure is what lies ahead . . . "

No. 1307
$17.95

GREENHOUSES:
FROM DESIGN
TO HARVEST
BY MARION WASENDA STEINBRUNNER

TAB TAB BOOKS Inc.
BLUE RIDGE SUMMIT, PA. 17214

FIRST EDITION

FIRST PRINTING

Copyright © 1982 by TAB BOOKS Inc.

Printed in the United States of America

Library of Congress Cataloging in Publication Data

Steinbrunner, Marion Wasenda.
   Greenhouses, from design to harvest.

   Includes index.
   1. Greenhouses.   2. Greenhouse gardening.
I. Title.
SB415.S734   631.5'83   81-18230
ISBN 0-8306-0056-6   AACR2
ISBN 0-8306-1307-2 (pbk.)

Cover Photo Courtesy of Lord & Burnham Irvington, NY 10533

Contents

Introduction

The home greenhouse is a warm, moist oasis of lush growth. It is a dream come true for the houseplant lover as well as the outdoor gardener. And it is a very practical addition for any residential dwelling.

If you think a home greenhouse is only for the privileged few, look around you. The number of such structures is increasing rapidly, and they appear in every imaginable size, shape, and price range. There are window greenhouses sprouting from the sides of high-rise apartments and miniature models on grandmothers' porches. There are lean-to nooks off master bedrooms and kitchens—and always the handsome, free-standing greenhouse in the center of a beautifully landscaped yard. Prices range from $100 to just about infinity. A good example of "infinity" is the lovely "antique-styled" greenhouse in Fig. I-1. It was copied from the elaborate structures built in England and France in the late 1800s, during the "golden age of greenhouses."

The benefits of a home greenhouse are both purely personal and highly practical. Let's explore both sides. Undoubtedly, the main reason a person decides to build a greenhouse is pure enjoyment. The greenhouse will be your refuge and your happy pill. The hours devoted to the care of your plants, whether many or few in any given week, will be some of the most enjoyable and satisfying hours you will spend. Family as well as friends will be drawn to this bit of the tropics in your home. It is a natural focal point and can be a true

Fig. I-1. This "antique" greenhouse is a smaller version of the elaborate greenhouses built in England and France during the late 1800s.

Fig. I-2. This lean-to greenhouse is also the family room. It covers a sunken patio that has been turned into a year-around room where people and plants thrive.

"family room." Figure I-2 shows a large, sunken patio covered with a lean-to greenhouse and turned into a very attractive family room. Everyday worries and cares seem to melt away as you watch plants thrive and bloom under your care. You will have a pleasant green garden to walk in and enjoy during the bleakest of cold winter days and the dreariest of summer rainstorms.

There is a practical side to all of this beauty as well. Any outdoor gardener can "get the jump" on spring with annuals and garden vegetables started from seed early in the season. Even plants normally impossible to cultivate locally due to a short growing season can fill your garden. With the new varieties of dwarf fruit trees and compact vegetable plants, it is possible to have a year-round supply of "home grown" produce. Wouldn't it be nice to serve fresh strawberries in January?

A greenhouse can also eliminate your florist's bill. A just-picked gardenia makes a wonderful corsage. Many seasonal plants usually purchased can be raised at home. Mums for Thanksgiving, Poinsettias for Christmas, and daffodils and tulips forced for early color while the ground is still covered with snow are just a few possibilities.

When your greenhouse is filled to overflowing, as it will be in an alarmingly short time, you are faced with a happy dilemma. What to do with the excess bounty? Plants can be given away to friends, shut-ins or the local hospital. They can be sold to area garden centers or florists. The sale can help raise money for the purchase of certain exotics that you may find hard to justify otherwise! Here is a hobby that can be rewarding in more than one way.

Now that you are thoroughly convinced that your own greenhouse will be an excellent investment in your happiness, as well as your practical success as a green thumb, let's begin planning.

Acknowledgments

I would like to thank Anna and Ray Lazarchic of Kirtland Garden and Gift, Kirtland, Ohio, for their invaluable assistance in writing this book.

A very special thank you to all the homeowners who allowed me to photograph and study their greenhouses.

Chapter 1

Greenhouse Origin and Development

Since the beginning of recorded history man has tried to outwit nature. We have used ingenuity to grow plants where nature never intended them to grow. We have found ways to raise fruits, vegetables and flowers in a climate or during a season where they could not be grown before. These attempts have sometimes been ridiculous and even disastrous, but the modern greenhouse marks a significant triumph.

The ancient Romans had many technical achievements without the knowledge of machinery. It is recorded that they even enjoyed hot running water in their homes. Their achievements extended to the cultivation of plants. The Emperor Tiberius so loved cucumbers that a method was devised so he could have them the year around. There is also evidence that peaches, grapes and roses were forced for a longer growing season. The Romans accomplished these feats by means of an early form of hothouse. They used a transparent substance, possibly talc, for part of the roof and walls. It is possible that the structures were also heated artificially as well. There are no ruins left for us to examine, but historians tell of a variety of "out of season" produce that was available to the wealthy.

The Middle Ages was a period when many earlier skills were lost. What lore and knowledge of plant care that survived was nurtured by monks. Every monastary had its garden where traditions in plant culture were passed on from older members of the order to younger ones. A major part of this tradition was concerned with herbs and their medicinal powers.

At the end of the 16th century, there was a renewed interest in forcing plants into early production. In order to ripen cherries early, hot limestones were spread in the orchard and the trees were watered with hot water. Favorite vegetables like peas were raised in boxes that were set out during the daytime and brought into a warm house at night.

In 1619, the orange trees of Heidelberg were covered with a portable "greenhouse" made of shutters. This structure was large enough to cover 40 large trees and 300 small trees. It was the chief concern of horticulturists of the day to protect the very fashionable orange. That fruit was the raging fad of the 17th century. Hence the creation of the "orangery," which was the ancestor of the greenhouse. These structures could have been a shed over the trees or a large room with windows for a southern exposure. Extra heat could be added if necessary.

In England, roses and carnations were brought into warm rooms for early blooming. Canvas tents were used as portable greenhouses. In order to receive maximum sunlight, a round greenhouse was built that "turned on a pin like a windmill and was full of glass windows."

Cold frames and hotbeds were starting to come into general use. These structures, along with the early greenhouses, were insulated with straw and hay. Double doors were built to keep out the cold. The basic idea of such buildings was to keep the plants just above freezing. Thus they could be started early and set out as soon as weather permitted.

The long-popular orange was replaced in the hearts of fruit lovers by the pineapple. This led to the construction of "pineries" that soon supplanted "orangeries" as the plant shelter of the day.

In 1699, King George I of England enjoyed cucumbers for Christmas. This feat was accomplished by the construction of a lean-to greenhouse. Slanted glass panels were used to build a shelter on the south side of a stable. Here the royal cucumbers flourished.

The 18th century marked a "golden age" in the history of greenhouses and plant culture. A combination of using glass for roofs and better artificial heating led to very large, elaborate structures. The royal and the wealthy collected tropical plants from all over the world and displayed them in huge greenhouses. Rare birds were often added to these exotic "playhouses'" of the rich. It was a privilege for honored guests to take a stroll through the tropics no matter what the season of the year. Czar Alexander of Russia had a greenhouse built for himself in St. Petersburg. It consisted of three parallel buildings, each 700 feet long, joined across the ends by two more of the same length. The whole structure was heated by wood-burning furnaces.

In the 19th century, the "home" greenhouse made its appearance in the form of the conservatory. This was a many-windowed room set aside for the cultivation of plants, especially flowering ones. It was part of any fashionable home to have such a room. Family and guests would stroll there and fresh flowers were available to fill the rest of the house year around. The American classic *Little Women*, by Louisa May Alcott, describes the delight Jo March experiences in the conservatory of rich neighbor Mr. Laurence.

> He said he had something more to show her, and took her away to the conservatory, which had been lighted for her benefit. It seemed quite fairylike to Jo, as she went up and down the walks, enjoying the blooming walls on either side, the soft light, the damp sweet air, and the wonderful vines and trees that hung above her—while her new friend cut the finest flowers till his hands were full . . . As he played the piano, Jo listened, with her nose luxuriously buried in heliotrope and tea roses.

This pleasant picture can be repeated today giving the same satisfaction it did when written 100 years ago.

Chapter 2

Site Selection

Once you have decided that a home greenhouse is for you, the next problem is where to put it. Take a long time for this step because your future enjoyment will depend upon finding that optimum location. Don't let your enthusiasm begin to overide good judgment and careful planning. If you build in a poor location, your joy will quickly become frustration and you will not use your greenhouse as much as you would have if it were in that best spot. Unused home greenhouses turned into storage are a sad monument to poor planning.

Your first step is a careful layout of your house and yard. Figures 2-1 and 2-2 are typical of the sketches you should make. Draw your property both from above and from ground level. Do this carefully and to scale so that the correct relationship to the size of your proposed greenhouse can be judged.

As you work on your sketches, ask yourself some questions. Where are the most frequently used entrances and walks? Do you want the greenhouse to be seen from the street? What large trees or near-by buildings will block the hot summer sun or the needed pale winter sun? Pay close attention to these patterns of light and shade. What plants you can grow successfully depends on how much light they will receive. Natural sunlight will save you the cost of much artificial light that you might need if you choose a shaded location. It is also necessary to consider prevailing winds as these can give natural ventilation and also raise your heating costs. An area of good

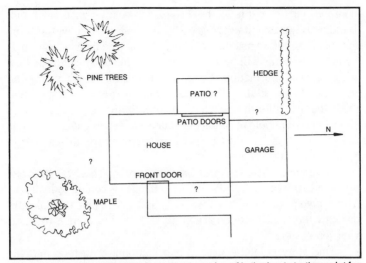

Fig. 2-1. An overhead sketch of your home and yard is the best starting point for deciding where to locate your greenhouse.

drainage is essential because a greenhouse has a great deal of run-off water. And, of course, there is your own convenience. What good is a greenhouse if it is an effort to enjoy? Draw your sketches and then consider the following points in detail.

BUILDING CODES

Be sure to contact your local building inspector before making any decision. Don't set your heart on a greenhouse off the master

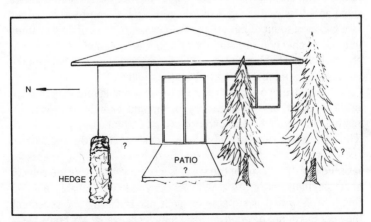

Fig. 2-2. Ground-level sketches of your house and yard will aid in determining the best location for your home greenhouse.

bedroom and find out it will be too close to your neighbor's lot line. Building requirements vary greatly, and you must know the rules for your area before making a choice for your greenhouse location. A building inspector will be able to supply some local expertise on a wide range of information. Things like foundation depth, prevailing winds, or the feasibility of extending your present heating system might be available through local building officials, or they might know the best people to contact in your area. You might also find out the best type of construction for your area and who has a nearby home greenhouse you could visit.

Remember that you will have to receive approval for your plans and a final approval after the greenhouse is completed. Make a friend of your local building inspector, and he will be a valuable ally during every phase of construction. Use his knowledge to make your job easier.

One other helpful source of information is your local agricultural extension office. These offices gather and dispense information under the U.S. Department of Agriculture. They can provide a wide range of free information (including greenhouse plans). They know your area's climate and soil conditions. It would be very wise to use the information that your tax money has provided for your benefit.

SUN AND EXPOSURE

For your plants to thrive and bloom, they will need lots of light—preferably natural sunlight. Light is essential for plant health and growth. Generally, the more light, the better. Blooming plants need about twice the light of foliage plants. Some plants can get along in an amount of light that would cause another plant to wither and die. Light requirements do vary, but no green plant can live in the dark. Artificial light can be added to any greenhouse, but first try to make maximum use of available sunlight.

There are two factors relating to light: one is intensity and the other is duration. The intensity or amount of light at any given moment is related to sky conditions (e.g., a cloudy day) and latitude. The northern latitudes receive less intense sun than those closer to the equator. The duration or length of time it is light relates to latitude and the season of the year. Winter always marks the time of short daylight hours. As a plant lover, you have probably noticed that a window that is suitable for your plants during one season of the year might not be good during a different season. My home has a nice dining room window that is great for my African violets during the summer. But as fall progresses, the amount of light that window gets is gradually reduced. The sun does not get as high in the sky during the winter and casts shadows from nearby trees to reduce the light. The plants that thrived in that window during the summer must be moved, or they will wither. Pay attention to the light for your chosen greenhouse location during all seasons of the year.

The direction of light must also be considered. In choosing between eastern and western exposures, choose the east. Plants are more productive during the morning hours. By afternoon, plant energy is slowing down. It cannot fully utilize the light it receives during the late afternoon. Plants are definitely "morning people."

In summer, the sun climbs high in the sky, but during the winter months the sun always hangs in the southern horizon. Therefore, it is generally agreed that a southeastern exposure is the very best for a greenhouse.

The various positions in which a greenhouse can be oriented are shown in Figure 2-3. The preferred position of professional greenhousemen is the roof ridge on a north-south axis. More specifically, they like 10 degrees northeast. An east-west ridge line will give a warm and a cool side to the greenhouse. The cool side will receive little or no direct sun. This will require special attention for the plants on the cool side to thrive. Artificial light can make up for the lack of sunlight, usually quite successfully. More on that topic later.

Remember when considering the best position for your greenhouse that surrounding buildings and trees can cast shadows from 50 or more feet away. That shade might be beneficial if it blocks the hot sun of a summer afternoon. However, it will not be very helpful if it blocks the limited winter sun. Also, trees near the greenhouse might shed leaves in the fall that will stick to the glass and present a clean-up problem. Be especially wary of any overhanging branches that could come down in a storm and shatter your greenhouse lites (as the glass or other light-transmitting material is termed).

Don't be discouraged if after reading this you find the only location for your greenhouse is north or northwestern. There are plants that will thrive in the cool light of a northern exposure (for example, alpine plants) and you can always supplement with artificial light. Today, the home greenhouse owner has a wide range of carefully developed products that can make any greenhouse a success if properly equipped. Find the "optimum" light for your situation and use your ingenuity to create the green world you want.

PREVAILING WINDS

When planning for your greenhouse, be sure to consider the prevailing summer and winter winds in your area. These winds are a mixed blessing. During the summer, they can help to cool and ventilate a greenhouse, but during the winter months, they can cause the temperature inside a greenhouse to plunge extra low.

It is possible to use a nearby building or a hedge row to block the harsher winds. The hedge row should be about 10 to 15 feet away from the greenhouse and should not be too dense. A very dense windbreak will cause the wind to skip over and rush down the far side to create worse conditions. Figure 2-4 illustrates various windbreaks.

There is also the possibility of using the land's contours to provide shelter. Building in a natural depression or beside a knoll will help protect a greenhouse. However, it is possible to "over-shelter" by building in a dead airspace where there is no natural ventilation. Cooling breezes will do a great deal to relieve the summer's heat. Just as you can supplement the sun with artificial light, it is possible to use a fan and vents to create artificial breezes. More on this later.

Take extra care to ensure that your greenhouse is not exposed to the severest winter winds. The wind-chill factor will greatly add to the strain of the heating system. Extra insulation will have to be added. To be energy efficient it would be very wise to build away from the coldest winds in your area.

DRAINAGE

The land your greenhouse is built upon must have very good surface and underground drainage. As with any structure, you do not want ground water pooling beneath the foundation and undermining your greenhouse. Also, pay attention to the runoff water if you are building on a sloping site. It can damage the foundation.

Surface water, as rain water, should be absorbed quickly and easily. The below-ground water should be deep enough not to interfere with construction. If your area has a high water table, perhaps special building techniques will be necessary.

Most greenhouses have no floor drains so the excess water from normal plant care must be carried off readily. To insure good drainage it would be wise to use the same methods used in new home construction for drainage. Figure 2-5 shows two common methods to aid drainage. One method calls for porous gravel at the

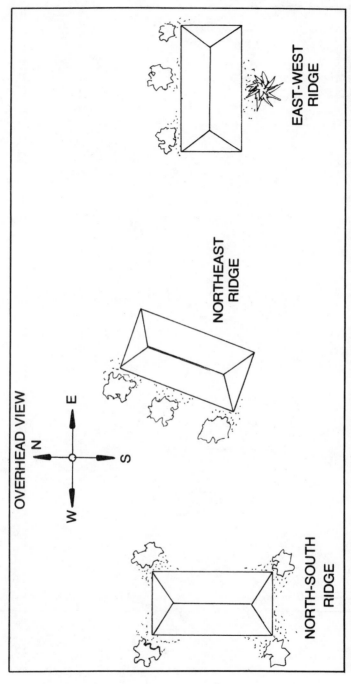

OVERHEAD VIEW

NORTHEAST RIDGE

EAST-WEST RIDGE

NORTH-SOUTH RIDGE

Fig. 2-3. There are several ways a greenhouse can be oriented. Among the views, above the northeast ridge line is the most desirable.

9

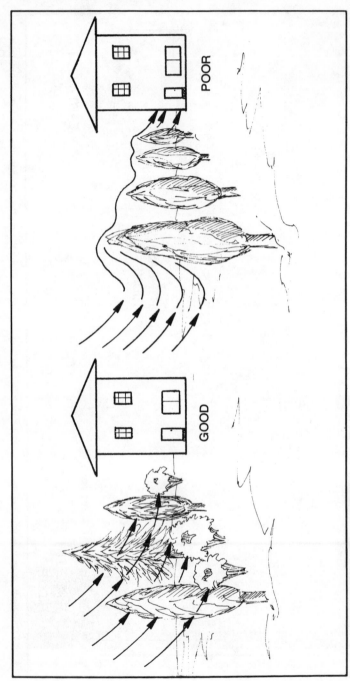

GOOD

POOR

Fig. 2-4. A wind break can be helpful if it is not too dense.

10

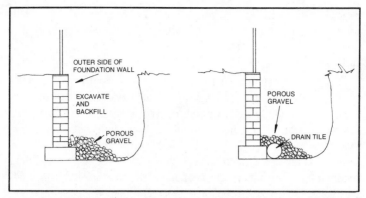

Fig. 2-5. To aid drainage around the greenhouse, gravel or a combination of gravel and drain tile are used. Always remember to place the drainage material at the base of the footers.

base of the foundation. The other method uses a combination of drain tile and gravel. Consult your local building inspector for the best drainage construction for your area.

It is possible to use some type of rain gutters if you anticipate a water problem. Figure 2-6 shows a gutter added to the top of the foundation wall of a curved eaves greenhouse. This is very functional and not at all unsightly as typical gutter additions would be on a greenhouse. Don't skimp when investing in good drainage. The

Fig. 2-6. This greenhouse has a gutter at the top of the foundation wall to carry off rain water.

problems that will result if you do will spoil your enjoyment and be much more expensive to correct after your greenhouse is built.

CONVENIENCE

A home greenhouse is there because you plan to use and enjoy it. You must give it daily attention to insure satisfactory results. Therefore, carefully consider your own convenience when building. The most expensive structure might become useless if it is just too much trouble to enjoy.

Consider the type of access you will have. A free-standing model means putting on your coat and boots to reach it during cold, wet weather. If your greenhouse is a small one, where will you do the potting and other related activities? Will you have to go up and down stairs to reach items that cannot be kept in the greenhouse? How close is the nearest outlet for hot water and cold water? If at all possible, water should be piped in all but the smallest greenhouses. Is your setup designed to make plant care easy and pleasant? If you want your greenhouse for a privacy spot, don't build it off the family room. Can it be closed off from the main living areas when you need to use smelly and dangerous insecticides? Think of all the possibilities and alternatives. Consider all the aspects—good and bad. Picture yourself using and enjoying your greenhouse, and tailor your construction plans to fit.

Fig. 2-7. A greenhouse should be attractive on the outside as well as the inside. This greenhouse has an exterior look you should strive for.

One additional point, your greenhouse, whether simple and inexpensive or elaborate and costly, should be part of the total look of beauty for your home. Do not let it become the neighborhood eyesore. It should be attractively landscaped and tended, outside as well as inside. Don't let it become a dumping ground for broken pots and "composting" plants. Figure 2-7 shows the well-landscaped look you should strive for. A beautiful greenhouse can add double its cost to the value of your home. It is an asset worth caring for as well as enjoying.

Chapter 3

The Basic Greenhouse

Today it is hard to think of a "basic" greenhouse; the styles are so very wide ranging. What comes to mind first is the traditional free-standing even-span favored by the commercial grower. Next, you might think of your neighbor's lean-to model that sprouts at his back door. The range is even much greater than this. In the next chapter, look at each of the many styles available and examine their good points and their drawbacks. For now, you have a basic choice to make. Shall your greenhouse be free-standing or attached to your home? There is a good case for each so consider the following points carefully.

FREE STANDING

The free-standing greenhouse is exactly what the name implies; it stands free, or separate, from any other buildings. With this type of greenhouse, you can let your imagination (and your budget!) run free. At one end of the cost spectrum is the simple plastic-covered frame pictured in Fig. 3-1. At the other end is the handsome glass even-span shown in Fig. 3-2. In choosing a free-standing greenhouse, it can be located almost anywhere on your property. It can be of any style such as an A-frame or geodesic dome. It can be situated to get the most out of the available light, space, and ventilation. You can even nestle it by the pond at the rear of your property, and as far from "civilization" as you can get.

It is usually more expensive to build and maintain a free-standing greenhouse than to build an attached one. Water and

Fig. 3-1. This simple greenhouse has a wood frame and a covering of sheet plastic. It can be erected for less than $100.

electric lines must be run from the main house or street-service lines. The heating system must be totally independent. There is also the matter of having to go outside to reach the greenhouse no

Fig. 3-2. This greenhouse has a permanent brick foundation and an aluminum frame. While costly, it will last for many years with little maintenance.

matter what the weather is like. This can be a very serious consideration if there is 3 feet of snow in January where you live.

The free-standing greenhouse is a favorite with many serious amateurs because it offers the most growing room per dollar spent on construction and can give the most success as well. With the best available orientation and maximum light, the free-standing greenhouse gives your green thumb its very best chance.

ATTACHED GREENHOUSE

The attached greenhouse or connected greenhouse shares a wall in common with your home or perhaps another building on the property. It offers easy access without your having to go out into the elements. It is usually easier to heat as your present system may be extended to supply all or part of the additional heat necessary. Water and electrical lines can be extended to the new addition with a minimum of cost and inconvenience.

One of the most popular home greenhouses is the lean-to. This attached model is inexpensive and versatile. Figure 3-3 shows a small, very attractive lean-to greenhouse. It is possible to attach an even-span style as shown in Fig. 3-4. Here only the short side of the greenhouse connects it to the home. This arrangement leaves plenty of growing room.

The more exotic styles in greenhouses, like the geodesic dome, are rather spoiled when attached to another building. An

Fig. 3-3. The lean-to greenhouse is the most popular type of attached greenhouse used by homeowners.

Fig. 3-4. An even-span greenhouse is usually attached by the short side as seen here.

attached greenhouse is going to be in the shade part of the day from the shadow of the building it is connected to. This often creates "cool" corners where some plants will not do well. To look its best, the attached greenhouse should be designed to blend in with the style of the house it is with. This will make the greenhouse look like it belongs with the home rather than like it was an afterthought.

When your greenhouse is attached, it can double as a family room or solarium. It can be designed to accommodate people as well as plants. It is less costly to build and maintain than a free-standing model. The attached greenhouse, and especially the lean-to, is the most popular with home gardeners.

A COMPARISON AND A COMPROMISE

To help you compare the free-standing greenhouse and the attached greenhouse, see Table 3-1. Carefully consider the differ-

Table 3-1. Comparison of Free-Standing and Attached Greenhouses.

	Location	Style	Utilities	Convenience	Cost
Free Standing	Anywhere on the property that is suitable.	Any except lean-to.	More expensive. Must be entirely separate.	Reached only by going outside.	Usually more costly.
Attached	Must have one wall in common with house or other building.	Some not suitable, e.g., geodesic dome.	More economical. House utilities can be extended.	Direct access from house.	More economical to build and maintain.

Fig. 3-5. This greenhouse is attached only by one corner to the garage of a century home.

ences in light of your personal situation. There is not one "best" style; there is just one that is best for you.

It is possible to do a little compromising if you want. An attached model could be attached to its own potting shed rather than to your house. This shed will provide work room and an area for the utilities. Placing it off the garage is also a very popular idea. Figure 3-5 shows a greenhouse attached only by a corner to the garage of a century home. This is a very effective compromise between the attached and free-standing types. Use your imagination to personalize a greenhouse for your needs.

Chapter 4

Which One Is for You?

Having considered where you should build your greenhouse and whether or not it should be attached to your home, now is the time to be more specific and decide which style and design of greenhouse is best for you. There are several common styles and some that are not so common. All can be built of less expensive materials or more costly ones. They offer a variety of usable space per area under glass. Each can be tailored to fit your site and your budget. There is no one style that is best. It is the taste and needs of the user that determines the "right" design. Consider the advantages and drawbacks of each type and consider each point as it applies to your particular situation. Look at the photographs of each style and try to visualize how it would look on your greenhouse site. Keep an open mind while enjoying a look at the wide variety of home greenhouses available to you.

MINIATURE GREENHOUSES

The miniature style does not really qualify as a greenhouse. Because it is highly impractical to use automated heating and cooling in it, it is more of a cold frame or large terrarium than a true greenhouse. However, it does have its uses.

As a cold frame, it can be used to give plants an early start before the frost season ends. During warm months, it can house delicate plants that would not normally be set outdoors. It can be especially useful for propagating rare plants that need extra attention.

As a terrarium, the miniature greenhouse becomes a green world in microcosm. It is possible to set up a miniature version of a tropical rain forest, temperate woodland, or arid desert. These can even be populated with small animals as well as plants. There are many good books available, which deal exclusively with terrariums. Keep in mind that a miniature greenhouse is also an excellent way for youngsters to learn about plant care under glass. Although not a true greenhouse, the miniature is certainly a fun extra for any green thumb.

WINDOW GREENHOUSES

The window greenhouse might be the perfect answer if your space, budget or needs are limited. It can be used in an apartment or condominium where there is no land for even the smallest regular structure. The window model is perfect in a bath or kitchen where the high humidity and need for a window covering make it a natural. Bay or bow windows can be created or enhanced with a greenhouse. Plant lovers are forever lining their window sills with as many plants as possible; the window greenhouse just goes one logical step further.

Fig. 4-1. This window greenhouse was installed on windows that are partially below grade. It prevents debris from filling the window-well area and solves a security problem at the same time.

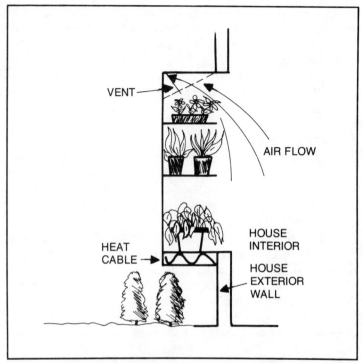

Fig. 4-2. This is the basic set up for a window greenhouse. Note the use of a cable for extra heat.

The versatility of a window greenhouse is shown in Fig. 4-1. Here it has been used to solve several problems. First, the windows were partially below grade and the window-well area kept filling with debris. Second, the below-grade aspect concerned the owners as a security problem. What could be done to solve these problems without detracting from the beauty of a costly home? This very attractive and useful window-well greenhouse was the perfect answer.

Window greenhouses can have some degree of automation. A top ventilation panel is a must as the heat builds up very quickly in these small structures. An electric heating cable on the bottom will give warmth in cold weather. Artificial lights can be added easily if your favorite window has a northern exposure. Figure 4-2 illustrates the basic set up for a window greenhouse.

The growing space in a window model is limited. Plants should not be crowded together here or anywhere else for that matter. Compact growing plants, like African violets, are ideal. Care and maintenance on such a small greenhouse would be minimal. Older or handicapped people could care for the plants themselves. Anyone with a demanding job outside the home would be able to manage a window greenhouse when a larger one would require too much time and care. If you are faced with an unattractive view from one of your windows, what better way to beautify it than a window full of lovely plants.

THE EVEN-SPAN DESIGN

When you ask someone to picture a greenhouse they will more than likely think of an even-span. This is the greenhouse with a roof of equal size and pitch on both sides similar to a residential house. This style is the traditional choice of the professional nurseryman—and with good reason.

The even-span design permits a maximum of interior growing room. Although it is more expensive to build initially, it does give the greatest growing area per dollar spent. Careful consideration should be given to this style if you are serious about the number and variety of plants you want to cultivate. You will not "outgrow" an even-span as readily as other styles and it is also the easiest to add on to in the future. If an even-span is to be attached to another

Fig. 4-3. This even-span greenhouse attached on the short side to a combination garage/potting shed.

Fig. 4-4. A small, free-standing greenhouse.

building, it is usually done so on the short side with the northern exposure as in Fig. 4-3. If it is to be a free-standing model, it will look similar to the small commercial greenhouse in Fig. 4-4.

One of the most successful amateur growers I know has an even-span attached to his garage. The garage is his potting shed and holds all utility equipment. He is a grower of the finest show orchids anywhere. He starts his orchids below the benches and moves them up as they mature. The walls are lined with benches and he is able to raise a great many plants in his greenhouse. He is convinced that the even-span is the very best style for his serious operation.

An even-span of the smallest practical size should be at least 8 feet by 10 feet. Benches can line all the walls except for the entrance. There will be room overhead for hanging baskets. If you build it as a glass-to-ground structure, as in Fig. 4-5, plants can be started below the benches as well. It is rather amazing just how much usable space there is in such a greenhouse.

The even-span is going to cost more to heat and maintain than other styles because it has so much exposed surface area. It will take more time and care to keep it looking right. It does take more plants to fill it up and that might be discouraging if your aspirations are small. But if you are professional about your plant hobby, then the professional greenhouse is the right one for you.

Fig. 4-5. This even-span greenhouse is a glass-to-ground design. Plants can be started below the benches in such a style.

THE LEAN-TO

If you want the greenhouse that is the most popular with home gardeners, the lean-to is for you. It is essentially an even-span cut in half lengthwise and attached to an existing building. It is practical, relatively inexpensive to build and maintain, and easy to enjoy. Figure 4-6 shows a very attractive, small lean-to greenhouse.

The same rules apply for locating a lean-to greenhouse as any other model; a southern exposure is best. Because it is closer to the house structure all along its length, be sure that shadows won't be cast over the lean-to for too long a time. You will find it less costly to build because one long wall is that of your existing home. It will be easier and cheaper to heat because home heating can be readily extended and the large area of attachment will reduce additional heating costs.

A lean-to can be built to cover the whole side of a home as seen in Fig. 4-7. If it is built around patio doors or a large window it can be an extra insulator. A small lean-to makes an excellent breakfast room or sitting room off the kitchen. When placed off the master bedroom, it can be used as study or personal hobby area. Covering an already existing patio is a popular way to use a lean-to greenhouse. Then it can add to the family room or den. It is a style that blends well with a home and does not have that "afterthought" look. The lean-to maximizes the advantages and disadvantages of an attached greenhouse. Carefully look over Table 3-1.

Care should be taken in situating your lean-to so that it does not block necessary windows or entrances that would be better left unobstructed. You do not want family members and guests making a thoroughfare out of your greenhouse because it is the only way to reach the back door. It is also true that a lean-to design has limited plant space with only one row of benches possible along the outside wall. If it is built very wide to accommodate a double row of

Fig. 4-6. The lean-to style is the most popular greenhouse for home use. This very attractive one shows why.

Fig. 4-7. Just about the entire back of this home is covered with a lean-to greenhouse.

benches, it will be more difficult to heat and maintain. Keep these points in mind, along with the advantages, when deciding if the lean-to style fits your needs.

PIT GREENHOUSE

The pit greenhouse is a rather old-fashioned style that is enjoying a revival in this age of energy consciousness. Basically, it is an evenspan with the walls and walks below grade. Only the sloping roof is above ground level. Figure 4-8 shows a pit greenhouse.

This style has the same advantages as an underground home. The surrounding soil has a natural insulating effect that will reduce heating costs. It also helps to keep the greenhouse cool during the warmest weather. Because of this, it is a natural for alpine and other cool-weather plants. Your growing space will be limited because so much of the greenhouse is below grade. Adding artificial light below the benches will reduce the savings gained in lower heating costs.

The major difficulty in building such a style is finding the right location. A natural slope would be ideal. Many pit greenhouses are built into a hillside with the entrance at or near grade. It is necessary to contact a professional to insure proper construction. In some areas with certain soil conditions pit greenhouses are just not feasible to build at all.

The pit greenhouse tends to be damp and musty and is often plagued with drainage problems. Try to contact someone locally who has one before you decide to build one yourself. Be sure to evaluate energy savings versus maintenance problems before choosing a pit greenhouse.

QUONSET HUT

This section describes a Quonset hut greenhouse constructed with plastic film. The Quonset hut is a very easy style for the do-it-yourselfer. It is constructed of very inexpensive materials. The frame is wood strips, light piping or plastic. The covering is a plastic film like Mylar. A backyard Quonset of PVC pipe and plastic film is shown in Fig. 4-9. An interior view of the same greenhouse is shown in Fig. 4-10.

There are several advantages to a Quonset-style greenhouse. Because they are so inexpensive to construct, it is possible to build a larger greenhouse than you might otherwise be able to afford. They are free-standing and usually don't have a permanent foundation even in cold climates. They are easily expanded or constructed

Fig. 4-8. Here is the unusual design of a pit greenhouse. The walls and walk are below grade (courtesy of Paul Bosley, Jr., Bosley Garden Shop, Mentor, Ohio).

Fig. 4-9. This backyard greenhouse is a Quonset covered in film plastic.

in pairs. They are a great way to experience greenhouse gardening with a minimum outlay of money.

This simple structure is going to suffer in severe weather and the plastic covering will probably have to be replaced every two years or so. There are several types of coverings that can be used on a Quonset structure. Leading plastic producers like Du Pont offer a variety of types. Some are thicker and longer lasting than others and they will cost a little more. Look into various brand names and the durability before choosing one. Thin film might only last one winter while a heavy type might last as long as five years.

A Quonset hut requires more maintenance and is much more temporary than a greenhouse of stronger construction. It is also not the most attractive addition to a homesite. It should be located away from public view. One problem when using a Quonset style is the lack of ventilation. The tunnel like design makes air flow difficult. This can be solved by cutting triangular "windows" in each section between the ribbing as shown in Fig. 4-11.

Table 4-1, lists various plastic types that can be used as greenhouse coverings. The costs figures are not current and you will have to update them. Note the great difference in durability among the various types. Table 4-1 will give you a starting point in choosing the best plastic type for your particular needs.

Fig. 4-10. The interior of a Quonset greenhouse shows the PVC framework and plastic film covering.

Fig. 4-11. The Quonset greenhouse is often difficult to ventilate. One solution is cutting "windows" in for film plastic covering.

Table 4-1. Comparisons of Plastic Materials for Covering Greenhouses (courtesy of the University of Illinois).

Plastic and Approximate Cost Per Square Foot	Available Thickness[b]	Available Width	Recommended Thickness[c]	Durability[d]	Notes
Polyethylene Regular (0.4 to 2.0¢)	1 to 10 mil	3 to 40 feet	4 or 6 mil, outside layer; 2 or 4 mil, inside layer	3–10 months	Polyethylene covered greenhouses are not suitable for continuous year-round use. Polyethylene breaks down rapidly during the summer, deteriorating first where folded. Unfolded rolls are available up to 14 feet wide. Application of an inside lining to form a 2- to 4-inch air space can reduce heating costs by 20 percent or more.
UV-treated (0.6 to 1.4¢)	2, 4, or 6 mil	3 to 20 feet	4 or 6 mil	6–12 months	Ultra violet resistant (UV-treated) polyethylene is recommended over regular polyethylene for covering during late summer or fall.
Vinyl (PVC) Film (3 to 10¢)	3 to 12 mil	4 to 6 feet (seamed to larger widths)	8 to 12 mil	2–4 years	Use only weatherable vinyl. Clear or translucent grades are available. Vinyl is pliable and contracts and expands with temperature. Vinyl becomes dirty easily.
Rigid (PVC) Panels (10 to 20¢)	4 to 6 oz.	28 inches	5 or 6 oz.	3–5 years	Available in 2½- and 1-inch corrugation. Susceptible to hail damage. Install properly. Poor grades may discolor in a few months.
Mylar (Polyester)[e] (13 to 15¢)	5 mil	36 to 52 inches	5 mil	3–5 years	Must apply correctly on rigid framework. Does not expand with temperature but "rattles" and can be quite noisy in wind.
Fiberglass (20 to 50¢)	.03 to .09 inch or 4 to 12 ounces per square foot	2 to 4 feet	6 oz. or heavier with durability guarantee	5–15 years or longer	Corrugated or flat available in panels 6 to 12 feet long, rolls, and glass-sized panes. Light is diffused, but clear grades generally transmit 80 percent or more of visible light. Shading often is not needed.

[a] For more complete information on plastics for greenhouse use and building tips, see University of Illinois, Circular 905, *Plastic Greenhouses*. For more sources of plastic materials, refer to Department of Horticulture, Vegetable Growing No. 13: Sources of Greenhouse Materials and Equipment.
[b] 1 mil = 0.001 inch.
[c] Thinner, less expensive grades can be used but they will probably be less durable.
[d] Properly installed for greenhouse use.
[e] Registered trademark for Du Pont polyester film, Type W.

A-FRAME

In recent years, there has been a surge in popularity of the A-frame. They first became popular as a vacation house and are now also seen in year around communities. Naturally, someone decided they would make enjoyable greenhouses. They would be especially appropriate if your home is a similar or complimentary style.

The A-frame greenhouse is very simple to build and is particularily suited to a glass-to-ground style of construction. The frame can be covered with plastic film or a more permanent covering. The foundation can be a simple wood frame or a regular concrete and brick affair. This style can be dressed up or down easily. Costs will vary according to size and permanence of the structure. Generally, an A-frame is most effective in a small size.

An A-frame has the same "dead" space at its base and the same limited headroom whether it is used as a home or a greenhouse. It is possible to put this style on a solid, straight-walled foundation which would greatly increase the usable space for plants. Figure 4-12 is a sketch of an A-frame greenhouse.

A friend of mine, who is a professional nurseryman, told me, "The only place I ever saw an A-frame greenhouse is in a book." It is certainly not a common style. But it is a simple, easy-to-build one and could be the eye-catcher you are looking for.

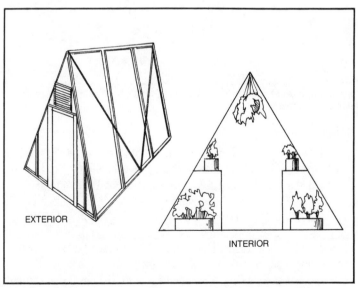

EXTERIOR

INTERIOR

Fig. 4-12. Exterior and interior views of the typical A-frame greenhouse.

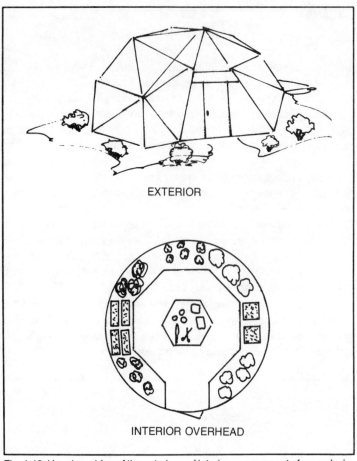

Fig. 4-13. Here is an idea of the exterior and interior arrangement of a geodesic-dome greenhouse.

GEODESIC DOME

As with the A-frame, the geodesic dome was a style of residential house before being introduced as a greenhouse. It is more practical than an A-frame because it has a good growing area.

Basically, the geodesic dome consists of triangular panels joined together to form a circular, domed structure. Inside, the benches can be arranged in a circle against the wall. If the dome is large enough, an hexagonal bench can also be placed in the middle of the greenhouse. Figure 4-13 shows a geodesic dome.

The design is a very easy one for the do-it-yourselfer to build. Assembly is relatively easy and fast. Many companies offer kits for the building of geodesic dome greenhouses. Construction can be of plastic film or a more permanent type. If you are building from plans, great care must be taken so that the triangles are of a uniform size for easy assembly. The geodesic dome is roomy and attractive and could be the answer for someone who wants a step up from the Quonset hut without the high cost of the more elaborate types.

Chapter 5

Greenhouse Construction

Once you have chosen the type of greenhouse you want, it is necessary to make another important decision. Will you purchase a prefabricated kit or build your greenhouse from plans? There are advantages and disadvantages to each method. It depends on your personal situation as to which is the best for you. Table 5-1 is a checklist to figure complete costs for a greenhouse. Use this table to figure your costs for buying a kit and building it yourself. Then you can make an accurate comparison on a cost basis.

There are other factors to consider besides cost. Do you have the skills to build it yourself or can you get help from a qualified friend? A kit is easier to put up for the unskilled builder. Time is also a factor. If you are anxious to have your greenhouse up and functioning, it will be completed sooner if you use a kit. What style greenhouse have you chosen? If you want a large, professional-looking structure, the chances are you will need professional skills to build it. A kit greenhouse will generally look more "finished" than a home-built one. Is that look important to you? Weigh all the factors involved and decide what will suit your needs the best.

Even if you choose to erect a prefabricated greenhouse, read this chapter over carefully. It will take you step by step through the building of a greenhouse. The basics are the same for any type or style and are useful to know even if you buy a kit. You cannot know if any structure is built properly if you don't know good building techniques.

Table 5-1. Greenhouse Checklist.

Size: Length_____ Width_____ Height to eaves_____
     Type of roof_____ Height to center of roof_____
Framing: Wood _____ Aluminum_____ Steel_____ Plastic_____ Other_____
Covering: Glass _____ Fiberglass_____ Polyethylene_____ Other_____
     Will it be double glazed?

Area: total surface area_____ sq. ft. Total floor area_____ sq. ft.
     Volume_____ cu. ft.

Utilities: Cooler size in CFM_____ Is it at least twice the volume?
     Heater: BTU rating_____ Is it adequate for coldest possible weather?
     Electric panel:ready___ available___ adequate_____
     Water lines: location_____ available_____

Foundation: Type_____ Adequate_____ Preparation needed_____

Estimated time to construct or erect _____
Special tools needed_____ Special Tool cost_____

Item	Cost
Basic greenhouse (materials or kit)	_____
Construction permit	_____
Plot plans (with utility plans as required)	_____
Site preparation	_____
Foundation or anchors	_____
Plumbing	_____
Electrical	_____
Heating supply (if not electrical)	_____
Water connections and piping	_____
Automatic watering system	_____
Heating equipment	_____
Cooling equipment (includes ventilation)	_____
Total labor costs	_____
All other costs	_____
Total cost of greenhouse	_____

Cost of Operation

Item	Cost
Increase in property taxes	_____
Heating cost for one year	_____
Cooling cost for one year	_____
Water cost for one year	_____
Electricity for one year	_____
Fertilizer, herbicides, pesticides	_____
Seeds, starter plants	_____
Pots, Flats, soil	_____
Other supplies	_____
Total operating cost for one year	_____

GREENHOUSE BLUEPRINTS

The greenhouse plans in this book are designed for the amateur builder. Most of the plans call for plastic or fiberglass coverings. These are the easiest to work with and they are the most practical for the homemade greenhouse. There are also plans for cold frame or hotbed use.

These plans have been developed under the guidance of the Department of Agriculture through their Cooperative Extension Service. They have been designed, built, and tested for home use. The construction materials are practical, inexpensive, and easy to handle. They are excellent choices for the first-time greenhouse user. Look over all the plans given with their respective design features and construction details. They can be incorporated into your own particular plan to insure good quality construction at a reasonable cost.

BUY OR BUILD?

Once you have decided you want a greenhouse at your home, there is a basic choice to be made. Should you build a greenhouse from scratch using plans or buy a prefabricated greenhouse kit and assemble it? Is one method better than the other? Is one cheaper, easier, or safer? The answers are not definite; it depends on the individual and your specific situation. Let's analyze the various aspects.

Cost is one of the primary concerns. Generally, it is assumed that a kit is cheaper. Because all the parts have been cut and fitted at the factory for mass marketing, the company has the great advantage of buying and cutting large quantities at a good discount. It would seem unlikely that a home craftsman could compete in any way. But when you are doing a cost comparison, be sure to calculate the total price of a "functioning" greenhouse. Most kits will make a completed shell and you will have to add a foundation, heating, cooling and humidifying units, benches, and other furniture. Don't be misled by the salesman who shows you a picture of a lovely 10 foot by 12 foot greenhouse and says it is all yours for $1000. Find out exactly what you are buying for your money. Add on all the costs necessary to really complete the greenhouse and you will have a figure as much as four times greater than the one you were quoted.

Use this figure to compare with the building costs of using plans and "stick building" from the ground up. It is likely that many costs will work out to be the same. The foundation cost is likely to be identical once you have decided on the type of foundation you want. Cost of benches and other furniture will be the same for a greenhouse of the same size and shape. The heating cost could vary a great deal from a homemade greenhouse of fiberglass and a commercial one with double-glazed glass. Will the extra cost of double glazing be made up with the savings on the heat bill? This can be calculated using the savings in Btu and your local energy costs. All factors needed to build and maintain a functioning greenhouse in your area need to be considered when you are comparing prices and costs. Look at the total picture.

Usually, with greenhouses of the same size and shape, a kit will cost less when built of the same material. Often, less costly material will be used for the home-built greenhouse. Instead of aluminum framing and glass lites, the do-it-yourselfer will use wood framing and fiberglass lites. The difference here will save money, but the resulting greenhouse will not look quite as finished or professional. Is that important to you? If it is, choose accordingly.

The main factor, besides cost, in the buy-or-build controversy is one of ease and speed of construction. The unhandy man will have an easier time putting a kit together than building from scratch. Also, a kit should assemble and be ready for use in a shorter time. How valuable is your time? Have you got the free evenings and weekends to build your greenhouse? Once you have made the decision to own a greenhouse, do you want it up quickly for immediate use? Are you handy with tools and you take pride in showing off what you have built from the ground up? These factors should be consider in making your decision. One way isn't better than the other, but it will be better for you and your particular circumstances.

A pre-fab greenhouse has to be adapted to fit your needs. The home-built one can be tailored to fit your preferences from the start. Don't make your choice because you assume it will save you money. Work up a complete cost sheet on each method and then compare to be sure.

If you want a large, elaborate greenhouse and aren't handy with tools, buy a kit. If you don't have free time to devote to construction, choose a kit. It is pointless to set yourself a task that has little chance of being completed without much aggravation and trouble. If you are impatient to have your greenhouse up and operating, go with a kit.

If you have the time and interest to construct exactly what you want in a greenhouse, then build it yourself. If you have compared prices and find you can build what you want for less, then do so. If you are handy with tools and want the pride of having built it yourself, then go ahead. A builder who lacks skill and experience, but still wants to do the construction, can do so by choosing a simple design and using easy-to-handle materials. Only you can decide whether buying or building is right for you.

CHECKLIST FOR A GREENHOUSE

Whether you buy or build, there are basics to be calculated before the first nail is driven. The checklist shown in Table 5-1 will give you a start in asking yourself the right questions and estimating costs before you begin. It is always better to figure things out on paper so there will be no surprises during construction.

With these lists you can get an accurate picture of what your greenhouse is going to cost to construct and use. If the numbers seem too large, you can reduce them on paper. That is far easier than reducing them after construction has started. Be as complete as possible in every detail. There are many costs, like the increase in your property taxes, that aren't readily apparent when you are doing an estimate.

If your budget is limited, don't despair that you simply can't afford any greenhouse. Material costs can be reduced substantially by intelligent substitution. Operating costs can also be slashed if you will set your thermostat wisely. As discussed in Chapter 6—the section on heating requirements—a small change in the warmest temperature required equals a big change in the number of Btu needed. Less Btu generated means a lower heating bill. A small, simple greenhouse is within the reach of every budget. If you do your paperwork first, you can own a greenhouse that is both satisfying and affordable.

READING PLANS

If you are building a greenhouse from a set of plans, it follows that you will have to be able to read those plans in order to use them. Good plans are not difficult to read and understand with a little time and practice. The plan should tell you what quantity of materials you will need and how they should be prepared. It should enable you to visualize the completed greenhouse and in what order it will be built and what materials will be used. You should also know what methods of building will be needed and what tools will be necessary. All these items should be worked out on paper with the help of the plan.

There are many sources of plans. The ones given in this book are a sample of those prepared and tested by the U.S. Department of Agriculture. There are various private sources for plans. Check a variety of plans and narrow the group to about three that are good for your needs. Look each plan over carefully and compare them. In most cases, the overall length can be increased or decreased easily by adding or subtracting to the number of sidewall components. If you have to make extensive changes in a plan, it would probably be better to find a more suitable one.

It is possible to draw up your own plans. Some basic knowledge of drafting techniques would be helpful. In order to draw plans successfully, you need an understanding of proportion, scale and an ability to visualize the completed structure. If you have no knowledge in drawing up plans, don't try. There are enough plans available that you will be able to find at least one that meets your needs.

Once you have found some plan or plans that seems suitable, it is time to read them. Begin by noting the title. It is usually fairly descriptive. For example, it might be titled "Lean-to Greenhouse for the Small Lot." Or perhaps "Inexpensive Plastic A-frame Greenhouse" might be the title. This will tell something about the style, type, and cost of building the greenhouse.

After the title, read all the printed instructions in the margin. These will help to explain construction points and methods. They will indicate the complexity of the building and the skill level needed to construct it.

Finally, look at the diagrams. With them, you should be able to visualize the finished greenhouse. The diagrams are usually keyed, by letter or number, to the printed instructions. This enables you to "see" the instructions by the diagrams. Key points of the units' features or construction procedures are usually shown in this manner.

A complete plan shows the structure from front, rear, and side elevations and also in perspective. A small key area will be "blown up" in a separate drawing inset to show the details. A materials list is often included in plans so you will know how much of what materials to buy. This list can be used as a reference point. It is possible to substitute for some materials in order to reduce costs or use those materials more readily available in your area. Consult with someone knowledgeable about building if you aren't sure about substitutions. Many substitutions are perfectly acceptable and others will spell disaster. Don't make any changes to a plan unless you are sure of them or have consulted with someone you trust who is sure.

Plan diagrams consists of several types of lines. Each type is used to represent one component of the diagram. Working lines are always the darkest, heaviest lines on the plan. They represent the actual structure shape or some part of the structure being built. Use them to visualize the greenhouse during construction and as a completed structure.

Dotted lines are used to indicate working lines that would obscure the view of some other feature. Visualize them as part of the total structure.

Dimension lines indicate the size of some part of the greenhouse. They are light, solid lines usually with small arrows at each end. The number shown along a dimension line states the measurement of that distance.

Extension lines are light, solid lines that extend some of the working lines. They are used so that a dimension line can be shown more clearly. For instance, from the ground to the peak of the roof, extension lines will come out horizontally with a dimension line between them to give the total height of the structure. Extension lines are very useful for making the dimensioning of a structure clear and easy to understand.

Additional data and measurements can be found in the margins of some plans. More complex plans might have a legend to explain construction terms.

Most plans are drawn to scale. This means that the size of a working line in the plan is in exact proportion to the actual part of the structure. For instance, if the scale on the plan says $\frac{1}{4}'' = 1'$, then each one-fourth inch in the diagram is equal to one foot of actual structure. A plan drawn to scale will have the size scale used indicated in the lower right-hand corner. If a plan has not been drawn to scale, it clearly should state so. Don't assume a scale is used if one is not clearly given.

Read the plan over several times. Use a pad to sketch out the basic diagram. If you don't understand something, read the plan again. There are books available on construction procedures and basic building terminology. Don't do any actual construction until you are sure you understand the whole plan from start to finish.

When building from a kit, there will be detailed instructions on assembling your greenhouse. Be sure you understand them thoroughly. If you can't figure something out, contact the manufacturer's representative who sold you the kit or write directly to the company. Don't start putting your kit up with the hope that all the pieces will fit. Know that they will fit in advance by knowing all of the instructions in advance.

Use all possible help when building your greenhouse. Ask questions of everybody who could possibly help. Ask the firms that make greenhouses. Ask the local nurserymen who use greenhouses. Ask private individuals who have already built one. Ask your county extension agent. If you don't know many qualified people, the local horticulture society should be able to give you some good contacts.

If you do all your homework on paper and in detail, you will build your greenhouse without delays, setbacks, and unexpected costs. The finished product will look good and function well. You will have justifiable pride in what you have built.

CONSTRUCTION MATERIALS

When building a greenhouse, there are several choices of materials available. Of course, a kit will have the materials chosen for you. You can compare kits and choose one made up of materials you prefer. Let's look at what is available.

For the foundation, the choice is all yours. Kits will only have recommendations but no actual materials. A simple, lightweight greenhouse might need only anchor pins to secure it. A more permanent structure needs a quality, permanent foundation. Poured concrete will probably be needed for the footers at least. The foundation walls can be made of concrete block, brick, or wood. If you cannot handle the foundation material yourself, hire a professional. As with any building, a greenhouse is only as good as its foundation.

The actual greenhouse is made up of two main components. One is the framing and the other is the lites or light transmitting material. Greenhouse framing can be steel, aluminum, or wood. Steel is just about unheard of for a home greenhouse. It is heavy, expensive, and it needs a good deal of upkeep.

Aluminum is an ideal material for greenhouse framing. It is strong, lightweight and virtually maintenance free. It is generally somewhat more expensive than wood. Most greenhouse kits have aluminum frames. For the home-built greenhouse, it is also an excellent framing material. Some types of aluminum cannot be shaped or worked with hand tools. When making a purchase, be sure to explain to the salesman what you want to do with the aluminum. He can advise you on which alloy is best and what tools will be needed to cut and shape it. Remember, aluminum will throw off a "hard sawdust" as you work; proper safety equipment is necessary.

Wood framing is the best for the greenhouse builder. The two best choices are cypress or redwood. Both are very long-lasting and free of rot. Use only the heartwood of each type. This means the oldest wood from the center of the tree. Sapwood is the new growth near the outside and is not suitable. Be very careful to buy the proper wood from your dealer. It is expensive and should be purchased with care. Treated pine can be used for framing although it will not last nearly as long as the others. Use it when you are building a more temporary structure (as one covered with sheet plastic). PVC or plastic pipe would also be suitable for framing for such a greenhouse.

For years, the only light-transmitting material for a greenhouse was glass. It is strong, attractive and durable, but it is also expensive and breakable. Modern science has provided several alternatives that have brought the price of a greenhouse down to a reasonable level. Plexiglass, fiberglass, sheet plastics and roll plastics are all suitable for covering a greenhouse. Some forms are supposed to transmit more light than glass. They are easy to cut and fit and won't break when a tree limb falls on them. Film plastics will wear out quickly and must be replaced every few years. Hard plastics wear well, but they will dull in time due to fine scratches from dirt and use. Shop around for various suitable plastics for the type of greenhouse you are building. Find out what tools are needed to cut and fit it and what anchors work best to secure it to the framing. Many large firms are constantly developing new plastics so check on them before buying.

Your greenhouse plans might specify what materials to use. You can make substitutions if you are careful not to sacrifice the quality you want. Whatever materials you decide on, be sure they fit your budget and your building skills.

RECYCLED MATERIALS

As an extra budget saver, consider used materials for part of your greenhouse or plant-support equipment. Used window sashes, with the glass intact, make excellent cold frame covers or hotbed covers. Used bricks can make up the greenhouse foundation. A sink, a heating unit or the water piping can come from a salvage company. Just be sure the item is the proper size and shape so it really will be useful. A "bargain" is worthless if it only gathers dust until your next garage sale. Purchase carefully and you might get good-as-new service for a fraction of the new price.

TOOLS

You will need a variety of simple hand tools and power tools to build your greenhouse. Most kits and those greenhouses built from simple plans will require ordinary tools. More elaborate designs might need specialized tools which will increase the overall cost of construction. If you are not familiar with such tools, don't try to build something that needs them. An elaborate greenhouse is not better or more enjoyable than a simple one. Plan on building a greenhouse that only requires the tools and building skills you already possess.

You will need tools and equipment to assemble your greenhouse whether it is a kit or not. You will need to make exact measurements. A good carpenter's rule (often called a "zig-zag") or a retractable steel tape is necessary. Some measuring jobs are easier with one rather than the other; having both would be a good idea.

In order to cut and shape the component parts, such items as hand saws or power saws, utility knives, and planes are needed. If you are working with aluminum instead of wood, tools designed for such use are required.

To fasten the greenhouse pieces together, some type of the following will be needed: nails, screws, bolts, glue or putty. A drill will be useful to start the holes for the fasteners.

Some people have grown up around tools and own a reasonable number of them before ever attempting to build a greenhouse. Others are all thumbs and have never hung a picture. But anyone who has the desire can learn to use simple, basic tools and build a greenhouse. Let an experienced friend watch over your work as you gain familiarity with the tools. There is no mystery to using them. Use common sense and follow a few basic rules. The more you use tools the easier it will become.

Abrasives, usually sandpaper, are used to smooth irregularities in wood or some other material before the final finish. Sandpaper is made of tough, thick paper or cloth coated with glue. Small particles of garnet, quartz or flint are spread over the glue. The size of the particles and their density on the sandpaper varies over a wide range. There are coarse papers to rough sand very jagged surfaces and very fine papers to rub out the finish on fine furniture.

Sandpaper is graded by numbers representing the range of surface from very fine to very coarse. The finer the paper the higher the number. Coarse papers will have low numbers. You will probably need two or three grades; it depends on the final finish you want.

There are many kinds of sandpaper. Check to find out which is best for the job you have.

Sandpaper is used to rub out the irregularities on a surface. This can be done by hand or with an electric sander. On wood, use the sandpaper with the grain—not across or against it.

A chisel is a type of knife used on wood. It chips away small or large pieces from the wood's surface. Generally, a chisel has a steel blade that is fashioned to a wood or plastic handle. The size is determined by the width of the blade.

For small cuts on softwood, a chisel can be used by hand. For larger cuts and those on hardwoods, a mallet is used to tap on the chisel. With the chisel held at a slight angle and regular tappings of the mallet, a series of short, even chunks can be removed from the wood. It is very useful for "fitting" pieces of wood without the use of expensive, speciality saws.

To cut the wood a saw is needed. A few hand saws in assorted sizes can do the job—especially a small one. A power-driven, circular saw is best for larger jobs. A circular saw is described by the size of its blade. A 7-inch saw uses a 7-inch blade. This size is right for most home projects.

Blades vary according to the job. A crosscut blade will be useful for most regular wood cutting. An abrasive blade will cut metal or masonry while a hollow ground blade will give very smooth, finished cuts. Choose the blade size and type for the job you have to do.

Use good safety practices with this power tool. It goes through fingers even easier than it goes through wood! Make sure the board you are cutting is held firmly in place where there is no chance of slipping. Keep your grip especially firm when you reach the end of a cut. A board jumps or drops when the cut is through if care isn't taken. Keep your free hand clear when sawing and wear glasses or goggles to protect your eyes from sawdust. A power saw will give you a cleaner, more accurate cut than a hand saw, but it should be used with care.

No matter what type of greenhouse construction you are doing, the one indispensible tool is the hammer. You will need a good one, suitable for the material you are using. For wood use a claw hammer. It is made for driving and pulling nails. The claw should be curved for easier removal of nails. A straight claw is designed for ripping apart boards. The hammer head should be convex or bell-shaped so it will not leave a deep mark in the wood if you miss the nail.

Buy a good quality hammer. Don't skimp on this most basic and important of tools. The best are made of drop-forged steel. One of rather heavy weight will have a larger striking face and be easier to use. Hold the nail right behind the head and lightly tap it into the wood with the hammer. When it is secure, pound it into the wood with straight, even strokes. Don't hammer at an angle; you will damage the wood. Don't hammer in light taps; this causes splintering. A nail driven in hard and straight will not tear the wood.

For metal work, use a ball peen hammer. A claw hammer is not suitable and might shatter, causing injury. As with all tools, use the correct one for the job.

Drills are necessary to start the holes to hold the frame anchors. A hand drill is used for small holes, usually in wood. It comes with bits of various sizes and a U-shaped handle. An awl, a small, pointed hand punch, can be used to start the holes before drilling. A hand drill must be held in a vertical position when you are using it or the hole will be too wide.

A power drill is best for most work. It is not costly and it often can be used for several other jobs. It can hold accessories for sanding, grinding, buffing, and other jobs. Power drills hold a wide range of bit sizes and can be used on metal and wood. Many have pistol-grip handles and variable speed control. They are very easy to use.

Before drilling, mark the exact location of the desired hole with a pencil and use an awl to give the drill a starting place. Power drills have a tendency to slip when first pressed against the wood. Increase the speed and pressure as the hole deepens. The harder the material, the more pressure will be needed. Use a few drops of oil on the drill bit to make drilling easier.

The screwdriver is one tool every greenhouse builder will need. Even the simplest kit will use screws to hold it together. Screws will hold more securely than nails and they are a must if there is the possibility you will want to disassemble your work one day.

It is helpful to start the screw hole with an awl or drill. Place the screw in the hole and turn firmly, from the vertical, with the screwdriver. The longer and heavier a screwdriver is, the easier it will be to use. Always choose one that is the proper size for the screws you are using. An incorrect one will be very difficult to use.

Good pliers will be helpful for bending and shaping wire and metal sheeting. They are used to grip and fasten or unfasten objects.

If your work involves nuts and bolts as fasteners, you will need wrenches to handle them. A wrench will hold, fasten, and lossen nuts and bolts. They might be a certain size or adjustable. Use a wrench that is the proper size. One that is too large will slip off and possibly hit you. Don't use pliers to grip the nut; the serrated jaws will cause damage. Once a damaged nut is in place, it will be very hard to remove.

A plane is used to create a flat, even board surface that is a must for accurate construction. The flat surface of the plane has an opening where the blade is located. This blade can be extended or retracted to take a controlled bite out of the surface.

Move the plane in firm, even strokes across the wood. Long ribbons of wood will be removed by the plane. Use it with the grain of the wood or across it, but never against it. The wood to be planed must be held securely by some device while you have both hands free to use the plane.

Various sawhorses, benches, and clamps will be needed to help you with your work. It is essential to have a suitable area with the right equipment if you are to build a greenhouse. Without them, every cut and hole will take an unreasonable amount of time and trouble. The mini work benches shown in many advertisements are very good for light construction. They will do several jobs without the addition of extra equipment. They are highly portable and can be stored easily.

STAKING OUT THE SITE

Once you have chosen the site for your greenhouse and the size and dimensions you want, it is necessary to stake out the exact site for the foundation. Many greenhouses are built to be rather temporary. They have no solid, permanent foundation. But even in that case, they should be properly staked so that they are square and true. Any structure is easier to build if it is square.

Use wooden stakes and strong twine for the job. Start at one corner and drive in the stake. Measure carefully for the next one and use the twine to connect the two stakes. Do the same for the other two corners. Remeasure to be sure the opposite sides are exactly the same length. Then measure, on the diagonal, an X through opposite corners. The two diagonal measurements should be identical in length. If they are not, then the stakes are not square. Relocate the stakes until the diagonals are exactly the same. Then remeasure the sides and across the front and rear. Be sure that your markers are correct in size as well as square. This will take up a little time and might involve several readjustments. A good greenhouse begins with a proper foundation. A mistake here will be very expensive; this is especially true when you are building a greenhouse with a full foundation. It is an old truism that any building is only as good as its foundation. Be sure your greenhouse foundation is sitting squarely on the ground.

EXCAVATION

When building for a permanent foundation, it will be necessary to excavate the site. This means removing enough of the soil cover to reach what is known as the undisturbed soil. The undisturbed soil is located below the soil layers that are subject to freezing and thawing during the winter months. A secure foundation must rest on this undisturbed soil or it will heave during winter weather. How deep you must dig to reach this layer depends on your location. In warm, Southern states only 12 inches or so might be necessary. In Northern states, it usually takes 3 feet of depth to reach undisturbed soil. In areas of severe winters, it might require 4 feet of depth. Be sure to check in your locale to find out what depth of excavation is best.

Even a temporary greenhouse will need excavation of a sort. Most people remove the top layer of soil from the area the greenhouse floor will cover and replace it. Clear that area of soil before any building begins. Usually a layer of 6 inches is sufficient. The flooring used to replace the soil can be anything from bark chips to poured concrete. It depends on your preference and what will be most suitable for the type of greenhouse being built.

Remove all the soil necessary to clear the area for further work. If concrete is to be poured for the foundation, there must be plenty of room for the forms. Excavate fully at one time so no further digging will be needed. Save the soil you have removed for backfilling after the foundation is finished. The rest can be worked into your garden or compost areas as needed. Part of your finishing work when the greenhouse is completed should include removing all traces of the excavation and leveling and landscaping the exterior.

FOUNDATIONS

Plan for a foundation that is suitable for the style and quality of the greenhouse you are building. Don't go overboard and don't skimp. The foundation should hold your greenhouse to the earth and last at least as long as the rest of the structure.

The simplest, least expensive greenhouse should be anchored to the ground rather than having a permanent foundation. The greenhouse with a framing of PVC pipe and a covering of film plastic is one of the simplest. It can be anchored to the ground with stakes driven in at least 2 feet at each of the four corners. Additional stakes can be used along the length if the greenhouse is more than 12 feet long. Any small greenhouse, one less than 10 feet on its longest side, can be anchored in a similar manner.

To do a more permanent job without a regular foundation, use treated wooden posts for the anchors. Drive them into the ground to a depth of 3 feet or 3 feet 6 inches for a good alternate foundation. It is also possible to pour concrete piers instead of using wood. Use 4-inch diameter piers with a three-eighth inch reinforcement rod in each. They should be poured to a depth of 2 feet 6 inches for best results. The frame is attached with 8-inch anchor bolts every 3 feet.

A traditional, permanent foundation comes in two types. One is the concrete slab and the other is the excavated one with concrete footers. Each is long lasting and suitable for permanent construction. The slab foundation is especially popular in the Southern United States for regular house construction and is less costly than an excavated foundation.

To build a slab foundation, use 1-inch by 6-inch boards to construct a form for the fresh concrete. Steel rods can be driven into the ground at regular intervals to act as piers throughout the poured area. Wire mesh is spread over the rods for additional reinforcement. The concrete is poured into the form and can be leveled by dragging a straightedge across it while the concrete is still wet. Most of the preparation for a slab foundation can be done by the average do-it-yourselfer with the concrete mixed and poured by a professional.

The traditional excavated foundation is the best for a quality, permanent structure. It will cost the most, but it will last the longest without maintenance problems. A trench must be dug for the poured concrete footers. The trench would be 2 feet deep in Southern states and about 3 feet in colder areas. It might need to be up to 4 feet in depth where winters are very severe. It is necessary for the trench to reach below the frost line to undisturbed soil so that it will not be affected by winter cold and ground frost. Figure 5-1 shows the correct excavation.

The trench is filled with poured concrete for a base known as the *footers*. These footers can be topped with additional concrete to ground level, as in Fig. 5-2, or hollow block can be used instead. The

Fig. 5-1. The kind of excavation necessary for the construction of a permanent foundation for a greenhouse.

diagrams in Fig. 5-3 give the correct construction. Bolts embedded in the wet concrete or in cement in the blocks will be used to hold the sill plates.

The foundation of any building is the key component determining the quality and useful life of that building. A greenhouse must have a foundation appropriate to the quality and expected usefulness of the rest of the structure. Plan for a foundation that will last at least as long as the rest of the construction. Overbuilding would waste money and underbuilding will reduce the useful life of the total greenhouse.

The plans given in this book, designed for the amateur builder, call for simple yet effective foundations. They are suitable for any greenhouse with similar design. Those with wood framing and flexible or rigid plastic glazing are right for use with these foundations ideas. Longer-lasting foundations of poured concrete are necessary for a greenhouse of larger size, metal framing and glass glazing.

A good, solid frame support shown in Plan 1 calls for 4-inch by 4-inch boards pressure treated with copper naphthenate and sunk 4 feet into the ground. Using posts of that size, sunk to a depth

Fig. 5-2. After a site has been excavated to the proper depth, it can be filled in with poured concrete.

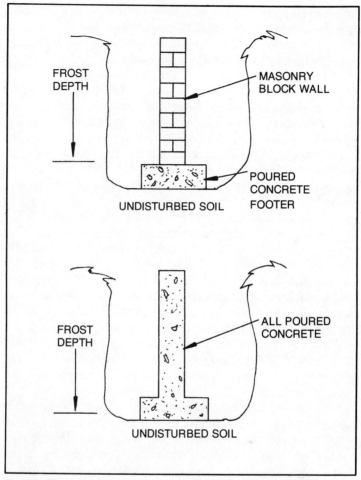

Fig. 5-3. When excavating for a permanent foundation, be sure to dig below the frost line down to undisturbed soil. Otherwise your foundation may heave during winter weather.

suitable even for areas of heavy snow, gives you a very sturdy support for a greenhouse with minimum expense. A similar anchoring, at the corners and centers, would be suitable for many greenhouses. Using 4 inch by 4 inch boards that are properly treated insures that they will last for many years. Setting them in the ground to a depth of 4 feet insures that they will not be affected by frost even in the coldest areas. For most of the Northeastern United States, the frost depth is 3 feet. In areas of extra cold, like the New England states, it is usually adequate to set support posts to a depth of 4 feet. By recommending that depth, the plan is suitable without special changes to accommodate a particular climate.

A similar foundation is used in Plan 2. Extra sturdiness is supplied here by backfilling the base of the posts, first with packed earth and then with a 1:3:5 mix of concrete, to an overall depth of 3 feet. This will secure the posts strongly and do just about the best job short of poured concrete footers with masonry construction. If you live in an extra cold area, it would be helpful to increase the overall depth of your posts to 4 feet. That will give you the needed depth below frost for even the coldest areas. This plan recommends soaking the post bottoms, up to the depth they will be in the ground, in copper naphthenate solution. Here the specific time of 48 hours is given.

The use of concrete for a foundation is given with Plan 3. The plan calls for digging anchor holes that are 8 inches in diameter. The recommended depth is 18 inches in firm soil and 24 inches deep in loose soil. The anchor stakes are set in the holes and supported by a one-half-inch-by-4-inch cross rods. When all are set, the concrete is prepared and poured into the holes. This will give secure anchoring with less cost for this unusual greenhouse shape than other foundation ideas. The small batch of concrete needed can be mixed in a wheelbarrow. Read directions on the bag of cement for the correct ratio of materials. These are often given in cubic feet. You can substitute a shovelful for a cubic foot using the standard shovel with a 6-foot handle.

A simple foundation is shown in Plan 4. This plan uses conduit for the framing and gives the option of corrugated fiberglass or 4-mil, clear polyethylene sheeting for the glazing. This gives a lightweight, easy-to-assemble structure. The anchoring is accomplished by means of G.I. pipe (black iron pipe) that is 1 inch in diameter and sunk 24 inches into the ground. This is sufficient anchoring for this style of lightweight greenhouse that has an easy-to-install and replace covering. This design should hold up well in most areas except where winters are severe.

The simplest anchoring goes with the simplest greenhouse. Plan 5 is a portable, plastic greenhouse. As the name implies, it can be moved to a different location after it is completed. It is wood-framed, covered with plastic sheeting, and about 8 feet by 12 feet in size. It has a curved eaved style made by bending bands of exterior grade plywood. For anchoring, sharpened stakes of 2-inch-by-4-inch lumber are used. They are located at each corner and at the door frame. They can be set into the ground from 12 inches to 18 inches in depth. The whole greenhouse can be lifted up and relocated after completion. Of course, this is done with a structure that does not have permanent heating and plumbing systems. It cannot have the permanent features of a greenhouse with a sturdier foundation.

WALLS

The walls of a greenhouse can be brick and 3 feet high or wood and just enough above ground level to anchor the framing. Or they can be anywhere in between. Which you choose depends on the climate where you live, the style of greenhouse you are building, and your personal preference.

In warm areas, wood or stucco are popular for greenhouse walls. Use treated redwood, cypress or pine (depending on the rest of the wood used in construction). If the greenhouse is to be glass-to-ground in design then the walls are only a few inches above the soil level. Figure 5-4 shows simple wood walls in such a greenhouse.

Masonry walls are more substantial and long-lasting. The least expensive of these is hollow block. Figure 5-5 shows the use of such block for the walls of a greenhouse. It would be more attractive

Fig. 5-4. This greenhouse has only a single board for its walls.

Fig. 5-5. Masonry block makes a sturdy and inexpensive wall for this greenhouse.

(and costly) to cover the block with a brick or stone veneer. Figure 5-6 shows a very fine greenhouse wall of cut stone.

The purpose of any wall in a greenhouse is to provide support, added strength and insulation. The more you need any or all of those elements, the higher and more substantial your walls should be. For added protection in heavy snow areas, the walls should be as high as the benches or a few inches higher. They shouldn't be much higher than the benches or they will block needed light. A high wall gives added insulation and protection from the weight of drifted snow. A cold-climate greenhouse with high, brick walls is shown in Fig. 5-7.

If your greenhouse is attached to or near any other structures on your property, try to coordinate the choice of wall material. The walls of all the buildings should harmonize so the entire property will look like components of a single whole. This will give the necessary eye appeal to your greenhouse and your entire homesite.

FRAMING

Framing is what holds the lites (light transmitting covering) of your greenhouse together. The most common framing materials are steel, aluminum, and wood. Other framing materials include plastic pipe (usually PVC, polyvinylchloride) and electrical conduit.

54

Fig. 5-6. The wall for this greenhouse is a handsome and durable cut stone.

Fig. 5-7. For severe climate conditions, this greenhouse has an unusually high wall of brick. Such a wall reduces heat costs and protects the glass area from drifted snow.

Steel framing is usually found on commercial greenhouses. It is high-strength and can support wide panels of glazing material. It is too expensive and too difficult to maintain for the average homeowner. Initially, it needs at least three coats of a rust inhibiting paint. During use, it will require constant repainting to fight the ever-present rust. Steel allows the most light to enter a greenhouse because its extra-strong structural members are thinner and less numerous than any other framing material. Its best use in the average home greenhouse would be in center supports or ridge supports. This use is shown in Figure 5-8.

Wood has been the most common framing material on all types of greenhouses for years. It is lightweight, easy to cut and assemble, and it comes in types and prices for every need and budget.

The top of the line in wood framing is cypress. To be more specific, it is the clear heartwood of swamp-grown cypress. This wood is by far the longest lasting and the most expensive. Do not use upland or highland cypress; they are unsuitable and quick rotting. Cypress can last just about indefinitely. I visited an orchid fancier who had constructed his greenhouse—about 20 years earlier—with good quality cypress. He had some scraps left on the ground at the rear of his property. They were still strong, clean and free of rot. However, such wood is difficult to obtain and very costly.

The second best choice for greenhouse framing is redwood. Use clear, heart redwood and not the sapwood for good results. It would be wisest to purchase the redwood from a greenhouse supplier so it will be of the correct type and properly kiln dried. This will insure its resistance to moisture. An acid preservative is used on redwood that will corrode iron and steel. When assembling redwood for framing, always be sure to use hot-dipped galvanized nails, bolts, and screws; they will not corrode.

After cypress and redwood, cedar is best for wood framing. It is naturally resistant to rot and insect damage, but will need paint or stain (redwood does not). Least expensive woods to use include fir and pine. But these two will not begin to last the long years of cypress, redwood, or cedar. All of these woods will need to be treated with a preservative to increase their useful life and to protect against insects and rot. Copper naphthenate is the recommended preservative for greenhouse use because it it harmless to plants. All wood (except redwood) should receive two coats (at least) of a good greenhouse paint. Select a paint designed for use in the high humidity of greenhouses. This is essential for proper wear and good durability. When building the frame, be sure to finish off all

Fig. 5-8. The best place for costly steel framing in a home greenhouse is in the center supports rather than the entire frame.

wood joints very smooth and tight and then paint so it seeps into the seams and seals as completely as possible. This will prevent moisture from gathering and giving rot and fungus a starting point.

Wood is a good insulator and won't transmit heat or cold the way metal will. It also will not "sweat" with condensed moisture like metals. But it requires periodic maintenance with regular painting if it is to look its best. Figure 5-9 shows what a wood-framed greenhouse looks like when it has not been properly cared for.

Aluminum is the most popular framing material for new greenhouses. Just like the aluminum siding used on houses, it is the

Fig. 5-9. To avoid looking like this, a wood framed greenhouse needs regular painting.

easy care and durable beauty that makes it so popular. Figure 5-10 shows aluminum framing before the lites were installed.

Aluminum framing is actually made of various aluminum alloys. It requires no painting, ever, and is impervious to moisture, fungus, or insects. It will not deteriorate in the weather so it stays new-looking over the years. Its framing members are thinner and much lighter in weight than the corresponding wood ones. It is sufficiently strong for normal home greenhouse size and shape.

The main drawback to aluminum is its excellence as a conductor of heat and cold. In winter, it will quickly conduct outside cold into the greenhouse and drive up the cost of heating. In summer, it will be hot to the touch on sunny days and cause heat build-up inside the greenhouse. But despite the increased utility costs, it is preferred by many due to its maintenance-free qualities.

A newcomer to framing use is plastic pipe. It is usually PVC (polyvinylchloride) or polyethelene water pipe that is used.It can be 1 to 3 inches in diameter. It is flexible, inexpensive and easy to work with. It requires no maintenance. Plastic framing does not need to be painted, does not rot or warp, and cannot be attacked by insects or fungus. An occasional cleaning is all that is necessary to remove dirt and algae.

The flexibility of plastic pipe makes it the best framing for Quonset greenhouses. It is also good for geodesic-dome construction where it is used for the struts that fit into hubs to form the triangular members. The struts must bend at about a 17-degree angle in the dome so that all members will fit together. With the use of flexible pipe, this is accomplished with ease. The pipe ends can be "squashed" between the hub plates and held in place with carriage bolts. This compression will make the bend of the pipe struts much simpler to achieve.

About the only drawback to plastic framing is its limitation to plastic glazing materials. It cannot hold glass panels satisfactorily.

Fig. 5-10. Aluminum framing is the number one framing material for home greenhouses.

But for rigid or flexible plastic glazing, it is excellent. For the individual who is building an entire greenhouse from scratch and wants to keep costs and maintenance to a minimum, plastic for the frame and the glazing are excellent choices.

One framing material you might not have thought of is standard electrical conduit. It does a fine job and is readily available to people in the building trades. Use 1-inch conduit and fittings that are galvanized and thick-walled. It is fastened together with U-bolts and set-screw fittings. Film plastic is used for the covering. For more permanence and better climate control, triangular panels of one-half inch plywood can be set under the roof peaks at one or both ends. These are secured with conduit clamps and screwed to the wood. Use the plywood area for ventilation screens or fans.

The conduit should be primed and painted after assembly. A light-colored enamel paint would be good. To attach wood for the door frame to the conduit, use a flat-headed stove bolt. If possible, use one large piece of plastic film to cover the greenhouse from the ground across one side and up and over the roof to the ground on the other side. Cut end panels to the size of the framing and seal to the main panel by heat. An electric iron can be used for this job. To avoid wrinkling the plastic, slip a piece of aluminum foil between the iron and the sheet. A simple and effective method for attaching the plastic sheet to the conduit involves using marbles or pebbles. Press these against the inside of the sheet and have someone tie a nylon cord around it on the outside to form a little bunch or gather with the pebble to secure it. The cord can then be used to tie the sheeting to the conduit (especially at the intersection of two tubes). This is very simple and it works quite well.

No matter what framing material you use, be sure that it is carefully and strongly secured to the foundation walls. This is usually done with bolts (see Fig. 5-11). Framing is attached by wood strips if it rests against another building as shown in Fig. 5-12. For the free-standing greenhouse without a regular foundation, sink the corner posts at least 2 feet and preferably 3 feet into the soil.

WOOD FRAMING

The plans in this book call for wood framing. It is the most frequently used material for framing a home-built greenhouse. Most home greenhouses with aluminum framing are made from kits. Wood is easier for weekend builders to work with and it makes very adequate framing. Here are a few suggestions for when you use wood for your greenhouse.

BOLT FOR
FRAMING
ATTACHMENT

Fig. 5-11. Aluminum framing is attached to the foundation wall with bolts.

The very best wood for greenhouse construction is the heartwood of cypress and redwood. The heartwood is the older wood at the center of a tree. It is the proper wood for this type of work. Do not use the sapwood. It is the new wood from the outside of the trunk and is not as resistant. Cypress will last just about indefinitely. It is naturally impervious to moisture, rot and, insects. A piece of cypress might lie on the ground for 20 years and be just as hard and solid as the day it was thrown there. It is the best choice if you can afford it. Redwood is almost as good. It is long-lasting and blends well with the look of many modern homes and yards. It is the second best choice for construction.

These two woods are costly and getting hard to find. You can substitute a properly treated fir or pine. They will not last as long and will need more maintenance, but they are satisfactory. Check with local suppliers and builders to find out what woods, available in your area, would be suitable for a greenhouse. You might find a good wood that will do the job and fit your budget.

Before you start to build, treat or paint all your lumber. It will be much easier to have the initial covering put on before assembly. Afterwards, a touch-up coat in the areas of joints and fittings will be all that is needed. At least two coats of wood preservative or paint are needed. Don't skimp here or you will have twice the work later on when the wood begins to weaken and rot. The moisture in a greenhouse is hard on wood. Try to protect your work from the start. If you use paint, check on those designed for greenhouse use that contain a fungicide.

The method used to anchor your wood frame to the foundation depends on the type of foundation used. Costs are reduced when using treated 4-inch-by-4-inch posts for a foundation. These can be set in concrete or sunk directly into the ground. Wood sill plates and framing members are easily attached with nails, wood screws, or bolts.

A concrete foundation gives you a trouble-free, permanent base for your greenhouse. Framing anchors or angle-iron braces are used to attach the frames to the sill plate and foundation. This is the method used for residential slab construction. Excellent anchors can be made from 3 inch angle iron cut 2½ inches wide and drilled for three-eighth inch bolts.

Generally, 2 inch by 4 inch wood members are the best for framing. They usually should be set no further than 36 inches on center. Use a jig or pattern for forming the dimensions of the framing. This will insure accurate and consistent results. Use the plan dimensions and build the jig by nailing boards in the proper configuration to other boards, plywood sheets, or a wooden floor. The actual framing members are cut and fitted in the jig. Frames can be secured by nails, wood screws, and glue in any combination you prefer. To add rigidity to the frame, use three-eighth inch plywood to form gussets over the joints. These are set by nailing and gluing. Use a resorcinol-resin glue for this work. It is waterproof and sets at low pressure under normal temperatures. It is recommended for greenhouse construction.

For even-span and lean-to greenhouses, size can be increased by adding extra framing members to the overall length. This allows

Fig. 5-12. When a greenhouse is attached to another building, the framing is secured to wood strips.

you to customize any size plan of those types without any basic plan changes. Conversely, you can make a greenhouse smaller by reducing the number of framing members. These styles are very flexible.

As discussed previously use the proper tools for working with wood and treat or paint the wood for long life before assembly. Use nails, screws and glue of the appropriate type and size for the job. Measure, cut and assemble the wood members in an accurate and workmanlike manner. You do not need expensive materials to do a high-quality job.

ALTERNATE FRAMING MATERIALS

Wood is the favorite framing material of most home greenhouse builders. It provides the ideal combination of ready

availability, ease of construction, and reasonable cost and maintenance. But there are alternative materials to use for framing. These
might suit your needs better and they are worth considering. Here
are a few possibilities.

Steel is rarely used in home greenhouses due to weight, high
cost and difficult maintenance. Steel is relatively costly and is used
mainly on commercial greenhouses. Its strength will support large
structures. It is not necessary for a home greenhouse unless it is
one of unusual size. With the high moisture level present in a
greenhouse, steel will rust even more easily than it normally does.
Thorough cleaning and removal of the rust and the application of
several coats of a rust-inhibiting paint are routine for a steel-framed
greenhouse. If you do want to consider using steel, the best thing to
do is have it cut and formed to your specifications at a local fab-
ricator's. Also, have as many holes pre-drilled as possible. It is not
to be recommended except under unusual circumstances.

Aluminum is very popular for home-greenhouse framing. It is a
good combination of strength, lightweight and low maintenance.
Most greenhouse kits sold today use aluminum for their framing.
You can use it for the home built greenhouse if you want to. Square
aluminum tubing, 1-inch by 1 inch, is good for a small greenhouse.
You could also use aluminum frames, similar to those that hold
house window screens, to hold the plastic glazing needed. The
aluminum frame material is readily available from screen manufacturers, suppliers, and repair companies. The panels can be made in
any appropriate size and attached to the square framing with metal
screws. You can make the panels yourself or have them made up by
the supplier. This type of work is not too costly. The greenhouse
will assemble easily and be virtually maintenance free.

The basic framing components in aluminum can be assembled
on site using sheet-metal screws. Corners are formed by corner
inserts. Wall ends are attached to the base and roof beams by
welding or by using 1-inch sections of U-bar brackets. The U-bar
section is screwed to the base or roof member and the end of the
wall tubing is inserted and held in place by sheet-metal screws.
Anchor bolts secure the framing into concrete anchor pads. Good
anchoring is essential because a lightweight greenhouse of this
design can be toppled easily in a strong wind.

A useful framing material you might not have considered is
electrical conduit. If you have a handy source for it, you have a good
choice for framing a simple greenhouse. Use the galvanized,
thick-walled type. Conduit that is 1 inch in diameter is satisfactory.

It is fastened together using U-bolts and set-screw fittings. Film plastic is the best covering for this type greenhouse.

When using electrical conduit for your framing, set it up for 24 inches on center. Frame the doorway in wood using flathead stove bolts to secure it to the conduit. This type of greenhouse is not fancy, but it can do the job at a very small cost.

Plastic pipe makes a good framing material for Quonset greenhouses where the pipe is bent to form the frame. It is also good for geodesic-dome styles where the struts are plastic pipe. Use polyethelene or PVC pipe in 1 or 2 inch diameters. These are flexible pipes that come in 300-foot rolls. They can be bent and formed easily. They are very lightweight and they are best with plastic film coverings. For the dome style, the pipe can be compressed into the hubs and bolted securely. There are also liquid solders available that melt the pipe pieces together to form joints. This is an excellent choice for the first home greenhouse. Cost is low and plastic pipe is easy to work with for the beginner.

COLD FRAMES AND HOTBEDS

These are the easiest items to construct for the budding greenhouseman. If you have little experience with tools or are uncertain about building a full-size structure for plants, begin with a cold frame. With the addition of heat, it automatically becomes a hotbed.

The cold frame is anchored by support posts. These can be 2 inches by 4 inches or 4 inches by 4 inches of redwood, cypress or treated wood of some kind. It is possible to use concrete block, but it is unnecessary. Sink the posts to a depth of 3 feet.

Sides of the cold frame can be 11-inches-by-6-inches boards and need to be coated with a suitable wood preservative. The sides should be 12 inches high in the front and rise to 18 inches at the rear for proper runoff. There is no bottom except the ground itself. The ground soil should be removed to a depth of 6 inches to 12 inches and replaced with a layer of gravel, then sand or peat moss, and finally good soil. The interior soil level will probably be above ground level on the outside. Straw or soil can be banked around the outside to provide insulation. The top of the cold frame is a window sash. Those commonly purchased are 3 feet by 6 feet or multiples of this. Used sashes from the wrecker are available at very low cost. Discarded storm windows are also a possibility. Attach the sashes by loose pin hinges for easy removal when necessary. A 1 inch by 2 inch board attached midway to the side of the cold frame and cut on a slant at the other end is ideal for propping up the sash as needed. Use 2 inch by 2 inch boards for framing in the top of the cold frame and the middle where two sashes meet (if preferred).

The interior should be painted white to reflect light as much as possible. The exterior can be finished in any manner preferred. The addition of soil-heating cables will turn the cold frame into a hotbed. It is possible to provide extra warmth with layers of manure. An excellent compromise between a cold frame and hotbed is to construct the frame against the foundation wall of your house where there is a basement window. The window can be opened in cold weather to allow basement warmth into the frame. It will stay above freezing at very little expense to your home-heating costs.

WINDOW GREENHOUSES

For those with limited space, the window greenhouse is the answer. They are especially good for apartment or condominium dwellers. But be sure to check with your landlord or property manager before building. Kit units are available, but a window greenhouse is easy and inexpensive to build from scratch.

For those of very limited skills and budget, try this bargain model. Get two metal shelf tracks of suitable length and screw them into the window frame. They come with brackets to hold the shelves. You could use wood for the actual shelves, but glass would be better to allow more light in. Cover the whole unit with sheet plastic tacked to the frame. It's not fancy but it works and costs less than $20.00 to build.

A cabinet-style model can be made of one-half inch plywood. Measure your window frame to determine the overall dimensions. The depth is up to you; 18 inches is satisfactory. Shelves can be set at various heights or use adjustable bracket tracks to allow changes in the shelves as preferred. They add a little to the cost but they are very convenient. Attach the plywood with L-brackets and flathead wood screws. The "door" that opens this window greenhouse is framed in 1-inch-by-2-inch fir or pine with flat L-brackets and flathead wood screws. Use rigid sheet plastic for the glazing with clear silicone tub sealer to eliminate air leaks. Nail the plastic to the wood frame with narrow, flathead three-fourth inch nails. Attach a knob for easy opening of your door.

In mounting this greenhouse to the window frame, more L-brackets are used. The weight of the greenhouse rests on the windowsill. Use the longest and heaviest wood screws possible to hold the unit. Be sure the window framing is in good condition. If the wood is weakened with rot, the screws will pull out and down will fall your creation. It is possible to overcome this difficulty by using three-sixteenth inch carriage bolts that go all the way through the sash and frame to the exterior. Be sure not to try to drill out the glass when you are preparing to use the bolts.

If you are an experienced builder, you might have other ideas on how to construct and mount such a unit. These tips are given as the simplest way for a novice to achieve success. If you have a better way, by all means use it. As anyone who has done any building knows, there are a variety of ways to achieve any end result in construction. Don't hesitate to use any skills or knowledge you have to build a unit in a manner you are most happy with.

A third possibility for a window greenhouse involves building a cabinet-like structure with legs to aid in support. The individual window will determine the dimensions you need. Use 2-inch-by-2-inch boards to frame in the window, the needed depth, and supporting legs. Enclose the top and sides with one-fourth inch plywood or one-eighth inch masonite attach with wood glue or nails. The bottom should be one-half inch plywood. Use white paint in the interior to reflect as much light as possible. Assemble the side frames and panels first and then the top and bottom connectors with their panels. A door similar to the one described above would be suitable here.

Plexiglass or other rigid plastic sheeting is the best choice for homemade window model greenhouses. They are lightweight and easy for the amateur to work with. Nail holes can be drilled into them for easy mounting. Their strength adds to the structural support of the whole unit. Cutting plastic is easy today because of the introduction of the plastic knife onto the market. It is made for cutting plexiglass, fiberglass, bakelite, and all similar materials. Lay the plastic on a smooth, hard surface. Place a metal straightedge along the line you want to cut. Run the plastic knife along the edge lightly and smoothly from end to end. Repeat this process several times until the score you have made cuts into the plastic about one-third of the total thickness. At this point, place the scored line over the edge of the work surface and sharply smack the overhanging area with your open palm. The plastic will snap in two with a sharp crack.

GLAZING

Glazing is the process of installing lites. It is the lites that let in the light; without them there is no greenhouse. Today, lites can be glass or plastic. The plastic can be transparent (clear) or translucent (cloudy). The plastic can also be rigid or flexible.

Glass has been the standard for years. It is the covering against which all other materials are judged. Its clarity allows the most light to enter and gives the owner and spectators the beauty of the plants as seen from the outside of the greenhouse. It has the best insulating qualities and wears the longest with the least maintenance. If you build a greenhouse of aluminum and glass, you will have the most durable and maintenance-free structure possible.

The glass used for a greenhouse should not be ordinary window glass or cheap imported glass with imperfections and discolorations. Only first-grade, double-weight glass should be used. It will weigh about 24 ounces to the square foot and will withstand falling branches, hail stones and snow loads the best. For extra protection against breakage, it is possible to buy thick glass with wire mesh embedded in it for superior strength. This glass will cost more. To add insulation and reduce heating bills, double-glazing with a "dead" air space in between the panes is very helpful. Purchase your glass from a greenhouse supplier to be sure of its quality and suitability for greenhouse use.

Glass panes should be set so that they are at right angles to the sun during the growing season. They should be secured as tightly as

Fig. 5-13. A greenhouse should be caulked neatly and tightly as this one is.

Fig. 5-14. A prefabricated greenhouse uses clips to secure the glazing.

possible with a minimum of overlap. Framing used with glass must be square and rigid. If not, there is the possibility it will heave in the frost or twist in a wind storm and the glass panels will shatter or loosen and fall. The best glazing compounds to use are the plastic ones. Mastic types are also good. Caulk tightly and neatly as in Fig. 5-13. The tape or bead forms of caulking are the easiest to use. They will stay soft and pliable for years with no shrinkage. Prefabricated greenhouses and kits come equipped with special clips to fasten the glass to the sash bars (see Fig. 5-14). A close-up view of a single fastening clip is shown in Fig. 5-15.

Fiberglass is the rigid plastic used in greenhouses. It is strong and adapts itself to curvilinear styles like the Quonset easily. It is lightweight, about 6 ounces per square foot, so it is possible to use large overhead sections with few supports. It is produced in large sizes just for this purpose (widths up to 40 inches and lengths to 12 feet).

Most fiberglass on greenhouses is corrugated or wavy-surfaced. It is a little difficult to seal well, but it is sturdy and easy to install. Flat panels of acrylic are also coming into use. They need some additional support members to prevent sagging. Although it comes in many colors, only clear or pale translucent types are suitable for plants. Other colors restrict too much light. Because they are translucent, rather than transparent, fiberglass panels emit a diffuse, shadowless light. This type of light is especially good for orchids and ornamental foliage plants. Its light diffusive qualities make extra shading during the heat of the summer unnecessary.

When first introduced on the market, fiberglass was tested extensively and found very durable. When properly installed and of high quality, it can last from 5 to 15 years in a greenhouse. It is subject to scratching and weathering. Some types can be refinished. The increased cost of petroleum has driven up the cost of rigid plastics, but fiberglass is still a better buy than regular glass.

Flexible film plastic is low on the glazing scale. It is low in both price and durability. It is best for seasonal use and temperate climates. There are a variety to choose from. They come in varying thicknesses and qualities. Look over what is available and pick what suits your particular needs.

Polyethylene film is the least expensive and the shortest wearing. It is really not suitable for year-around use. It deteriorates rapidly in the summer heat. Several layers work better than one. Generally it has a useful life of one year or less.

Vinyl (PVC) film is better quality. It will last about twice as long and will cost over twice as much. Choose only the weatherable grades for greenhouse use. Also look for fungus-resistant types. They are available in both transparent and translucent varieties. Drawbacks include a tendency to attract dirt and to expand and contract during temperature changes. This makes it brittle and easily torn in cold weather. The best thicknesses are 8 mil to 12 mil and it can last up to 4 years.

Mylar is a tradename for Du Pont polyester film. It is fairly durable, lasting up to five years, if properly installed. It must be stretched tight for optimum performance. This usually means stretching the film over the frame by means of a wooden batten applied to one end of the unrolled film. The batten is used to provide equal stress at all points of the tightening film to eliminate sags and wrinkles. This inhibits the destructive and annoying "snapping" which plagues film plastics in high winds. Batten boards are also used to secure the film to the frame members (see Fig. 5-16). This reduces the stress caused by nail holes. Any film used will benefit from tight installation in this manner.

In the Quonset style, the plastic film is laid over the framework and only secured at edges and ground level. Such securing at the doorway to a Quonset is shown in Fig. 5-17. To help hold the plastic

Fig. 5-15. A close-up of the glass holding clips supplied with a prefabricated or kit greenhouse.

film down over the main portion and the wind from ripping it free, flexible cables are used as in Fig. 5-18.

The plastic glazing called for in the plans in this book is either corrugated fiberglass or film plastics. But the smooth rigid plastics can be substituted as preferred. Generally, they are interchangeable in most plans calling for one or the other.

Plans that allow for rigid or film plastic are Plan 1 and Plan 4. In each case, the rigid plastic specified is corrugated fiberglass. The film plastic for one (Plan 4) is 4-mil, clear polyethylene. In Plan 1, however, it is two layers of 6-mil plastic that is air-inflated between the layers. This air space is very helpful for insulating the greenhouse and reducing heating costs. The air in such a space inhibits the passage of outside temperature conditions to the inside. Such a design is good for Northern states.

Plans usually give suggestions for how to secure the film plastic to the framing. Plan 3 calls for 6-mil, poly film ordered in 100-foot rolls. To secure the film, this plan calls for redwood stock molding that measures 1 inch by 3 inches by 10 feet. It is to be used as the batten boards over the plastic and the framing members. With redwood, there will be no maintenance needed against weathering.

A less expensive idea is shown in Plan 7. Here the batten boards suggested are wooden strips measuring three-eighths of an

Fig. 5-16. When a greenhouse is glazed in film plastic, the plastic is secured with long, thin batten boards.

inch by 1 inch by the preferred length. Such small boards will be harder to work with and more subject to wear and stress. This plan is designed for the very minimum of costs for a functioning greenhouse.

Good notes for lapping the plastic film are given with Plan 4. To install plastic covering run sheets from the ground on one side up over the plate, ridge and down over plate to the ground on the other side, lap joints on rafters. Another suggestion is to dig a trench around the sides, run the plastic into the trench, and then backfill against the plastic to make the covering tight around the bottom. This is an excellent idea! It will secure the plastic along the ground to keep it tight and prevent drafts of outside air from entering the greenhouse. This will give you the best return on plastic-film glazing.

GLAZING COMBINATIONS

It might be worthwhile, in your particular greenhouse setup, to use more than one glazing material. In combination, it is possible to maximize the advantages and minimize the defects of various cover-

Fig. 5-17. This shows how the film plastic is gathered and secured at the doorway of a Quonset greenhouse.

Fig. 5-18. Light, flexible cables are used to prevent wind damage to film plastic greenhouses.

ings. For instance, use film plastic for the sides and rigid plastic for the roof of a greenhouse. The roof takes much more abuse and weathering so the stronger material belongs there. Glass walls could be combined with a rigid roof. Here the beauty and clarity of glass can be enjoyed while the less expensive plastic will do fine for the roof. Also, if it is translucent, the plastic roof will eliminate the need for shading in hotter climates where it is generally necessary.

Glazing combinations will save on your heat costs. A double layer of glazing, with a "dead air" space in between, will give valuable insulation. Researchers estimate that a 20 percent heat saving can be realized with a 2 to 4 inch dead airspace between glazings. This can be accomplished in several ways. Double layers of glass are nice, but they are quite costly. Two layers of rigid plastic work well and are cheaper. The best way to achieve the insulating effect at minimum cost is with a combination of film plastic under the regular glazing material of glass or rigid plastic. There are also some recent innovations in greenhouses that involve two layers of soft plastic formed into "pillows" that are inflated with air. Whatever type of double glazing is used, it will be effective in reducing heating costs in cold climates.

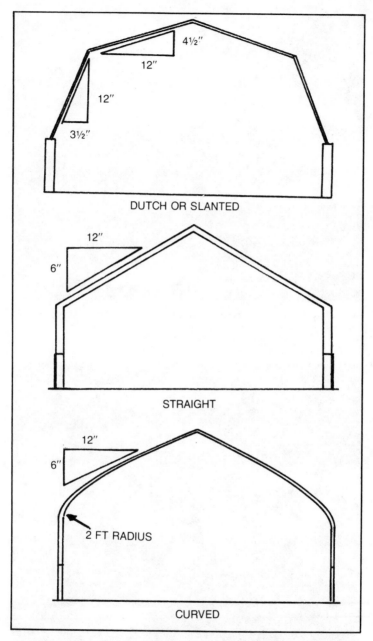

Fig. 5-19. Here are the three styles of greenhouse eaves. The Dutch or slanted eaves is at the top. The straight eaves, best choice for the do-it-yourselfer, is next. The bottom style is the curved eaves, it is very graceful and attractive.

Fig. 5-20. This straight-eaved greenhouse is the easiest to construct. It is the best design for a stick-built greenhouse.

Fig. 5-21. The curved-eaves greenhouse is especially graceful. It is available from most kit manufacturers.

EAVES STYLES

There are a variety of eaves styles available and each will add a certain look to your greenhouse. Most style variations are merely a matter of esthetics, but there are some practical considerations. The amount of "headroom" plants have can be greatly effected by the eaves style and proportions. An extreme example would be the A-frame. It restricts plants set on its benches by the continuous slope of its walls. The three basic and most common eaves styles are Dutch, straight, and curved eaves. They are illustrated in Fig. 5-19.

The greenhouse with straight sides and eaves is shown in Fig. 5-20. This type is the simplest to construct and very practical. An identical greenhouse in size has a very different look by changing the eaves. Figure 5-21 shows a low-walled, curved-eaves model that has a greater amount of ridge room for hanging plants. This type of extra space would be wasted if you grow African violets.

If you are building the greenhouse yourself, stick to the straight-eaves style. For the purchaser of a prefab unit, consider what eaves variations companies offer. Then decide if one style will suit the plants you plan to cultivate or the overall architecture of your property better than another.

Chapter 6

Climate Control

Within the glass walls of your greenhouse exists a miniclimate that might be wildly different from the natural climate that surrounds your greenhouse. Picture orchids blooming while a raging winter storm is killing evergreens on the other side of the glass walls. This delicate internal climate is created by the greenhouse itself, but also by the automated equipment and human care that are essential to maintain it.

There are four factors that make up the climate. These are temperature, water, light, and air. The four strike a delicate balance and one cannot be changed without effecting the others. For example, if you raise the temperature in your greenhouse, it will need more water (humidity) because heat dries the air. It will take time and practice to learn how to maintain the best balance for your plants. Each greenhouse is unique in location and outside factors that effect inside performance. How to control the various factors will be discussed in this chapter. These factors will have to be tailored to your particular situation.

VENTILATION

Any greenhouse will have air in it but that is not enough for plants. They need moving, fresh currents of air and not just a stagnant mass. Without an exchange of air, the heat buildup from the summer sun would soon wilt all the plants in a greenhouse. Ventilation can be achieved by using nature's air currents or by creating some of your own.

Fig. 6-1. The ridge vent, at the top of the greenhouse ridge, is the best way to remove super-heated air and keep the greenhouse cool on summer days.

The one essential for ventilation is the ridge vent. This opens the very top of the greenhouse to allow the hottest air to escape. The ridge vent on a lean-to greenhouse is shown in Fig. 6-1. If natural breezes are to be used to draw fresh, cool air into the greenhouse so hot air will be pushed out the ridge vent, windows are one answer. Figure 6-2 shows a lean-to greenhouse with windows and the ridge vent open. To be effective, the window area should be equal to the 60 percent of the ridge vent area. A similar benefit can be derived from side vents. These can be placed in the foundation wall—below the benches—so cool breezes won't blow directly on plants. Figure 6-3 shows foundation venting.

In a very small greenhouse, the doorway will serve to admit cooling air. A small exhaust fan at the ridge vent will aid in the transfer of heated air to the outside. Automated opening and closing of the ridge vent is very helpful. Figure 6-4 shows the control mechanism for an automated vent. It is a small, electric motor that drives the grooved blades that control the amount the vent is open. These are shown in Fig. 6-5. Remember to screen doorways and vent openings to prevent insects from entering the greenhouse.

When vents are not feasible to build in a greenhouse, as with plastic film construction, then the answer is to use fans. Intake fans,

Fig. 6-2. With windows and ridge vent open, this lean-to greenhouse is cooled and ventilated naturally.

Fig. 6-3. This vent in the foundation wall allows cool air in without chilling blasts blowing directly on plants.

Fig. 6-4. A small, electric motor automatically controls the opening and closing of a greenhouse ridge vent.

exhaust fans, and circulation fans all have places in venting the greenhouse. The most important of these is the exhaust fan. It draws the superheated air out of the summer greenhouse. The fans will have to be powerful enough to completely change the inside air about 150 times on a warm day. Always choose a fan system for the very hottest weather possible in your area. The exhaust fans are located near the roof ridge (see Fig. 6-6).

For the smaller home greenhouse, a reversing fan can be located in the side to take air in or exhaust air as necessary. Such a

Fig. 6-5. The grooved blades are used to provide precise control of the amount a ridge vent is open.

fan is shown in Fig. 6-7 in an attached, even-span greenhouse. It is wisest for exhaust fans to have thermostatic, automated controls. Heat build-up can be very dangerous in a greenhouse.

The intake-only fans are located in the lower third of the side of a greenhouse. These could be over jalousie window openings that can admit cool air without turning on the fans on breezy days. All the fan openings need to be properly screened.

The circulating fan is placed below the ridge area, but not too close to plants. The purpose is to move air about. This is an aid to preventing disease and fungus growth.

Fig. 6-6. Exhaust fans, mounted near the roof ridge, pull the hottest air out of a greenhouse in summer, Such fan openings should always be screened to prevent insects from entering.

Fig. 6-7. For the home greenhouse, a small reversing fan, mounted in a sidewall, can do a good job for both cooling and ventilation.

83

The right combination of vents and fans depends on the individual greenhouse and where it is built. To test the air currents and air flow in your greenhouse, place smoldering wood or rope in a couple of cans. Put these in the greenhouse and open and close the vents; turn the fans on and off. You will know where the currents are and if they are weak or strong. The air flow currents for a greenhouse using side and ridge vents is shown in Fig. 6-8. The current flow for a greenhouse using fans is shown in Fig. 6-9.

HEATING

The most expensive and crucial factor in the greenhouse climate is heating. All areas of our country have some below-freezing weather that the plants in the greenhouse must be protected against. The cost of heating will be the highest item on your greenhouse maintenance list. In planning for the type of capacity heating system you will need, be sure to take two factors into account. One factor is the coldest possible temperature your area might experience and the other is any future expansion of your greenhouse. In this way, you will be sure to have adequate heating now and in the years ahead.

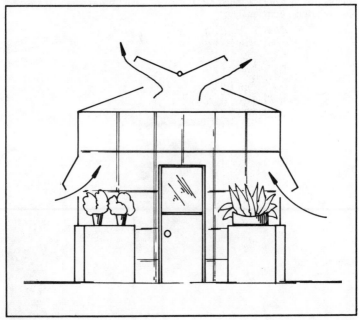

Fig. 6-8. This is the way air currents flow in a greenhouse that uses side and ridge vents.

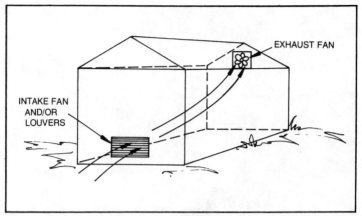

Fig. 6-9. The air flow pattern for a greenhouse using fans for ventilation.

The first thing to do when planning for heat is to figure how much you will need. This is done by calculating the British thermal units, or Btu, your greenhouse requires. You can ask a heating contractor to advise you, but it is possible to do the calculations yourself. You will need two numbers. One is the greatest temperature difference possible between the outside temperature and the temperature you want to maintain in your greenhouse. The other number is the square feet of exposed glass in your greenhouse. Let's look at an example.

The coldest temperature for your area = $-15°$
Your greenhouse should be = $+65°$
Temperature difference = $80°$
Your greenhouse has 1000 square feet of glass surface
Temperature difference × square feet × 1.2 = number of Btu required

$$80 \times 1000 \times 1.2 = 96,000 \text{ Btu}$$

How can you reduce the number of Btu required? There are three ways. One is to reduce the temperature of your greenhouse. Do your plants really need to be at 65°? Many houseplants will do fine at 50°. If you do the above calculation with a greenhouse temperature of 50°, the Btu required drops to 78,000. How about reducing the glass area? Consider a foundation wall as high as the benches. What about a slightly smaller model? If you reduce the square footage from 1000 to 750, the same calculation gives you 72,000 Btu. Use an insulating layer of plastic film inside your glass area. This layer is shown in Fig. 6-10. The plastic layer creates a dead air space between itself and the glass that has good insulating

Fig. 6-10. It is possible to insulate a greenhouse. Here a layer of film plastic is secured beneath the glass. The dead-air space created by it cuts down on heat loss to the outside.

ability. Using this or a double pane (more costly), will reduce the heat factor from 1.2 to 0.8. Substituting above, the required Btu is now 64,000. By combining all the heat reducing possibilities—lower temperature, less glass area, and insulating plastic film—the new answer is 39,000 Btu. This is less than half the original number! Use a sharp pencil and clever building techniques and your heat bills will be well within your budget.

Once you have decided how much heat you will need, the next decision is how the heat is to be supplied. There are a variety of alternatives. Factors in this decision are the size and location of the greenhouse and cost and availability of fuels.

First, consider the small, attached greenhouse. The simplest method in this case is to extend the home heating system. If windows or doors open into the greenhouse, there might be sufficient heat flowing in to handle the load. Figure 6-11 shows a home's double doors and the framework where a small lean-to greenhouse will be attached. A slightly more sophisticated approach is shown in Fig. 6-12. An extra duct has been run from the furnace to an opening in the house's foundation where a large lean-to greenhouse is

Fig. 6-11. The small greenhouse that will be built over these double doors can be heated simply by keeping the doors open.

Fig. 6-12. An extra duct from the home's furnace will blow heated air into the bottom of an attached greenhouse.

attached. The owner reports this is sufficient to keep his greenhouse at 40° or higher in the coldest weather. This is warm enough for the plants he raises. Always check with a competent heating contractor before extending the home heating system. Many systems are simply not adequate for the job no matter how small. Extra equipment will be needed. If you do extend the house's hot air system, be sure the discharge duct is below the benches and well away from any plants. Also remember that this air is very dry and additional humidity will be needed.

A space heater or soil cable heat can do the job in a small greenhouse when extending the home heat isn't possible. The best space heater for a small job is electric. If more power is needed, consider bottled gas, kerosene, or light fuel oil for power. Coleman, Mayflower, and Duo-Therm are some of the better makers of space heaters. When installing, make sure the chimney is high enough to insure an adequate draft. Also be sure a ridge vent left open will not extinquish the pilot light with its downdraft. No-vent and Saf-Aire are two brands of heaters where the gas is burned in a sealed chamber and no chimney is required. Two small heaters will probably do a better job than one large one. They should be placed opposite each other so the airstreams will meet, circulate upward and around to the place of origin. If you use one heater, place it under the bench opposite the door to help create a circular motion of air.

For larger heating requirements, there are three choices: hot water, steam, or hot air. Hot water provides safe, even heat that is non-drying. The boiler is located out of the greenhouse and the water is circulated through finned tubing as shown in Fig. 6-13. It is important that this tubing be located low on the foundation wall and away from the wall so that heat can radiate from all sides of the tubing. Circulation of the heated air can be aided with a small fan. Steam heat is excellent, but it is rarely seen in a home installation today. Steam boilers require expert installation to insure proper circulation of the water. Steam heat is efficient and faster than hot water. There are water-heated systems that hang from the greenhouse roof and eliminate the need for piping. The units heat their own water and blow the air warmed over the hot water coils down and horizontally for even distribution.

Hot air systems are the most popular for the home greenhouse. They do not need costly boilers and piping. Most homeowners are familiar with how they work because of the resemblance to their house heating system. Be very sure to add the extra humidity needed when you use a hot-air system.

Fig. 6-13. When a greenhouse is heated by hot water, the finned tubing will aid in distributing the heat.

Radiant type heaters are not usable in a greenhouse. They heat objects directly in line with their rays, but do not heat the air itself.

Consider an alarm system for when the temperature in your greenhouse reaches a dangerous low. You can install a back-up heating system to use when normal power fails if your plants are delicate and valuable. Have an electric heater powered by a generator for your standby unit. A hot-water system could have a manual pump for gravity feed in case of an emergency.

Use a good thermostat, centrally located out of the direct rays of the sun. Consider a thermostat with the contact points sealed in mercury tubes. These are moisture proof, dust proof, and dirt proof and there is no danger that the points will corrode or oxidize.

COOLING

It is not usually a problem to keep a greenhouse at a low enough temperature in the summer heat. Two climate control features, ventilation and shading, do much of the job of lowering the temperature. However, if your area has very hot, dry summer weather or you are growing plants that need cool conditions, there is a way to automatically cool off your greenhouse.

You can use an evaporative cooler. This is not like a home air conditioner; that would be totally unsuitable for plants. The evaporative cooler draws air across a dense filter pad that is continually moistened with cold water. There are two types of setups that provide evaporative cooling.

One type has the moistened pad at one end of the greenhouse and a very powerful exhaust fan at the other. This is shown in Fig. 6-14. During this procedure, all other vents and louvres are closed.

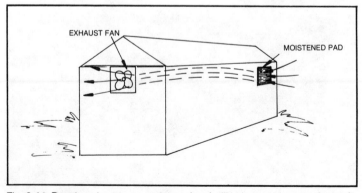

Fig. 6-14. Drawing air across a moistened pad will help to cool a greenhouse in the summer.

Fig. 6-15. This is an evaporative cooler. It is the best method to artificially cool a home greenhouse.

Only those in direct line with the air flow are used. Water drips continously on the spongy filter pad that is usually made of aspen fiber. The cooled, moistened air is drawn into the greenhouse by the exhaust fan opposite.

The home greenhouse is cooled easier by an all-in-one evaporative cooler. The unit is a rectangle about 2 feet by 3 feet. The drum-shaped fan it contains draws outside air through the moistened pad and pushes it into the greenhouse. The ridge vents are left open so the displaced heated air can escape. This type of cooling unit must be placed outside the greenhouse with an intake pipe to draw in the cooled air. Such a unit is shown in Fig. 6-15.

There is a rough formula for calculating the capacity cooler needed; it is provided by the U.S. Department of Agriculture. Calculate the total volume of your greenhouse (length × width × average height) and then multiply this figure by 1½. This answer represents the cubic feet per minute (CFM) air-capacity rating you should look for in an all-in-one evaporative cooler. This style is the preferred one for the home greenhouse. The pad-opposite-fan setup is best in large commercial greenhouses.

WATER

The water needed by the plants in a greenhouse comes in two forms. One is the actual water used to moisten the roots of the plants and the other is the water, better known as humidity, that is in the air in a greenhouse. Maintaining both at the correct levels are essential for healthy plants.

The best answer to the question, "How often should I water?" is "As often as your plants need water." Unfortunately, making the correct judgment takes a practiced eye. A simple moisture tester would be a good investment when you are a novice gardener. Do not put your plants on a watering schedule. "Every third day I will give them a thorough watering."

A plant's water requirements will vary from day to day as the temperature, light and ventilation varies. As the temperature increases, so will a plant's need for water. If there is strong ventilation, the air currents will cause plants to dry out faster. When it is cloudy plants use less water. Until you have developed a good eye for judging water needs, check the potting soil with your finger. It should be moist about half an inch below the surface. Consider your individual plants. A gardenia can almost never receive too much water, but a cactus must be allowed to dry out between waterings.

What are the consequences of watering mistakes? It is easy to tell if your plants are underwatered because they will wilt. This is not serious unless it occurs repeatedly and weakens the plant. Unfortunately, it is much more difficult if you are guilty of overwatering. This is the most common cause of death for houseplants. Soil becomes saturated and the plant's root system cannot "breathe." The roots begin to rot and fungus diseases take hold. A plant's soil should be thoroughly moist, not soaking wet.

Your plants can be watered via a simple watering can, a garden hose or an automated system of pipes. It is probably best to use a combination of methods. A good, large capacity water can is essential. Buy one with a long spout so individual plants anywhere in the greenhouse can be reached easily. Garden hose should be sturdy rubber or plastic and not the shoddy plastic that splits after a short period of use. Hoses should always be equipped with shower or spray water breakers to cut the force of the water. Figure 6-16 shows some watering equipment ideas.

Automatic waterers are a nice extra for the larger greenhouse or one where the owner cannot give much personal attention. A series of pipes runs around the perimeter of the greenhouse above the benches as shown in Fig. 6-17. The water comes through sprayer heads located along the pipe. A close-up of such a head is shown in Fig. 6-18. The waterer is controlled automatically by a humidistat that will turn the water on when the humidity in the

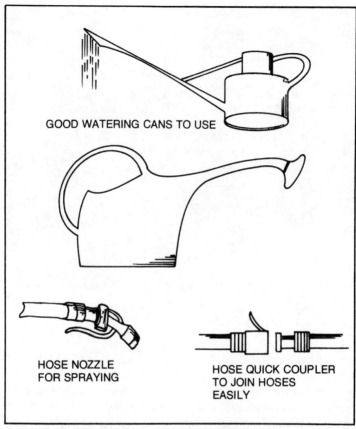

GOOD WATERING CANS TO USE

HOSE NOZZLE
FOR SPRAYING

HOSE QUICK COUPLER
TO JOIN HOSES
EASILY

Fig. 6-16. Here is some of the equipment that will make watering your greenhouse easier and faster.

greenhouse reaches a predetermined low. The waterer can also be manually operated as needed.

In winter, it would be wise to let a tub of water stand overnight to use for the next day's watering so your plants won't be chilled by the very cold water right out of the pipes. When using a hose or automatic system, arrange for a hot water access to mix with the cold.

Humidity levels are naturally tied into the watering process. Plants can be misted separately or, when watering, the benches and aisles can be watered down so they will dry off slowly during the day to supply needed humidity. The automatic watering system can be started briefly when the humidity drops. Never do any manual humidifying in the late afternoon or evening. As the sun goes down

Fig. 6-17. This greenhouse has an automatic watering system. The pipes have sprayer heads that produce a fine mist of water.

and the temperature drops, humidity comes out of the air and a heavy "dew" can form on your plants. An overnight wetness on the leaves is an invitation for insect pests and fungus. A regular humidifier can be installed to keep your greenhouse properly moist. Humidifiers come in a wide range of sizes and degrees of sophistication to fit in any greenhouse.

If humidity balances are delicate for the type of plants you are growing, then condensation might become a problem. This was partially solved by one orchid fancier with an inside gutter system. As shown in Fig. 6-19, a gutter was run a few inches below the eaves where water condensed on the glass could be trapped there and carried off before soaking the plants or the bench edges.

LIGHT AND SHADE

All plants need light to grow and thrive. Flowering plants generally need twice the light of foilage plants. Certain types of plants will do fine in diffuse, Northern light while others need plenty of full sunlight. Consider what plants you want to grow, how much light your greenhouse receives, and whether or not there is going to be a discrepancy. Generally, three hours of good morning sun will fulfill most plants' light requirements. Artificial light can be added in a shady location or plants can be chosen for less than average sun requirements. If your greenhouse receives strong sun all day, some shading will probably be necessary.

Try to build the greenhouse so the most light rays possible enter the glass at right angles. That way the fullest spectrum of the sun's rays enter. As light rays move from right angles to parallel with the glass, more of them will be reflected. Remember to keep the glass of your greenhouse clean. Algae and dust can reduce the amount of light entering by as much as 50 percent. To judge if extra

Fig. 6-18. This is one of many water-spraying heads that is located on the automatic watering system of a greenhouse.

INTERIOR GUTTER

Fig. 6-19. The problem of interior condensation was solved with a gutter on the inside wall of the greenhouse.

light is needed, use a photographer's light meter. Take a light reading outside on a cloudless summer day. Then go into your greenhouse and take another reading. The outside reading will be the control figure representing the maximum amount of light available. The inside figure will show what is actually reaching your plants. If the numbers are considerably different, you might want to consider the addition of artificial light.

Artificial light can be in the form of incandesent or fluorescent lighting. Fluorescent lighting gives more light per watt and does not give off the drying heat of incandesent light. However, a combination of the two will give light that is the closest to full sunlight. The recommended ratio of light is 1:3, incandesent to fluorescent. It is a good idea to have adequate lighting in your greenhouse even if it is used only occasionally. There will undoubtedly be times you will want to work in your greenhouse after dark or show it off to evening visitors.

When your greenhouse receives full sun the entire day, your problem will be too much light and some shading is advisable. Heat will build up and present a real problem under a full day of summer sun. This is especially true of the hot afternoon sun. There are several shading methods available. However, be cautious about overshading. Plants will become long and leggy as they stretch out seeking more light.

One solution to the shading problem is a "paint." This is actually a commercial shading compound that coats the glass with a translucent film. Figure 6-20 shows a greenhouse so treated. There are several commercial shading compounds on the market. If your greenhouse is plastic, be sure the solvents in the compound will not harm it. A homemade shading compound consists of 4 pounds white lead, one-half gallon of kerosene and one-eighth pint linseed oil. Apply your first coat in early spring, with a brush or sprayer, and subsequent heavier coats as the summer lengthens. Shading compounds can be washed off in the fall or allowed to wear off.

There are rolls of green vinyl sheeting that are cut to the size of the glass panes. These are applied by wetting the glass, placing the plastic sheet against it and squeegeeing out the excess water so the plastic adheres. They will remain in place until peeled off and they can be stored for future use.

Shade nets can be used on the inside or outside of the greenhouse. These are of some weather resistent, non-rotting

Fig. 6-20. This greenhouse has been painted with a shading compound. It will shade and cool the greenhouse during the hottest weather (courtesy of Paul Bosley, Jr., Bosley Garden Shop, Mentor, Ohio).

Fig. 6-21. Shade netting is tied to the exterior of a greenhouse to shade and cool the greenhouse.

material such as nylon or fiberglass. Exterior netting is shown in Fig. 6-21. Interior netting is shown in Fig. 6-22.

Roller blinds make an ideal shading method because they can be varied from day to day. They do not give the static shading of

Fig. 6-22. Shade netting is used on the interior of a lean-to greenhouse.

Fig. 6-23. Roller blinds on the interior of a greenhouse are an excellent way to shade it. They can be changed daily while the shade netting and paints are on for the entire season.

compounds or plastic sheets and they are easier to remove than netting. An example of roller blinds is seen in Fig. 6-23.

SOLAR GREENHOUSES

Solar energy is an alternative to soaring energy costs. It is not yet perfected for home heating, but it is very effective in a greenhouse where the sun's heat on all the glass surface has long had a solar effect.

The purpose of the solar greenhouse is to use only the heat of the sun for fuel and hopefully to have extra heat to supplement your home's system as well. Using it for plants is logical, but to be truly effective the energy benefits should take precedence over plant culture. The solar greenhouse can be a free-standing structure, but it is much more sensible to have it attached to your home to enjoy some cost savings on your heating bill. How it is designed and built and of what materials is not a matter of personal choice. It must be constructed to very specific standards or it will not be solar in nature.

The basic design for a solar greenhouse is shown in Fig. 6-24. It must be a lean-to style with the foundation walls and roof very well insulated. It must be oriented within 40° of true south to take full advantage of the winter sun. It must be double-glazed to hold the heat entering and protect that heat from cold winds. There must be some materials designed to hold the heat that enters—some thermal mass construction.

The lean-to design is essential so that maximum benefit is derived from the sun's heat that enters at the best angle and is stored in the thermal mass units on the far wall. In regular, even-span construction, too much of the sun's heat is dissipated. The thermal mass storage is usually containers of water stored on the back wall and a flooring of insulated rock. Air-filled containers or loose stone flooring will not work. You need substances that will hold the heat build-up and release it slowly as the night progresses. Plastic jugs or 55-gallon drums make suitable containers for the water. Styrofoam is a good choice for insulating the rock bed. The surfaces that will absorb the heat should be painted black or a very dark color. This will help them do their job. All other exposed surfaces in the greenhouse should be painted a light, reflective color.

To make use of the heat build-up in the greenhouse some method of bringing it into the home is necessary. This can be simply leaving a door or window open that connects the two or having a fan and duct work that adds the heat to the home's central heating system. An intake fan can be the best method for a modest-sized solar greenhouse. Be sure whatever openings that draw the warm air in can be tightly closed when it is very cold outside and all the heat of the day must be shut in to maintain the proper temperature overnight. It is also wise to have a thermal shutter for such nights. This should be an additional insulating layer on the inside of the glass. Styrofoam panels or an inside "storm window" of two plastic layers with a dead air space are possibilities.

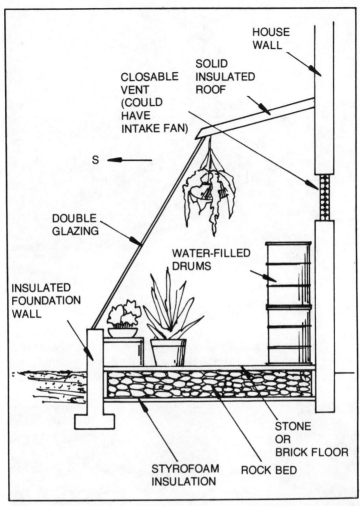

Fig. 6-24. This diagram shows the proper setup for a solar-heated greenhouse. It can save you money in heating costs rather than costing money.

Because this greenhouse is designed to build up heat, it will need shading in the summer and good ventilation to remove the heat. A really sophisticated design could carry the heat build-up from the rock floor to the home's hot water supply for use there.

THE TOTAL CLIMATE

In planning for the year around climate needs of your greenhouse, consider every possible weather condition in your

Fig. 6-25. Even when there is snow on the ground, a greenhouse is a tropical paradise.

area. Will summer hail stones endanger the glass? Are winters very windy or summers very dry? These will require a very tight-fitting structure. Are there many dark, cloudy days suggesting the need for

Fig. 6-26. A greenhouse must be kept cool and moist during the hot, dry days of summer.

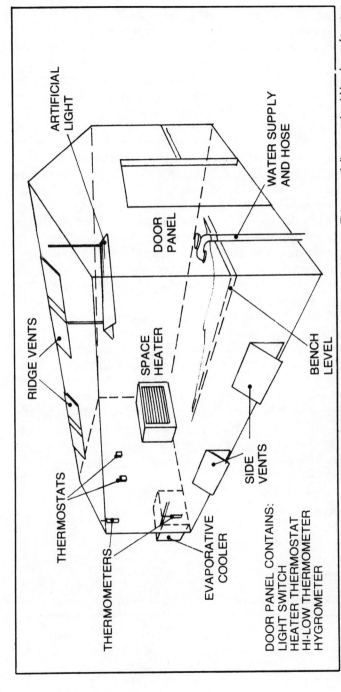

ARTIFICIAL LIGHT

RIDGE VENTS

THERMOSTATS

THERMOMETERS

EVAPORATIVE COOLER

DOOR PANEL CONTAINS:
LIGHT SWITCH
HEATER THERMOSTAT
HI-LOW THERMOMETER
HYGROMETER

SIDE VENTS

SPACE HEATER

DOOR PANEL

WATER SUPPLY AND HOSE

BENCH LEVEL

Fig. 6-27. There are many pieces of equipment necessary for climate control in a greenhouse. This type of diagram should be drawn for your greenhouse before building begins.

103

artificial light? Be sure to plan for extra capacity of the heating and cooling units in case the weather is extreme or you plan on expanding. Figure 6-25 shows a greenhouse in winter while Fig. 6-26 shows the other end of the scale—summer's sun and heat.

There are cool and warm greenhouses. These depend on the temperature ranges maintained (which in turn will depend on the type of plants grown). The cool greenhouse has a nightime low of 45-50°. The warm-climate greenhouse has a night temperature range of 60-65°. The cool-climate greenhouse is suitable for azaleas, camillias, and alpine plants. The warm-climate greenhouse is best for plants such as orchids and African Violets. The daytime temperatures will run 10-15° higher than those at night. The climate you choose will help decide what capacity heating and cooling units you will need. When the internal climate is closer to the one outside the greenhouse, fuel costs are cut. Always position several thermometers, some recording the high and low extremes, at various locations throughout the greenhouse. This will give the best picture of what the climate is really like and how close you are to the temperatures you want.

Plan for all the climate-control equipment you need and where it should be placed in the greenhouse. Certain equipment must be placed in a specific location or much energy will be wasted. Heating units must be low to the ground because warm air rises. Evaporative coolers must be set outside the wall or they will not cool. Exhaust fans need to be high at the roof ridge to expell the hottest air. Figure 6-27 shows the placement of climate control equipment in an average 9 foot × 12 foot even-span. Do this type of equipment locating on paper, before construction begins, to insure against costly mistakes.

Chapter 7

Arranging Your Greenhouse

A greenhouse is a shell in which you must plan, arrange, and install all the fixtures and equipment necessary to successful gardening. First, decide on paper how you want to arrange benches and aisles. Decide where potting and plant care chores will be done and where soil, tools, pots, and hoses will be stored.

The amount of available bench space depends on the width and design of your greenhouse. Usually benches are placed around the perimeter of the greenhouse. If it is wide enough, there could be a center bench as well. Benches are usually 36 inches wide. Aisle width can be as narrow as 18 inches, but 2 to 3 feet is much easier to work in with comfort. Arrangement for a sink and potting area within the greenhouse is a good idea. They would generally be placed in the northwest corner where the least amount of light is available for plants. The most luxurious setup uses an attached potting shed so all the greenhouse is devoted to plants. For a very small greenhouse, a potting tray—which is portable and stored under the bench area—is an excellent space saver. Various ideas for greenhouse interiors are shown in Fig. 7-1. Draw up this type of plan first and then decide on the materials and construction techniques described in the following sections.

THE WORK AREA

A permanent, well-designed work area will make all your greenhouse chores a lot more pleasant. This area might be in the greenhouse itself or close by. Here is where all plant-related activities and the equipment for them are located. Potting, sowing seeds, mixing soils, and cleaning pots are just a few of the many activities carried on in a greenhouse. The size of the area needed can be very compact with the right planning or as generous as an ample budget will allow. Every area needs to contain pots and soils, tools, and chemicals and some space to work with the plants.

For the very smallest greenhouse, a potting tray is the answer. It is built of heavy, tight-fitting lumber. It should hold up to plenty of pounding and be tightly made so soil won't build up in cracks and spaces. The sides should be about 6 inches high so soil won't spill over. Design it as a tray without legs. When you want to use it, place it on a plant bench that has been temporarily cleared or between benches bridging the aisle. When not in use, it is stored under the benches along with the pots and soils. Potting soils can be stored in large or small plastic trash cans. They can be mixed in a three-sided box with a round hole for pushing the soil to a waiting storage can below. Figure 7-2 shows the type of setup to use when space is at a premium.

When there is some extra space available, a potting bench should be installed. It should be the same width as the plant benches and 3 feet to 4 feet long. The bottom should be five-eighth inch waterproof plywood or tongue-and-groove flooring. If an opening is cut in the bottom, any debris can be brushed to a waste can waiting underneath. The chemicals cabinet, and pegboard for tools can be above the potting bench and bulkier items, such as the soil cans, can be beneath it. An adjacent sink is an excellent idea if at all possible. The best location for this work area is the northwest corner of the greenhouse. Here light for plants will be the least desirable and cabinets will not cast shadows over nearby plants. Figure 7-3 gives an example of a potting area arrangement.

For the ultimate in a greenhouse work area, the attached potting shed or work room is the thing to build. It can be a separate room designed and built right along with your greenhouse or the conversion of the room nearest the greenhouse's site. A garage makes an excellent potting room. Besides holding equipment and work areas, it can also house the utilities for the greenhouse, outdoor garden tools, furniture, and even a general workshop as well. An area 8 to 10 feet long and as wide as the greenhouse itself is ample. One side can be used for the potting bench and the other side can be used for a general work bench. Shelves, cabinets, and a large

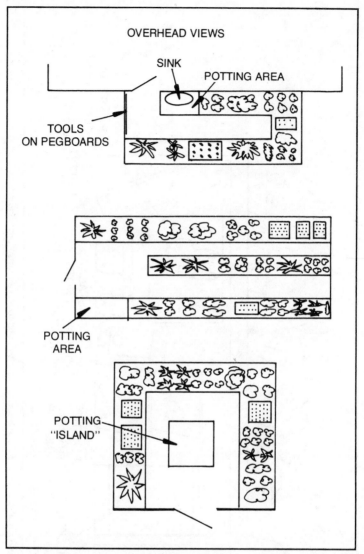

OVERHEAD VIEWS

SINK

POTTING AREA

TOOLS
ON PEGBOARDS

POTTING
AREA

POTTING
"ISLAND"

Fig. 7-1. Here are a few of the ways benches may be arranged in a greenhouse. Plan to have as much bench space as possible.

sink or stationary tub complete the picture. Figure 7-4 shows a possible arrangement for a potting shed.

If plant-related activities must take place away from the greenhouse, do try to set up a permanent, well-organized location.

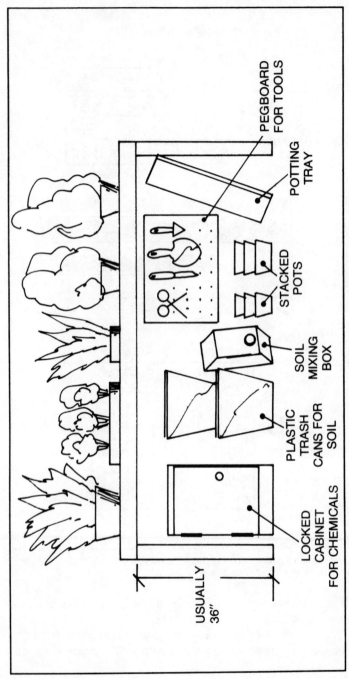

PEGBOARD
FOR TOOLS

POTTING
TRAY

STACKED
POTS

SOIL
MIXING
BOX

PLASTIC
TRASH
CANS FOR
SOIL

LOCKED
CABINET
FOR CHEMICALS

USUALLY
36"

Fig. 7-2. In a small greenhouse, the area under the benches can be used to store many gardening needs.

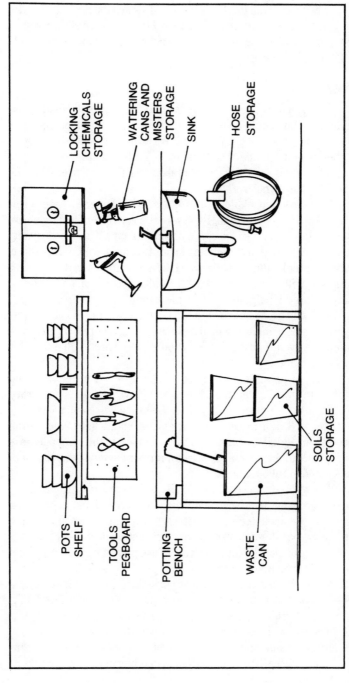

Fig. 7-3. The potting area should be arranged to neatly hold all potting needs. Make use of the space above and below the potting bench.

LOCKING
CHEMICALS
STORAGE

WATERING
CANS AND
MISTERS
STORAGE

SINK

HOSE
STORAGE

POTS
SHELF

TOOLS
PEGBOARD

POTTING
BENCH

WASTE
CAN

SOILS
STORAGE

109

Use a plastic carryall for toting tools and sprays that must be used in the greenhouse itself and then returned to your work area. Keep all your gardening needs in one area so plant care will be an enjoyable task and not a burdensome one.

TOOLS

There are a variety of tools needed in the greenhouse. Those made of metal should be quality stainless steel or galvanized steel to resist moisture. Thinly plated ones will soon rust and those of aluminum will corrode. The basic tools are listed here, but you will probably be able to think of several others that are useful for the types of plants you work with.

Everyday household tools are essential. Different size screw drivers, pliers, and a hammer are necessary. Scissors and twine are useful. Do not use scissors for pruning plants. Use good quality shears; the type that resembles small tin snips are best. A sharp, stainless steel knife is essential. Hand-size shovels, a trowel and a cultivator will be necessary. A good cultivator is made by fitting a sharp-pointed single hook into a file handle.

A plastic garden hose with the necessary spray nozzle, watering cans and a mister will handle watering chores. A separate sprayer or two for pesticides is a good idea. A water bulb is used for syringing plants.

Besides pots, you will need tampers or a potting stick and markers to complete potting chores. A stiff wire brush is necessary for cleaning clay pots and a larger bristle brush will clean the potting bench as well. For mixing up your potting soil, a set of measuring spoons, various size sieves and scoops for each of the components is necessary. Rubber gloves are useful for handling poisonous insecticides and scrubbing pots.

You will need several pots in all sizes from 2½ to 10 inches. If you are growing plants unusually small or large sizes these, extra sizes will be included. Clay pots are still the favorite of many gardeners, but the lightweight, non-breakable plastic ones are increasingly popular. It would be wise to use pots of various materials and decide which you prefer.

Keep all tools and equipment clean and in good repair. Use a light oil for tools as well as lubricating motors and ventilating equipment. Scrub up pots a few at a time so they will not pile up to a full days work. Keep a regular schedule for hosing down your greenhouse inside and out. Dispose of all out-of-date sprays and chemicals. Always practice good housekeeping in your greenhouse.

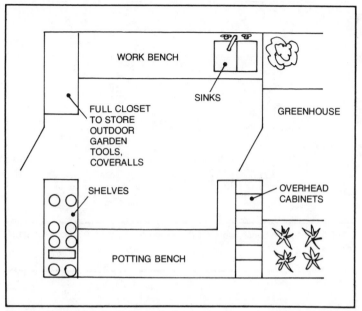

Fig. 7-4. The potting shed allows for the most room to do all greenhouse and gardening chores. Here is a possible arrangement for a potting shed.

BENCHES AND SHELVING

The bench area is where plants will be placed for growing. The more bench space you have the more plants you can grow. After your greenhouse work area has been set aside, all the remaining space should be used for benches. Plant benches are generally set at the same height as counter tops (about 36 inches or so). They can be customized if you are shorter or taller than average. The width is usually 36 inches maximum. Remember all the bench area must be within easy reach. If you have to lean and stretch to reach a plant, you might end up damaging others in the process. Center benches can be 6 feet wide because they are accessible from both sides.

There are several materials suitable for bench construction. The least expensive is wood slat or lath fence which is essentially a snow fence. It is usually available in 4 or 6 foot widths. A diagram of such a bench is shown in Fig. 7-5. For plants that need good air circulation from below, a bench of welded wire fabric is the best choice. A construction diagram of such a bench is shown in Fig. 7-6. Such a bench is shown in use for orchids in Fig. 7-7. Another good bench material is corrugated or flat asbestos sheets or *Transite*. Figure 7-8 shows two construction possibilities using asbestos

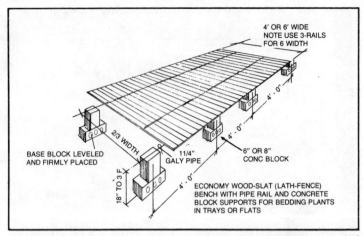

Fig. 7-5. This plant bench is the most inexpensive to build. It is constructed of wood lath.

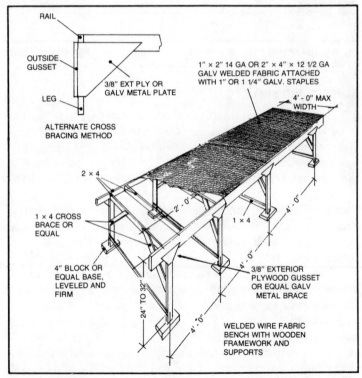

Fig. 7-6. A plant bench of welded wire fabric allows for good air circulation beneath the plants.

Fig. 7-7. This wire-fabric bench is used in a greenhouse of orchids.

sheeting. The sheeting is usually covered with loose, light stone to absorb water. Such a bench system in use is shown in Fig. 7-9.

Last, but certainly not least, is the all-wood bench. The wood should be 1 inch thick and properly treated with copper naphthenate for long life. The boards can be from 1½ to 6 inches wide and should be placed with regular spaces to allow for drainage. A basic construction diagram for a wood bench is shown in Fig. 7-10. A wood bench in use is shown in Fig. 7-11. Benches are usually designed with 6 inch sides to protect plants from being knocked to the floor and to hold any absorbent material if so desired. Be sure to leave a space between side benches and the wall.

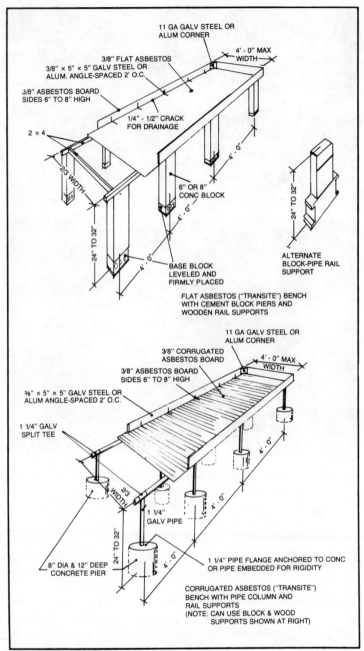

Fig. 7-8. These diagrams show the use of flat and corrugated asbestos sheeting for greenhouse benches.

Fig. 7-9. Asbestos sheeting was used for the benches in this greenhouse. The sheeting is covered with gravel before the plants are placed on it.

Bench supports can be wood, piping or block. Any material used should be treated to preserve it in the moist greenhouse atmosphere. The under-bench area can be utilized for plants if the greenhouse is of glass-to-ground construction. If not the room under benches makes an excellent storage area and is also good for starting seeds and bulbs.

Shelving can be used in the greenhouse to increase the growing room, but remember that the more shelving there is the more shade there is. Shelving should be of a material that will allow some

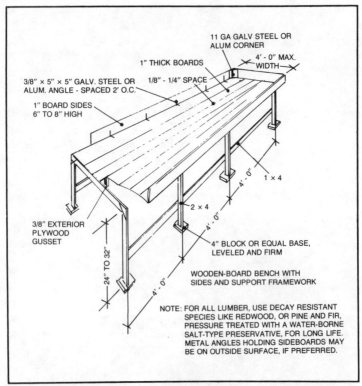

Fig. 7-10. This diagram shows the use of 1-inch thick boards for the benches. Remember to use treated, decay-resistant lumber.

Labels in figure:

11 GA GALV STEEL OR ALUM CORNER

1" THICK BOARDS

4' - 0" MAX. WIDTH

3/8" × 5" × 5" GALV. STEEL OR ALUM. ANGLE - SPACED 2' O.C.

1/8" - 1/4" SPACE

1" BOARD SIDES 6" TO 8" HIGH

1 × 4

3/8" EXTERIOR PLYWOOD GUSSET

2 × 4

4' - 0"

24" TO 32"

4" BLOCK OR EQUAL BASE, LEVELED AND FIRM

WOODEN-BOARD BENCH WITH SIDES AND SUPPORT FRAMEWORK

NOTE: FOR ALL LUMBER, USE DECAY RESISTANT SPECIES LIKE REDWOOD, OR PINE AND FIR, PRESSURE TREATED WITH A WATER-BORNE SALT-TYPE PRESERVATIVE, FOR LONG LIFE. METAL ANGLES HOLDING SIDEBOARDS MAY BE ON OUTSIDE SURFACE, IF PREFERRED.

Fig. 7-11. This bench is made of narrow boards installed lath style.

Fig. 7-12. The welded wire screen seen here is a good material for plant shelves in a greenhouse.

light through as the welded wire seen in Fig. 7-12. For most standard greenhouses, the shelf hangers and the shelving can be purchased disassembled. Plants can also be hung from the ridge. A very imaginative use for a standard wooden pallet is shown in Fig. 7-13. The pallet is hung by chains and eye hooks are inserted across the bottom. Several plants can be hung from it over the ridge area. Another idea for expanding plant room is shown in Fig. 7-14. This "plants rack" of treated lumber holds many hanging plants and also has a lower shelf for additional ones.

Fig. 7-13. An ordinary wooden pallet makes a imaginative hanger for several hanging plants.

Fig. 7-14. This "plant rack" holds hanging plants and free-standing ones as well.

FLOORS AND AISLES

The greenhouse floor is usually made up of some loose, porous material laid over the actual soil. The aisles might be of the same material or a more solid one. Rarely is an entire greenhouse floor done in a finished manner as poured concrete. It is expensive and unnecessary unless your greenhouse is a room used by the entire family. Occasionally, local building codes will require a solid floor; if not, it should be avoided. It is less expensive and more useful to have a loose floor covering that can provide growing space beneath the benches and, when hosed down, supply extra humidity.

Flooring can easily be done by the most inexperienced handyman. Simply purchase the desired material, spread, and smooth out. Some common floor coverings for greenhouses are stone or gravel, shedded bark, and sawdust. You could leave the soil uncovered and construct aisles only. The aisles can be of the same material as the floor covering, but they are usually more solid. Some good choices are concrete, brick, building blocks, stone, or wooden slats. If concrete aisles are used, they are poured when the foundation is installed. The concrete should not be finished off flat or water will puddle and make a housekeeping problem. They should be finished so that water is carried off.

Figure 7-15 shows three ways to finish concrete aisles to aid water run-off. Brick, flat stone, or block aisles are set in sand and tamped down. A brick aisle is shown in Fig. 7-16. There are a variety of patterns that brick may be laid in. Four such patterns are shown in Fig. 7-17. Aisles and flooring of the same gravel are shown

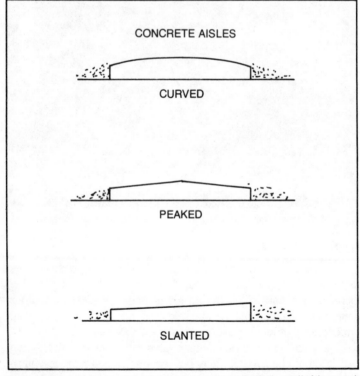

Fig. 7-15. Concrete aisles should be finished so that water will run off of them and not form puddles.

Fig. 7-16. This greenhouse aisle is made of large bricks tamped into the base soil beneath.

in Fig. 7-18. Whatever the aisles are constructed of, be sure they will not become muddy, form puddles or become slippery underfoot. A porous material can be hosed down and the moisture will slowly evaporate and help raise the humidity in the greenhouse.

Aisle ways can be as narrow as 18 inches. If possible, making them at least 2 feet wide is better. If you expect to need a wheelbar-

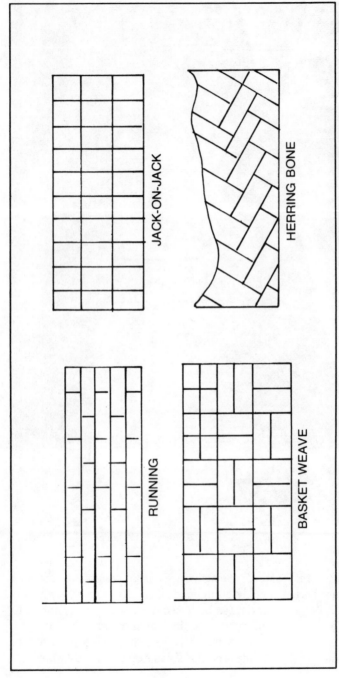

Fig. 7-17. The bricks used to make up the greenhouse aisles can be laid to form various attractive patterns. Four of the most popular patterns are shown here.

JACK-ON-JACK

HERRING BONE

RUNNING

BASKET WEAVE

Fig. 7-18. This greenhouse uses gravel for its floor and aisles. It is inexpensive and practically maintenance free.

row in your greenhouse, plan the aisles accordingly. Try to use aisle and flooring materials that blend into the appearance and natural surroundings of a greenhouse.

Chapter 8

Helping Plants Grow

A greenhouse gives plants the climate they need to thrive and bloom. The pot a plant goes in and the contents of that pot do the rest to insure success. Experienced gardeners develop personal formulas for soil mixtures, fertilizing schedules and "tricks of the trade" to insure their success. This chapter explains the basics of potting and give some good formulas to start with while you are developing your own secrets for plants everyone will admire.

SOILS

The roots of plants must be anchored in a growing medium. This medium supplies nutrients, moisture and support to the roots. Soil of the right composition is the prefered medium. A word about words! *Dirt* is what you sweep under the carpet; *soil* is what a plant grows in. The two words are not interchangeable.

Soil needs to be of the correct texture and composition for balance. If it is too loose, water will run right through it and the plant will dry out quickly. If it is too heavy, water will be held in the soil. This causes the roots to become water logged and to rot. There are three basic components to soil: clay, sands and organic matter. The ratio between the three will determine the type of soil you have and which plants will do the best in it.

The clay component gives soil its adhesion properties. However, too much clay makes soil heavy and will water-log plant roots. In a heavy clay soil, roots cannot be properly aerated and they are susceptable to fungus and rot. Most houseplants are better off in a soil that has too little clay rather than too much.

Loam is a term that usually describes a garden soil that is richer in organic components than ordinary soil. A good compost can be used to make loam. This should consist of sod to leaves and manure in a ratio of 3:1. Be sure the compost is well rotted and decomposed before use. It will contain desirable bacteria that contributes to plant growth. But there is a school of thought that recommends not chancing the introduction of a harmful bacteria by using anything from the compost pile that has not been sterilized. More about this later.

Organic matter in soil is that material that was once living and is rich in nutrients. In a decayed and well-rotted state it supplies many nutrients that nourish plants. It also retains moisture in the soil. There are several types of organic matter that I will discuss.

Leaf mold is decayed leaves. It is an excellent source of organic material. This is especially true for the leaves of oak and beech trees. Any gardener can gather leaves and compost them. Already rotted leaves can be found on the floor of the forest. Leaf mold can also be purchased commercially. *Humus* is the same as leaf mold, only finer. It can be purchased as well.

Manure is the decomposed feces of cows and horses. Today, most gardeners buy dehydrated manure that is ready to use. It has less odor and better consistency than manure composted by the gardener. However, it is possible to obtain fresh manure and use it. First it must be composted at least six months; a year is better. Fresh manure will burn plants and should never be used. Horse manure is superior to cow manure because the higher straw content gives it better moisture retention.

Peat is usually bought by the bag or bale as peat moss. Sedge peat is black in color and has a fine texture. Sphagnum peat is red-brown and much coarser; it supplies more fibrous material. Imported peat is usually sphagnum. Michigan peat and other native peats are sedge. Sphagnum peat is an excellent mulch and ground cover. It will retard the growth of weeds and give a neat appearance to a flower bed. Today, decorative bark is becoming quite popular for this purpose. For use in a soil mixture, the sedge peat is best.

Sand is needed for the opposite reason as organic matter and clay. It is light and non-absorbent to keep the soil from packing down. It is necessary to insure proper drainage. Sand to be used in a soil mixture should be builders' or masons' sand—never beach sand.

Perlite is a commercial substitute for sand. It is light, porous bits of volcanic material that never absorbs water or decomposes. I prefer it to sand in home soil mixtures and I use it to lighten up commercial potting soil which is so fine it might otherwise pack down too much.

Vermiculite is the name of another commercial product used in potting soil. It is a very lightweight material that looks like bits of cork. It absorbs and retains moisture but never packs down or rots. Therefore, it does double duty in soil; it lightens the mixture while adding moisture retention. I like to use it as a top layer in the pots of moisture-loving plants. It retards evaporation and the plants do not have to be watered as often.

There are a few other ingredients used in soil mixtures. Charcoal is supposed to prevent fungus from starting in the soil. Lime is bought as ground limestone. A small amount is useful for sweetening the soil (reducing the acidity). Some plants need an alkaline soil and some soil mixtures are too acidic and require lime for better balance. Bone meal and various commercial fertilizers are added for their nutrient content. It is a matter of personal preference as to how much of what type is used. Be sure to store these products in waterproof containers and label them carefully as to composition.

SOIL MIXTURES

Most gardeners have a special recipe for potting soil that they have developed over a period of time through trial and error. Different plants do have different soil requirements. There is not a best soil for all plants. The gardener's individual care will also influence what soil mix he has the most success with. Someone who waters with a liberal hand would do best with a loose, porous soil that does not retain moisture. Cacti and succulents need a very light, fast-draining soil while a gardenia needs an acid, moisture-holding mix. There are some hardy souls like the pothos vine that will grow in just about anything!

In general, the best soil texture for greenhouse plants is moist enough to form a solid mass when pressure is applied, but will crumble easily afterwards. "Friable" is a good word to describe this condition.

The following soil mixtures are a starting point for your greenhouse plants. Try various ones and develop your own that is tailored for your watering habits, the plants you grow, and the area you live.

■ Standard traditional mixture of equal thirds:
  1 part garden loam.
  1 part leaf mold (or other organic matter).
  1 part sharp, clean sand.
■ Mixture for extra moisture retention:
  1 part loam.
  1 part peatmoss.
  1 part leaf mold.
  1 part sand.
■ Acid mix (good for gardenias, azaleas, camiallas):
  6 parts peatmoss.
  3 part sand or perlite.
■ Commercial mixture (rich in nutrients, but too fine in texture):
  2 parts packaged potting soil.
  1 part perlite.
  A pinch of charcoal.
■ Nutrient-free mixture (use water with liquid fertilizer for every watering):
  1 part vermiculite.
  1 part perlite.

This last, nutrient-free mixture is popular with the gardener who wants to control exactly the amount and type of nutrients his plants will receive. Therefore, he mixes a liquid plant food and waters his plants and fertilizes them together in whatever program or schedule desired. This type of arrangement is popular with a more exacting gardener.

The commercial mixture blended with perlite is a favorite of mine for most common house plants. The perlite prevents the fine, packaged soil from packing down too much. Using a good quality commercial soil gives a uniformity that is hard to duplicate by home-mixed soils. It is usually rich in nutrients and gives plants a fine start without any initial fertilization needed.

There is also an alternative to using soil. This is called *hydroponics* and it means raising plants in water only. Plants are grown in water and liquid fertilizer is added. Additional water without fertilizer is added as necessary to keep the level up. Plants can be left unattended for days without hurting them with this setup. There is also the advantage of watching the complex root systems develop in the water before your eyes. This is an excellent way for children to raise plants.

STERILIZATION

Many gardeners sterilize the soil that they use for potting plants. This process rids the soil of harmful bacteria, weed seeds, and insects. It can be done with a commercial sterilizing unit, but this is not necessary for the home gardener. The kitchen stove makes a fine sterilizing unit. However, it will leave an earthy, pungent smell in the kitchen for a day or two afterwards.

Fill a shallow pan or roaster with garden soil for your home potting mixture. Cover the pan tightly with aluminum foil and then poke a few holes in it for ventilation. Bake the soil for 30 to 45 minutes at 180° F or the lowest setting on your oven. Cool completely and stir the soil before using it.

There are many gardeners who use soil taken directly from outside without treating it by sterilization. They have good results using this soil and merely pull up any weeds that appear. You can do the same thing, but you should be aware that there is a risk in doing so. If you happen to use a bad batch, disease or insects could be transmitted to your greenhouse and be troublesome to eliminate.

Almost all the commercially packaged soils and those sold by florists or nurseymen are already sterilized. This saves you the time and trouble of doing it yourself. Commercial mixtures are usually quite uniform from batch to batch so you are working with the same soil each time. Buying prepared soil might be the best idea for a small-scale greenhouse operation.

FERTILIZATION

Fertilizer (plant food) nourishes plants the same way the food we eat nourishes our bodies. Plants need nutrients to live and these nutrients are usually supplied through a program of regular fertilization.

Soils that are "rich," or high in organic components, already contain many of the nutrients a plant needs. On the other hand, perlite, vermiculite and sphagnum moss contain no nourishment for plants. Most soils lie somewhere in between; they contain some but not all of the essential nutrients. It is possible to take a soil sample to your local agricultural extention office and have it checked for nutrient content. This should only be done for a large batch of soil that will be used for many plants. It is not very sensible to bring in a sample that represents only a small amount of soil. In such cases, it is better to add fertilizer to the soil as it is used.

There are three basic plant nutrients that are supplied by commercial fertilizer. These are nitrogen, phosphorous, and potassium. A fertilizer will list these three components, in the order given, with a numerical ratio. This ratio might read 5-10-5 or 4-12-4. The numbers represent the percent of the component in the total mixture. For example, 4-12-4 means 4 percent nitrogen, 12 percent phosphorous and 4 percent potassium in the fertilizer with the balance made up of inert ingredients or filler to equal 100 percent. Often necessary trace elements, like iron or manganese, are added in minute quantities.

Nitrogen is necessary to stimulate plant growth and promote strong stems and healthy green color. A lack of nitrogen is characterized by weak spindly stems and yellow-green leaves.

Phosphorous stimulates root growth and the production of flowers and seeds. A plant that loses its lower leaves and has yellow edges on its remaining leaves indicates a lack of phosphorous.

Potassium, also known as potash, builds up disease resistance in plants. It also helps to stabilize growth and improve color and productivity. When potassium is lacking, plants have a dull and listless appearance with mottled-colored leaves.

Fertilizers come in dry bulk, soluble powder or paste, and slow-release pellets and rods. The safest and best application involves dissolving a soluble fertilizer to the proper dilution and fertilizing your plants as you water them. This gives the plants a light and uniform feeding without the risk of burning them through too much feeding. If you do apply a dry fertilizer, do so after the plant has been watered. Do not apply fertilizer to bone-dry soil. You greatly increase the chance to overfeed and damage the plant by doing so. Give a light watering first and then work a pinch of fertilizer into the soil.

The various new *slow-release fertilizers* allow one feeding to work over an extended time period. Food capsules or rods are placed in the soil and dissolve slowly and release a little food at a time. However, if the feeding seems too strong for any reason, it is difficult to undo before the alotted time is up. Food sticks can be removed and a good drenching with plain water will help wash away accumulated nutrients. With time capsules it might be necessary to repot the plant and dispose of all the old soil.

Whatever type of fertilizer you use, be sure to establish a regular feeding schedule and follow the directions for application carefully. During periods of active growth, the plant needs to be fertilized about every two weeks. I use a weak feeding solution for every watering during the late spring and through the summer months.

During the time of least natural light (the months of December and January), I do not feed the plants at all. Plants do go through cycles of growth followed by a rest period. They especially rest during cloudy weather and short winter days. Plants need sunlight to make use of the nutrients they are fed, so it is useless and sometimes harmful, to feed them during low-light conditions.

Watch your plants and their individual reactions to feeding. Try several different types of fertilizers to find what is the best for you to use and which your plants seem to respond to the best. There are plant foods designed to feed a certain type of plant like those for acid-loving gardenias and camellias. Ask other growers which fertilizers they have had the most success with. Stop feeding plants that appear to be losing vigor. Find the cause of the problem and correct it before starting to feed again. Fertilizers are an enormous help in raising healthy plants, but they must be used wisely.

POTS AND POTTING

Each of your plants will have to have an individual pot. All pots must meet certain basic requirements. First, they must have a drainage hole in the bottom to insure proper drainage and root aeration. Second, certain plants do their best in a specific type of pot. Be aware of your plants' needs. All potting containers need to be thoroughly scrubbed and sterilized between plantings. The best way to do this is to scrub the pots in a solution of bleach and water. If the weather permits, letting the cleaned pots stand out in the sun helps kill any fungus spore that might still be in tiny crevices.

The longtime first choice in greenhouse pots has been the familiar red clay. They come in a wide range of sizes and their appearance compliments any plant. Clay pots are porous. This allows them to absorb and release moisture and "breathe." This has two advantages. First, it is difficult to overwater a plant in a clay container because excess moisture is readily evaporated. This is an important point because overwatering is the number one killer of houseplants. Secondly, this moisture evaporation adds needed humidity to the air of the greenhouse where it is beneficial to all plants.

Clay pots have the disadvantage of being rather heavy once they are potted up. A whole bench of clay pots makes up a heavy load to be supported. Also, clay pots break and crack easily and this can be a nuisance. Excess salts will build up on the outside of the pots as a crusty tannish, white film. In a humid greenhouse, moss will grow on the outside of clay pots. These coverings should be scrubbed off to keep the pot porous.

In recent years, plastic pots have become very popular with greenhousemen. They are bright and attractive and come in a wide range of colors, shapes and sizes. Plastic pots are lightweight and easy to handle. They are just about indestructable and clean up quickly. The primary disadvantage is that they are completely nonporous. Any water that does not flow out the drain hole will stay in the pot until it is absorbed by the plant. This makes overwatering a very easy thing to do in a plastic pot. Be sure to check such pots carefully for moisture before adding any water. This characteristic can be a help for the gardener who has a problem watering his plants as often as they need to be. It will take fewer waterings to keep a given plant healthy in a plastic pot.

There is a third type of pot made of pressed peat. These come in small sizes and are designed for starting seeds or cuttings. When the roots begin to poke through the bottom, the plant (pot included) is transplanted to a larger pot or to the outdoors. These pots are a real help in starting delicate plants without having to handle them during transplanting. When preparing a peat pot for use, remember to wet it thoroughly, but do not soak it as you would a clay pot. They are delicate and will simply fall apart if they are too wet.

The alternative to growing each plant in an individual pot is using a flat tray or seed tray. These broad, shallow containers are best for starting seeds and cuttings. In bygone days, whole benches were turned into giant flats to raise plants. This practice is uncommon today, but smaller tray flats are still used. Because all the plants in a flat will receive the same care, it is best to raise identical plants in a flat. If you make a mistake in care, all the plants will suffer for it. Don't attempt to raise a flat of seeds or cuttings until you have some experience with that type of plant and can be confident of the care needed. The flat method is an excellent way to propagate from a large, healthy "parent" plant you own. Also, it is good for starting flowers and vegetables in the early spring that are to be set outdoors when the weather permits.

There is a procedure to follow when potting a plant. First, be sure to choose a pot of the proper size and type for the plant that will be put in it. Don't stuff a large plant into a small pot or place a little plant in a huge container hoping it will "grow into it." The plant and its pot should compliment each other. Generally, when the roots of a plant fill the pot and begin to grow out of the drainage hole, it is time

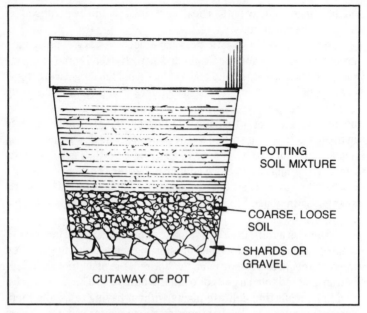

POTTING
SOIL MIXTURE

COARSE, LOOSE
SOIL

SHARDS OR
GRAVEL

CUTAWAY OF POT

Fig. 8-1. These layers in a pot help roots to breathe and prevent waterlogging.

for a new pot that is one or two sizes bigger than the current one. Some plants, like African violets, do better when they are somewhat rootbound. Others need plenty of growing room. Even if you are doing everything else right, the wrong pot can greatly hinder the plant's health and growth.

A pot's drainage hole must be kept open to insure proper drainage for the plant. This is done by placing a few pieces of broken clay pottery, known as *shards,* in the bottom. Some pebbles or coarse gravel could also be used. For a small pot with fine soil, a little piece of screening could be used. Above this goes a layer of extra-coarse potting medium. Adding something for the extra coarseness will help the roots develop freely and not become waterlogged. Then the plant with its own root ball and any additional potting soil are placed in the pot. The soil is gently, but firmly, tamped down around the plant. Water the plant thoroughly, but do not fertilize it for a few weeks. Give the plant some time to adjust after the shock of transplanting. See Fig. 8-1 for a diagram of the proper "layers" in a potted container.

Chapter 9

What to Grow

When your new greenhouse is complete and you are ready to fill it with lovely plants, you are faced with a question. What plants will you grow? This might seem a little silly because you must have quite an interest in plants to bother with a greenhouse in the first place. But when you are confronted with all that new growing area, it is sometimes difficult to decide just what you want to grow. Without a plan and some specific goals, you could find yourself rather dissatisfied with your greenhouse. You might have plants that require very different care and cause confusion and trouble. You might have chosen some warm-climate plants for your cool-temperature greenhouse and they are not doing well. You might find it hard to fill all the new space you have or that the space has filled up too quickly without leaving space for some special favorites you wanted to cultivate. All this confusion can be avoided if you plan in advance just what you want to grown.

Consider the reason you wanted your greenhouse in the first place. Is it going to be a pleasant garden room for family and friends or a place for the serious cultivation of your prize orchids? Do you want it to cut the family food bill by raising fresh produce the year around or would you rather feed your soul with fresh flowers the whole year? Is your greenhouse a family project where everyone's favorites will grow or your private green thumb center? Consider what you will grow before the first plant is ever set inside.

Many greenhouses are used to grow just one type or family of plants. By survey, the spectacular orchid is the most popular greenhouse plant grown in this country. A close second is the ever popular African violet. Other plants popular in the single plant greenhouse are cacti, bromeliads or alpine plants. This could be the best idea for you if you are very fond of a particular plant. If you want your greenhouse to generate some income, you could raise cut flowers or starter plants to sell. Fresh vegetables and herbs are available the year around if you want to raise them in your greenhouse. If you really aren't sure what to concentrate on, don't worry about it. Many home greenhouses are used for a pleasant mix of plants that vary with the seasons and the interests of the owner. In the beginning, try a few different types and don't fill your greenhouse to capacity. Give yourself time to get used to maintaining it and explore its possibilities. Experiment with a wide range of plants as you allow your skills and tastes to develop. Always remember that your greenhouse is suppose to be a pleasure and a joy; don't let it become drudgery. Some of the favorite plant families for greenhouse cultivation are discussed in this chapter. They will help give you ideas and whet your appetite for further study and actual cultivation. Consider them all and begin with those that appeal to you the most.

BULBS: TENDER AND HARDY

Tender and hardy bulbs are so classified according to the care they need. Hardy bulbs require a period of cold darkness to form adequate roots before any foliage grows. Cold—below freezing—is fine for them. Tender bulbs cannot survive in cold or subfreezing temperatures. Therefore, they are the "tender" ones. Hardy bulbs are true bulbs. They have fleshy scales that protect the bud at the base. An embryo flower forms inside the bulb which is encased in a very thin, dry skin. Many of the tender bulbs are not true bulbs at all. They grow from corms, rhizomes, tubers, fleshy roots or some other form of underground stem. All are handled in much the same way and hence, are classified together.

I will discuss the hardy bulbs first. With them, you can fill a greenhouse with bright and beautiful flowers throughout the winter. These are the bulbs that become daffodils, tulips, and fragrant hyacinths. When planted on a staggered scheduled, it is possible to have continuous blooming for weeks. Most hardy bulbs are the spring-flowering kind after a period of winter cold to enable the roots to form. You must duplicate these conditions to *force* or coax the bulb into early blooming.

Forcing simply means supplying the proper conditions of winter cold that will enable the bulbs to form the necessary roots and then bringing them into warm temperatures where they will bloom. These blooms will mature weeks or months before they would if grown "naturally" outside. They must be kept covered in a cold, dark location for 8 to 12 weeks. The exact amount of time depends on the variety of bulb and the specific rooting conditions. When they have formed a pot full of roots and the shoots are sprouting, they are ready for warmer temperatures. Generally, the best temperature for rooting is between 40° and 50° F. If they are kept any colder, it will take longer for the roots to form. If bulbs are kept warmer than this, roots will not grow. Pots of bulbs can be set outside in a trench about 1 foot deep and covered with straw, leaves, or salt hay. They may also be set in a cellar, garage, or shed. Be sure to keep them covered in some manner so they stay in darkness. Water the bulbs very thoroughly when they are first set out. Check them periodically so they do not dry out. The best potting mixture for hardy bulbs is:

- 2 parts rich loam.
- 1 part peatmoss or leaf mold.
- 1 part sharp sand or perlite.

Bulbs contain their own food supply for the first year of bloom and do not need any special additives. Some experts recommend the addition of one-half cup of bone meal per pail of potting mixture.

Pot your hardy bulbs in regular pots, shallow bulb-pans that are wider than they are deep, or 4-inch deep flats. Be sure to fill the pot with as many bulbs as possible for a fuller effect when in flower. Use at least three to five of the larger bulbs and about 10 of the little bulb types for a good display. Place a layer of shards or gravel across the bottom of the pot with a pinch of charcoal to "sweeten" it. Add soil mixture and judge the depth so the bulbs can be placed with their tips at the top of the pot. Place soil around the bulbs; don't force them into the potting mixture because they might be damaged. Label the pots to keep track of varieties and colors. You might want to force them in a certain order. Don't skimp when buying bulbs to force; always buy the best quality. The work to prepare bulbs to bloom will be wasted on cheap, "bargain" bulbs with few blooms.

The small hardy bulbs for forcing include the crocus, snowdrop, muscari (grape hyacinth), and scilla. These do best if planted six to 10 in a pot. They should be kept cool throughout the blooming period. They can be planted in a very shallow pot with just enough soil to cover the corms. After the necessary rooting period, they will bloom very quickly. They are usually the earliest to bloom.

Hyacinths are especially desirable to force because of their wonderful fragrance and the fact that they are about the only hardy bulb to come in blue. Buy larger-sized ones and place them close together in the pot. Their grass-like foilage allows them to form a very compact display. They will have to be staked once they bloom because the flower stalks are so heavy. They usually bloom about three to four weeks after being brought in from the cold.

The iris family has several good bulb varieties for blooming. These include the Dutch, hybrid Wedgewood and Spanish iris. These bulbs should be potted early, preferably in September, to allow plenty of time for the roots to form before forcing. They need about 10 to 12 weeks for root formation.

Daffodils are one member of the narcissus family that are classified as hardy. Others will be discussed under the tender bulbs. Daffodils do best planted three to five in a 6-inch pot. They need about eight weeks of cold for root development. Once brought into warm temperatures, they will bloom in about three weeks. There are many varieties used for forcing. The most common in the Trumpet type. But consider others if you are fond of these bright harbingers of spring.

Tulips present the largest variety of types to force among the hardy bulbs. These include Early (single and double), Breeder, Cottage and Darwin. The early tulips are the easiest and quickest bloomers. Check with your supplier for which bulbs do best; some force much better than others. Plant them so the tips of the bulbs are slightly below the soil level. Be sure that there is at least a 3-inch shoot growing from the bulbs before bringing them in to force. There is a little trick to raising a pot of full, symmetrical tulips. Plant the bulbs with the flat sides to the outside of the pot. This side is where the first large leaf will develop. With all these leaves drooping gracefully outward as the tulips bloom, the whole pot will look very elegant and decorative from any angle.

Once a hardy bulb has been forced, it should not be forced a second time. Either discard the bulb or plant it outdoors after all danger of frost has past. Once outdoors, the bulb needs water and sunlight until the foilage has fully developed and begun to wither. This will insure a bloom for the next year.

Tender and half-hardy bulbs might need a short period of cool temperatures to set their root growth, but they cannot tolerate the cold and subfreezing temperatures of the hardy bulbs. The tender "bulbs" include many types of underground stems like rhizomes, corms, tubers and fleshy roots. In most cases, all of these tender bulb varieties are handled in the same manner and can be potted up and enjoyed at any time of the year. The fact that they can be started immediately makes them easy to plan for any time of the year. Another plus is the wide variety of plant and flower types among the tender bulbs. There is everything from the huge blossoms of the amaryllis to the delicate freesia. Pot tender bulbs in the same mixture used for hardy bulbs:

- 2 parts garden loam.
- 1 part peatmoss.
- 1 part sharp sand or perlite.
- A pinch of bone meal.

Screening the potting mixture is helpful so the roots will form without obstruction. Pot in the same manner as for hardy bulbs with a bottom layer of gravel to aid drainage. Water thoroughly after potting and place the pot under the greenhouse bench for two weeks. Then move the pot out into good light. Proper watering is very important. After the initial soaking, water lightly until the foliage is well started. Then increase the water as the bulb matures and the blooming begins.

There are several types of tender bulbs that do not need soil at all. Simply set the bulbs in a shallow container of pebbles and fill with water. The pebbles are used to support the bulbs which should protude about halfway above the pebble line. Keep the container filled with water and there will be plenty of moisture for a well-developed root system. A piece of charcoal will help to sweeten the pot. Paperwhite narcissus and French-Roman hyacinths do very well when raised in this manner.

After blooming, the tender bulbs vary considerably in the kind of care they require. Some bloom almost all year and some have evergreen foliage. Others require a period of dormancy. None can be set outside for additional blooming except in the deep South. Refer to a plant care book or your local bulb supplier for specific care of your tender bulbs.

The following list of plants offers some suggestions for you to raise. They are among the most popular families of tender bulbs. Do not try more than two or three types your first year (along with a few hardy bulbs). Try different ones over the next few years while deciding if you want tender bulbs as part of your regular greenhouse plants.

Achimenes (magic-flower)
Agapanthus (lily-of-the-Nile)
Alstroemeria (Peruvian lily)
Anemone
Begonia, tuberous
Clivia (Kafir-lily)
Cyclamen
Dahlia
Eucharis (Amazon-lily)
Freesia
Gladiolus
Gloriosa
Haemanthus (blood-lily)
Hippeastrum (amaryllis)
Iris
Ixia
Lachenalia (cape cowslip)
Lilium
Nerine (Guernsey-lily)
Oxalis
Ranunculus
Sinningia (gloxinia)
Tritonia
Tulbaghia
Vallota (Scarborough lily)
Zantedeschia (calla-lily)

VEGETABLES AND HERBS

Even the most ardent flower lover is likely to have a few tomato plants tucked away somewhere. It is enjoyable to raise food for your family and it is practical to be able to cut food costs with home-grown produce. Just about any plant raised in your garden can be raised in your greenhouse if you want to devote sufficient room for it. Some vegetables do best in a cool climate greenhouse while others need a warm climate to thrive. It is also possible to raise herbs and even dwarf fruit trees. For limited space, there are several types of miniature and dwarf vegetable plants so that even a small greenhouse can be a source of fresh vegetables for your family. Let's look at some specific possibilities.

Tomatoes are probably the number one favorite plant for garden and greenhouse alike. To grow them, you will need a warm-climate greenhouse. It is best to sow the seeds in July. The plants need to have fruit well set on the vine before the short days of fall. Plant on a staggered scheduled to insure tomatoes throughout the winter. Only a few plants will be necessary. Grow them to a single stem that is staked for support. For good tomatoes that take up less space, consider the "Patio" varieties that were especially developed for raising in tubs in a confined area. For very little space, there is the Tiny Tim and other types of cherry tomatoes. These grow to be about 15 inches tall with a fine-flavored fruit only three-fourths of an inch across.

Lettuce is a good companion for the tomatoes. Bibb lettuce requires the same 60° F temperature. Sow it about every two weeks beginning the first of September. There are head and loose-leaf varieties that do well. Among these are Bibb Forcing, Burpee Bibb, Butter King and Grand Rapids Forcing. For those who want a minicrop, there is Tom Thumb with a crisp, sweet head about the size of a tennis ball.

Carrots grown in a greenhouse should be of the smaller size because greenhouse bench will not have sufficient depth for an 8-inch root. Burpee's Goldinhart and Chantenay varieties will mature at 5½ inches in length. Little Finger carrots are only 3 inches long when ready for harvest and they mature in 60 days. To use larger varieties, they should be harvested when half-mature. For the best growth when forcing in winter, carrots need a temperature of 50° F and bottom heat (if possible).

Cucumbers need lots of room and warm temperatures to grow. The best plan might be to start them early and let them mature inside faster than they would if outdoors. Use the wall or ridge supports to train your cucumbers and other vining plants.

It is even possible to grow watermelons and sweet corn in your greenhouse. The New Hampshire Midget is a small, tasty variety of watermelon. For sweet corn, try Golden Midget with ears 4 inches in length and a plant just 2½ feet tall. This corn will be ready for harvesting 60 days after planting.

There are varieties of dwarf fruit trees available for every popular fruit. Some of these will mature at 6 feet and can be further reduced in size if kept in tubs. It will take a good-sized greenhouse to accommodate even the smallest tree, but it is possible. Check with major fruit tree suppliers like Stark Brothers.

All fruits and vegetables will need artificial pollination because you will not have any insects in your greenhouse to do the job. This can be accomplished by using a camel's-hair brush, gently shaking the plant, or running a fan. Using a brush is the most reliable method. Be sure to do something for pollination or you will have no harvest for your efforts.

Be very careful when treating your vegetable greenhouse plants for pests. Many pesticides are not to be used on food plants. Read the label carefully and check with your local garden center and agricultural extension office. If you are having trouble with pests, don't try to raise any edible plants until the problem is completely solved. It is very disheartening to raise a crop you will not be able to eat.

Herbs in your greenhouse are a good addition or alternative to a crop of vegetables. The plants are generally small and easy to raise. They add a pleasant fragrance and have delicate blossoms. They add an exciting dimension to cooking. Every cook uses and enjoys some herbs. Being able to pick then fresh and to dry sweet bunches for using and gift-giving is a real treat. Any greenhouse can accommodate herbs even if there is no room for larger vegetable plants. Let's look at a few.

Most herbs do well under glass with moderate temperatures and rich, well-drained soil. Be sure to keep them clean with syringing because they will be used for eating. Herbs are available through larger garden centers and by mail order as both seeds and started plants. Begin with a few that you cook with now and add others as you want to try them out in your cooking. They can be dried for ornamentation and gift-giving if you do not want to cook with a certain one. Also, herbed vinegars are delightful to make, enjoy, and give. The popular herbs, shown in Table 9-1, will give you a good start in gardening and cooking:

FAVORITE PLANT FAMILIES

At the beginning of this chapter, I discuss the popularity of devoting an entire greenhouse to one type of plant. Many people enjoy becoming an expert on their favorite plant and raising as many varieties as possible. It can be the most rewarding and challenging way to increase your knowledge and fill your greenhouse. Some plant lovers specialize from the onset and others try many types of plants and gradually concentrate on the one they like best. There are so very many plants in this world and they are all beautiful in their own way. It is possible to achieve great satisfaction as a grower of many varieties and as a grower of one special family. This section will briefly cover several of the most popular plant families. Go to your library and to successful growers to get more information. A separate book could be written for each of them. Because

Table 9-1. Popular Herbs.

Name	Plant Type	Uses
Basil	Annual	Leaves in soups, meats, salads and omelets
Caraway	Annual/biennial	Seeds in breads, cakes and cheese
Dill	Annual/biennial	Leaves to flavor pickles, sauces
Fennel	Perennial	Dried leaves for fish, fresh for garnishes
Rosemary	Hardy evergreen	Leaves in soup, ham-loaf, white vegetables
Summer Savory	Annual	Leaves in consomme, soup, eggs
Sweet Marjoram	Annual	Leaves in beef broth, over fried chicken or fish
Thyme	Evergreen	Leaves - all seasonings

these are such favorites with gardeners, consider trying a few plants from each group at some time in your gardening career so you won't have to wonder what you have missed out on. This overview is just enough to whet your appetite for more knowledge and growing experience.

BEGONIAS

The begonia family is a plant lover's dream come true. There is great beauty and diversity among begonias, yet they are easy-care plants anyone can enjoy. Such a combination is hard to pass up. The great diversity of begonias comes from the various root types they have. There are tubers, rhizomes, and fibrous-rooted types. They are small, windowsill-sized and very large as well. The flowers come in every color but blue. I will discuss begonias according to their root and stem type rather than foliage or flower form.

Tuberous begonias give a glorious display of flowers through the summer. The flowers ressemble carnations, roses and camellias, and can grow to 8 inches across with proper cultivation. Start the tubers in early spring when the first tiny pink shoots have appeared. Cover it completely with only the shoot tips visible. Use a mixture of leaf mold and sand or milled sphagnum moss to start the tubers and transplant them to a fibrous, well-drained potting soil after the roots are well established. Keep them moist and place them in filtered sunlight; too much light burns the blossoms and too little light makes the plant leggy. Don't let water collect in the depression of the tuber where the stem grows. This causes the tuber to rot. Pinch off the first few buds to insure a strong root system so the blooms will continue, uninterrupted, throughout the summer.

When the plants start dying off in the fall, withhold water and allow the pots to dry out completely. Remove all the roots and dead foliage and store the tubers at 40 to 50° F in dry sphagnum moss or dry sand. Continue this storage until new pink shoots appear and then start the process all over again.

Pendent tuberous begonias are ideal for hanging baskets. This variety comes in several colors and in single and double flowers. Start the tubers in January using the same procedure as for the regular tuberous begonias. They will be ready for transplanting to a basket in about four weeks. Space them evenly using three or more tubers (depending on the size of the basket). Pot in a mixture of 3 parts leaf mold, 1 part well-rotted manure, and 1 part sharp sand. They should bloom through the summer in filtered sunlight. When they die off, cut them back and store in the same manner as the other tubers.

The beautiful Rex begonias grow from rhizomes. These are thick stems from which the roots and foliage grow. The rhizome creeps on top of the soil rather than through it like roots. These begonias bloom through the spring in filtered sunlight. They will become inactive during the short days of winter or die back completely, but they will be blooming again in the spring.

The begonias with regular fibrous roots are the ever-popular wax begonias. These grow easily in a mixture of 3 parts good soil with 1 part peatmoss. They do well under varied conditions and can be cut back for a fresh start at any time. Three common types are the sprawly angelwing, small-leaved branching, and the hirsute (hairy) begonia. All can be easily propagated anytime by taking a stem cutting and rooting it in water. Plants can be pinched back to keep them more compact and encourage blooming. All types of begonias will reward you very well for the minimum care that they need.

BROMELIADS

If you want visitors to your greenhouse to think you went to Mars, or at least the Amazon jungle, to find your plants, try Bromeliads. This plant family contains more than 40 genera and 1000 species. All are native to the tropics in the Western Hemisphere and most are very exotic looking with tough, spikey leaves that form graceful arches. Two bromeliads known to most people are Spanish moss and the pineapple.

Most plants in this family are tree dwellers, but they are not parasites. They are true epiphytes or "air plants" that use the rough bark of trees to anchor their roots. Some can grow on bare rocks and a few grow in jungle soil beneath the trees. In the greenhouse, they need warm temperatures (not less than 60° F at night). Most cannot tolerate full sun so shading is necessary. They may be potted in peat or sphagnum moss, charcoal pieces, Osmunda fiber, or ground fir bark. The latter two are potting material for orchids. Many bromeliads need not be potted at all. They may be fastened to chunks of bark and hung in the greenhouse.

Most members of this family grow in a rosette that forms a water-tight vase at the center of the plant (hence the common name vase plant). In nature, the "vase" collects and stores water for the plant's use. In home culture, this vase should be filled with enough water so some runs over onto the potting material. Leaves like to be misted or syringed regularily. They are hardy plants that can withstand neglect and adverse conditions. They will grow to a very large size in many cases and form an intriguing combination of tough, often spiney leaves, that are very graceful and delicate looking.

The simplest way to raise your first bromeliad is to lop off the top of a pineapple. Let it dry for a day or two and then root it in sand. When ready, pot it a rich, humus soil. It grows easily and becomes very full and green. Another interesting plant for your greenhouse is the common Spanish moss of the deep South. A few strands hung in a warm, moist greenhouse will grow long and luxuriant.

Bromeliads can be propagated from the offsets that start at the base of the parent plant. These often appear after a blooming period. Root them in moist vermiculite or sphagnum moss. Keep them in very warm temperatures (75° to 85° F), high humidity, and shade. Rooting is usually accomplished quickly. The parent plant will often die after flowering and producing offsets. They can also be grown readily from seeds. These can be sown on moist blotting paper and kept covered during germination.

Bromeliads are interesting and dependable plants to use in a home greenhouse. They do very well when grown with orchids; both need warm, moist conditions. If you have a warm-climate greenhouse, try a few bromeliads and enjoy the comments from startled visitors.

CACTI AND SUCCULENTS

This family of unusual looking, easy-care plants are an attractive addition to your greenhouse. However, many people are reluctant to try them due to the really undeserved reputation that they are difficult to grow and impossible to coax into bloom. The problem here is one of too much care rather then neglect.

All members of the succulent family (the cactus is one) are plants designed to survive periods of drought and harsh weather.

The plant lover who gives them "a little extra" drink is doing them more harm than good. These plants have fleshy leaves and stems in which to store moisture. They have a tough skin or wax layer over their skin to prevent moisture from evaporating. Plants like the barrel cactus have a very small surface area in relation to their size; this conserves water. Cactus spines replace leaves to reduce surface area. These plants can shrivel up during extreme drought and save themselves. The moral of all this is to water them very sparingly. During winter dormancy, just mist them every few weeks and withhold water from the soil altogether.

Generally, succulents will do well in a greenhouse, but most desert cacti will not tolerate the high moisture in the atmosphere. There are "jungle" cacti—the Christmas cactus is a good example—that will do well in the typical, humid greenhouse. These are epiphyes that grow in the notch of jungle trees using the decayed leaves gathered there for the soil. To raise them, you must use a very rich, but porous, soil that drains easily. Allow them to dry out between waterings.

Desert cacti need a very loose, porous soil. It must drain well and be non-acid and non-caking as well. Use a good loam with sharp sand and a pinch of leaf mold. Fill the lower half of the pot with coarse gravel only. Place the cactus in the soil mixture at the top and do not tap down the soil. This could cause damage to the plant. Withhold water for the first two or three days after potting. To save your hands when potting cacti use thick gloves or rubber-coated tongs to handle the plant.

Keep your desert cacti on a very sparse watering schedule. For the resting period of January and February, give no water at all. In March a light spraying will do. For the growth season of April, increase the water, but allow the plant to dry out completely between waterings. Reduce waterings to once a month in the fall as the hours of daylight decrease.

Other succulents need water regularily, but most dry out in between. They can be killed with kindness, but rarely die of neglect. Allow them to dry out completely during winter. Succulents need this resting period when there is low light and no growth. Do not try to force continued growth with water and fertilizer. This could injure and finally kill the plant.

Most succulents can be propagated very easily. A cutting or offshoot should be taken and allowed to dry and callous over. Then set it in barely moist sand for rooting. The ease of propagating succulents can be shown by cutting off a leaf and pinning it to a curtain. Soon it will be edged in tiny plants. One extra in growing cacti is the ease with which they can be grafted. It is a very rewarding aspect of cacti culture.

One warning is that root nematodes are a very common pest for cacti and succulents. Always be sure to use pasturized soil for potting and repotting such plants. If nematodes take hold, the plant will probably have to be destroyed.

Cacti and succulents are easy-care plants. Try them in your greenhouse or, better yet, in the driest corner of your home. They can add interest anywhere.

FERNS

If you want to enjoy a greenhouse that is lush, warm and very much like a South Sea island, consider filling it with ferns. These beautiful plants can grow to very large sizes and give a wonderful tropics quality wherever they are. Most do very well in a greenhouse and need less care than many other plants.

Grow your ferns in a highly organic medium that has good drainage. They need much moisture, but will rot if their roots are water-logged. A good mixture is:

- 2 parts peatmoss
- 1 part rich loam
- 1 part sharp sand

Ferns are easy to propagate by several means. Many send out runners that will root and become a new plant. Others "walk" by sending out plants at the tips of their fronds where they touch the soil. Some have tiny plants that develop among their fronds. Several do best when propagated by division. New ferns can be raised from the spores of the parent plant. These are a more primitive form of seed. However, because a thousand baby plants may be grown from one plant's spores, this method is not necessary for the hobby grower. With correct care, ferns in the home greenhouse will become very large and additional plants will not be needed in large quantities.

The following lists a few of the favorite ferns grown in the home. There are many others to choose from for the interested grower.

Maidenhair. This fern is from Brazil and has been a favorite for many years. It's stems grow delicate wedge-shaped leaflets in several types and colors. Grows one to two feet high in a warm greenhouse.

Bird's Nest. This fern grows its fronds from a center of brown hairs that resemble a nest. Care should be taken so water does not stand in the "nest" where it could cause rot. This fern is very attractive and does well in a warm-climate greenhouse.

Rabbit's Foot. This fern has brown hairy rhizomes that give it it's name. These creep along and grow over the side of the pot or basket. The fronds are very graceful also. It makes a real conversation piece for any greenhouse.

Boston. This fern is a perennial favorite. It appeared as a chance seedling among a shipment of Sword ferns sent to Boston in 1894. It was a beautiful plant that grew several mutations in the next generation. There are dozens of varieties of Boston fern and all are attractive and easy to grow.

Staghorn. This fern is an epiphyte that grows on the rough bark of jungle trees. In a greenhouse, it is often grown in a manmade pocket of Osmunda fiber or bark that is fashioned on a board. Then the fern is hung from the wall of the greenhouse in a moist, shady location. The fronds are broad and flat with deep indentations that strongly ressemble a stag's horn. It is unusual and easy to raise.

Table. These ferns come in dozens of leaf types. Some are fine and delicate, others have crested fronds, and still others have streaked and colored fronds. They are low growers, easy to care for, durable, and relatively inexpensive. They make excellent "fill" with other plants and in a fern specialty greenhouse.

GESNERIADS

If you want your greenhouse to be filled with flowers that grow in every size and shape, raise gesneriads. This family contains the most popular of the flowering houseplants, African violets, as well as many beautiful bloomers like Sinningia and Streptocarpus. They are all natives of tropical regions and do very well in a home greenhouse. Most have been hybridized into hundreds of varieties for you to choose from.

The growing requirements for gesneriads are similar for the whole family. They need warm, humid conditions with night temperatures of 65° to 70° and humidity of 50 to 60 percent. Good bright light is needed to go along with this. Strong direct sunlight will cause discoloration and sunburn. They do very well under artificial lights as well.

Soil should be very high in organic matter, but must be well drained. It needs to form the proper balance between moisture retention and porousity. Many home growers use loam and leaf mold with sharp sand. I have good success using the commercially prepared potting soil designed specifically for African violets. This soil is very rich in nutrients but is usually too fine to be used alone. When combined with perlite in a 2:1 ratio, it is excellent for African violets and other gesneriads.

The rich potting mixture will supply nutrients, but a fertilizer supplement is helpful. Gesneriads are not heavy feeders so a mild, liquid fertilizer given with the regular waterings is best. This should be discontinued during periods of less light or cool temperatures. Also, stop feeding during dormancy such as gloxinia have when they die completely back to their tubers. It is important to recognize the resting stage of these plants so they do not become weakened by feeding they cannot use.

Propagation is a simple matter as anyone who has cut an African violet leaf knows. They root easily in water, moist vermiculite, or regular potting soil. Often one leaf can be used to start several new plants. Other gesneriads can be raised from stem cuttings and the division of tubers. Also, they can be raised from very fine seeds for the careful grower.

Saintpaulia. The every-popular African violet is the number one houseplant in America. If you move these into a greenhouse you will be amazed at how large and lush they will grow. African violets have been heavily hybridized for years and the new plants available bare little ressemblance in the native species introduced from Africa years ago. They now come in standard and miniature varieties in every imaginable color except a true red. New varieties have flowers of one color that are edged in two other colors. Some have the so-called "fantasy" markings that are streaks of one color through petals of another color. Blossoms are single, double, and triple with plain and ruffled edges. They can measure up to 3 inches across. Foliage comes in several colors and is quilted and ruffled as well. The endless variety and constant introduction of new ones makes it very easy to fill any size greenhouse with African violets.

Sinningia. This is a group of lovely plants with bell-like blossoms that usually die back to their tubers during a dormant period every year. Some of the newer varieties will stay green all year around. The large, popular gloxinia is a tuber type that does go dormant. The blossoms are large, velvety and bell-shaped and they are held high above the foliage. Other sinningias are miniature with pretty bells of white, pink, and blue. One type, S, pusilia, can be raised in a thimble with tiny trumpet flowers only one-quarter of an inch long. It does best when grown in a terrarium.

Among other favorites in the gesneriad family are achimenes, episcias, Streptocarpus (Cape-primrose), kohlerias, "temple bells" and the "lipstick plant." All have similar growth requirements and bloom profusely when these requirements are met. They form a family with enough beauty and interest to keep a plant lover busy for a lifetime.

ORCHIDS

Elegant, exotic orchids are considered by many to be the king of flowers. There are over 10,000 species of orchids that grow from the Artic to the tropics. The lady slipper our American woodlands is a member of the orchid family. Most people who begin to raise these beauties end up specializing in them. They are so lovely, it is very hard to resist them.

There are many groups within the orchid family. Some are terrestrial and others are epiphytic. Among the terrestrial, some have both underground and aerial roots and are called semiterrestrial. Orchids are further divided by the type of growth they have. Cattleyas grow from a horizontal rhizome that sends out roots from below and a "lead" each year from above. The lead curves upward to an erect growth from which the flower bud emerges. The lower part of the lead enlarges to become the pseudo bulb. This type of orchid is called *sympodial*. Others are known as *monopodial* and have a stem where leaves develop. At the leaf axil, the flower spike emerges. Vandas are an example of this type. Some orchids are classified as evergreen or deciduous. Dendrobiums are an example of this type. Many large books are devoted to orchids and their culture so I will just touch upon a few key points here.

Because orchids come from all over the world and have several growth patterns, they all do not need high humidity and high temperatures. You can raise orchids in a cool or moderate greenhouse with good success. Merely choose varieties that grow in such climates naturally. Most do not need full sunlight and will do better in filtered light. Humidity can be supplied by wetting down the benches and walks in the morning and allowing the water to evaporate during the day. Good air circulation is essential for orchids throughout the year.

Until recently, Osmunda fiber was the only recommended potting material for orchids. Now white firbark is available. It is easier to handle, comes in graded sizes, and is suitable for epiphytic orchids. This is true even for those that naturally cling to rocks rather than tree limbs for support. They will need frequent waterings after potting until the bark has been saturated. Also the bark is low in organics so feeding is essential. Terrestrial and semiterrestrial orchids need a very rich soil that drains well and does not become soggy. They need frequent waterings except during cloudy weather. The soil must drain freely so the roots can breathe properly.

For those who are patient, orchids can be propagated from seed. However, you will have to wait five to seven years before your first flowers appear. It is best to start off with mature plants so you can enjoy the blossoms and know what you have right away. They are expensive. Check carefully for reputable growers in your area. When repotting is necessary, they are usually divided by using a sharp knife. Those with pseudo bulbs need at least three with each section of rhizome. Make sure the new pots they are started in will allow for two years of growth or more to cut down on repotting.

Chapter 10

Care and Maintenance

When you step into your just completed-greenhouse, what do you think is the most important thing you can do to insure its success and your satisfaction? Fill it full of your favorite plants and flowers? Buy the best equipment to use in it? The one thing that can make the difference in enjoying your greenhouse is how it is cared for and maintained. If little cleaning jobs are allowed to grow into time-consuming tasks, your greenhouse activity will turn into drudgery. If discarded potting soil and dead leaves accumulate into a breeding place for pests, you will quickly tire of a constant battle against bugs. If dirty glass reduces the amount of light your plants receive—so that they begin to sicken and die—you will soon become thoroughly discouraged. To insure success for you and the plants you grow, start off with the best habits of cleanliness and good maintenance. When your greenhouse is clean, neat and well-organized, it is a pleasure to care for your plants and do the necessary potting jobs.

DAILY MAINTENANCE

You are bound to spend at least a short time every day in your greenhouse. You might just check your plants and perhaps mist them. You could water them and remove dead or yellowing leaves. When there is more time you can do some repotting or start seed flats. No matter what the job or how much time you spend in your greenhouse, always put things back where they belong and leave everything "company ready."

Replace watering cans and hoses. Pick up any spilled soil and put in in the trash container immediately. Do the same with any leaves or stems you have removed. If you pick up after each job, you won't be faced with a messy greenhouse and hours of work to put it right.

Get in the habit of doing greenhouse work before gardening outside. Don't wear the same clothes and shoes for outdoor work and then walk into your greenhouse. It is very easy to carry in pests that cling to your clothes or shoes. If you begin with these good habits, they won't seem like trouble to switch to later on. It is a good idea to be sure other family members follow the same procedures.

Keep separate tools for greenhouse work and outdoor use. This will cut down on the transmission of pests and diseases. Tools in the greenhouse should be sterilized after each use. They can be passed through a flame or gas jet or rinsed in a solution of 1 part bleach to 4 parts water. This is another good practice to get into the habit of doing from the very beginning.

Empty your greenhouse trash container frequently and not just when it is overflowing. It is easier to handle when only partially full and used potting soil and decaying plant material is a wonderful breeding ground for all sorts of things you don't want in your greenhouse. Discard various chemical pesticides that should be removed from the area promptly. One very handy setup is a potting bench with sides to prevent any soil from spilling and a hole cut in the bottom. A lined trash receptacle is placed directly beneath the hole. As plants are potted, all old and excess soil is swept off the bench and into the waiting trash can below. Your bench is always clean and old soil is not left to accumulate until you have time to pick it up. Such a potting bench is one of the best investments you can make. It makes potting such a pleasant and easy task, you will be able to enjoy your greenhouse that much more.

SEASONAL MAINTENANCE

The most important season for greenhouse maintenance is summer. That is the time when the entire greenhouse should be cleaned and scrubbed. It can also be fumigated if necessary. It is best to choose a cool, cloudy day in June for your summer cleaning. Many people wait until August to do their complete cleaning, but June is preferable because plants can be set out for the day without the danger of burning in the strong sun.

Begin in the morning by setting outside as many plants as you can. For complete cleaning or fumigating, all the plants should be removed. Place delicate ones under trees or in a sheltered corner where wind or sun should not harm them. A shadehouse or lath house is a fine summer home for your greenhouse plants.

Next, sort and remove pots, tools, chemicals (and soil if it is not stored in permanent containers). Clean all the dirty pots or set them elsewhere for cleaning before returning them to the greenhouse. Clean and oil the tools and remove any rust spots. Sort through all your chemicals; any with expired dates should be discarded in the manner described on the label. Old solutions of pesticides and fungicides should be thrown out. They usually settle out and lose their potency a short time after being made up into a solution. They are of no value and just cause clutter in a storage area. Remove hoses and watering equipment and check for leaks and bad valves. Put them in good working order.

If your greenhouse has soil-filled benches, empty them out and clean and scrub the benches. Replace bad boards as needed. Benches made of other materials will need a thorough scrubbing. If you do not want to change the soil, turn it over well and remove any weeds and debris. Add any components to bring the soil to the right consistency and composition. Then cover the benches with plastic so any cleaning solutions or paint you will be using to finish your maintenance job will not fall into the soil.

Now you are ready for the major work of a summer greenhouse cleaning. Begin with the frame of your greenhouse. If it is wood, it might need scraping and painting. Check for any rotted or damaged pieces. A steel frame needs to be wire brushed and painted with at least two coats of a rust-inhibiting paint. A primer paint is often helpful on steel to prevent rusting. An aluminum frame probably will not need any maintenance.

Next, carefully examine all the glass in your greenhouse. Cracked and broken lites must be replaced. Look for deteriorated glazing or missing clips that secure the glass. Reglaze as necessary. Use a glaze designed for the high humidity of a greenhouse. It will last longer and stay pliable. After the glass has been repaired and secured, it needs a thorough cleaning. Dirt and algae can reduce the amount of light being transmitted through the glass by 30 percent. Scrape and then wash until the glass is clear and sparkling.

If you have interior gutters and drip basins, they will need a good cleaning to remove accumulated salts. Check the foundation for cracks or settling. Some repair work might be called for. The floor of the greenhouse should not be overlooked. If it is dirt and gravel, the weeds will need to be dug up. Don't just pull them out because the roots you don't get will soon be new weeds. Always dig them out and get every bit of the plant. After removing the weeds, smooth the floor and add a fresh layer of gravel. Concrete floors need to be scrubbed and cleaned. Brick floors need to be checked for loose bricks and worn mortar. Bricks set into soil will have weeds nearby to be dug out.

On the inside of your greenhouse is all the important mechanical equipment that keeps your plants healthy. It needs good care in order not to suffer a breakdown when it is most needed. Ventilators and their automatic controls should be cleaned and checked. Do any lubrication called for by the manufacturer. If you have a cooling system, this is a good time for a complete inspection before the hottest part of the summer puts it to the most severe test. Go over your heating system, but save any major work until fall cleaning so it will be in peak condition at the start of the heating season. Carefully check all the electrical wiring and controls. Greenhouse fires are most always caused by the heating system or the wiring. Have you overloaded your wiring? Are you trying to use more equipment than you know the wiring can take? Now is the time to add an extra circuit and the necessary breaker connections. Do not ever skimp on your electrical service; to do so is foolish and dangerous.

When you have finished with the inside of the greenhouse, look all around the outside. Check the foundation and glazing from outside. Clean the walkways and remove any accumulation of old pots and "spare" equipment from around the exterior. Get into the habit of keeping the outside of the greenhouse as clean and neat as the interior. Have attractive plantings and compatible landscaping. Don't let the outside of your greenhouse become a dumping ground for what is unwanted on the inside. It is very important that your greenhouse be an attractive addition to your property and not the neighborhood eyesore. The habits of neatness and cleanliness are ones you should cultivate right along with your plants.

After this major summer cleaning, your other cleaning bouts will be fairly minor. In the fall, at the start of the heating season, give your heating system a very thorough check and cleaning. Do any and all recommended maintenance. Test the thermostat and controls and any warning alarms. Alarms, along with some form of back up heating, are a good idea if you raise rare or valuable plants. You should have one heating system that will work manually when there is a power failure. The thermostatically controlled alarms will give you enough advance warning so that your plants can be saved. Fall is the time to test and check all systems and do any repairs or changes as they are needed. Remember to keep some basic spare parts on hand for all your important control systems. If you are really careful, a complete second system will be ready in case of emergencies.

Midwinter maintenance involves a close look for any pests or diseases that are taking hold in the hospitable environment of the winter greenhouse. Many plants will be coming into bloom at this prime season for a greenhouse so you must be especially careful that pests don't spoil your pleasure. Keep after pots that need cleaning and remove weeds from benches and the floor.

Spring cleaning means getting ready for the warm weather ahead. Check whatever method you use to provide shade and see that it is ready. Move your bedding plants and others outside when possible. Empty the greenhouse slowly as the weather warms. Lush plants from a greenhouse really add glamour to a home and patio. Prepare your greenhouse for the major summer cleaning by sending as many plants as you can out to the fresh air. Just be careful they do not pick up pests while soaking up the spring sun. Treat for any pests as needed.

PEST CONTROL

There are many different insects that enjoy greenhouse plants for their food. It is your job to be able to recognize pests and to use the proper treatment to destroy them. If pests are allowed to get a firm hold before any treatment, they might be impossible to eradicate and your plants will have to be destroyed.

The best cure for pests is prevention. Always check new plants carefully for insects and disease. Never put a new plant directly into your greenhouse. Keep it segregated from all your other plants for the first few weeks to see if any problems develop. Even the finest supplier will have an occassional problem crop up. Check all incoming plants to be sure. Another preventive step is to cover your ventilators and any other greenhouse openings with screens. Don't ever let your greenhouse stand open to the outside air. It is a sure invitation to every bug in town. If it is open for your thorough summer cleaning, spray or fumigate before replacing your plants.

General cleanliness will always deter insects. Debris piled in corners is a wonderful breeding ground for pests. That is another reason to practice good greenhouse keeping. Removing weeds also removes another hiding place for insects. Keeping dead leaves and stems trimmed off and taking out the trash every day eliminates another source of trouble.

When you do see an insect problem, it is most important to diagnose it correctly and apply the proper remedy for it. If you make a mistake and use the wrong substance, the insects might take a stronger hold and be that much more difficult to eliminate when you begin using the right insecticide. If you are not sure what is bothering your plants, call the local agricultural extention agent or a reputable nurseryman and show him a sample of your infected plants. They can identify your problem and recommend the best corrective treatment. It is important for your continuing success with plants to identify the problem and remedy it as soon as possible.

When you are using a pesticide. Don't make the mistake of thinking that if a little of a pesticide does some good, a lot will do that much more good. You can seriously overdose with any chemical and harm yourself and your plants. *Always* follow label instructions to the letter. Don't invent any new dilution or method of application that will work better (so you think). There is a serious risk in such activity. Always dispose of old and unused chemicals according to product information and instructions. Some of these products are highly poisonous and all should be treated with the upmost respect. Use eye and hand protection while mixing and applying your pesticides. Always follow label instructions.

When you purchase any pesticide, be sure to date the package so you will be able to tell at a glance if it is outdated and should be discarded. Always store your weed killers away from any pesticides and fungicides. They give off fumes that might injure the plants.

Some of the most common insect pests are aphids, nematodes, mealybugs, red spiders, thrips and white flies. Among the popular pesticides to use for their control are Malathion, Chlordane, Diazinon, Systox, Rotenone, and Lindane. One pesticide is often effective against several types of pests. Consult local nurserymen in your area to learn what has proven successful for them. Many people use a good general spray occasionally as a preventative measure when there are no pests in their greenhouse. You might want to establish a similar practice.

DISEASE CONTROL

Many diseases that plants are subject to can be prevented if good greenhouse management is followed. One important thing to do is keep a balanced atmosphere between the temperature and the humidity in your greenhouse. If the temperature drops when the humidity is high enough, condensation will form on the leaves and stay there, This is an open invitation to many leaf diseases. Balance the elements of climate control to prevent this from happening.

Along the same lines, always water plants in the forenoon when temperatures are rising. This will allow any water droplets on the leaves to evaporate before cooler, nighttime temperatures. On cold and cloudy days, be extra careful about getting any water on the plants to begin with. It will not evaporate on such days; care should be taken during regular watering chores. A help in preventing condensation buildup in good ventilation. Moving air currents around plants are much healthier than still, stagnant air. Be sure to open the ventilators some time every day. Even on the coldest days, the fresh air will be good for your plants. Just be sure it does not cause a severe drop in the temperature. Maintaining good ventilation is one of the secrets of successful plant culture.

The rules for treating diseases are the same as those for treating insects. Know what particular disease is affecting your plants and use the correct fungicide to treat it. The list of diseases is, unfortunately, a long one. No effort will be made to list them all here. Some are peculiar to one variety of plant and some are common to all plants. Consult your library, extension office, and local professionals to find out about specific diseases and their treatment. Buy the proper fungicide and use it exactly according to directions. Always put your spray equipment away clean and ready for the next use.

One thing that is essential for good disease control is the awareness that there is a disease problem. For this, you must be tuned in to your plants. know what they normally look like and behave like. Observe them closely while you are doing your regular greenhouse activities. Pay attention to your plants and they will tell you when something is wrong and in enough time to make it right.

HANDLING POISONS

Always remember when you are using pesticides and fungicides that you are indeed handling poisons. Many are very toxic and they can cause burns to the skin and severe irritation if inhaled. Use the right equipment when preparing and applying your chemicals. Wear old clothing that can be washed as soon as you are finished. Use gloves and goggles to protect your hands and eyes. Wear a face mask or respirator to protect your lungs from inhaling the dust or spray. Clean all measuring utensils and the sprayer as soon as you are finished. Make sure everything is ready for the next application.

Date every chemical as it is purchased. Some can be stored for years and others lose their effectiveness quickly. Discard emulsions that salt out and any powders that are caked and lumpy. Keep all products of this type under lock and key and well out of the reach of children. Be careful of storing herbicides with other chemicals as they might give off fumes that effect other chemicals they are near.

When using these potent products, it is wise to have someone nearby in case of an accident. You could be overcome by fumes or blinded by spray and unable to help yourself. Treat these chemicals with respect and you will enjoy their effectiveness without endangering your safety.

SPRAYING AND FUMIGATING

Anyone that owns a greenhouse is going to have to battle some bugs and diseases at one time or another. To fight this battle, you are likely to spray and fumigate with various chemicals. This does not have to be a difficult chore if you plan ahead and follow some basic steps.

■ Know what pest or disease you are combatting and choose the proper chemical that will do the best job.

■ Read the directions carefully and then follow them to the letter! There are no exceptions to this rule. Always use accurate measures and apply as directed.

■ Keep a set of measuring utensils just for your pesticides and fungicides. Clean them thoroughly after each use and never use them for anything else.

■ Do a thorough job when you are spraying. Many sprays kill by contact and must reach the trouble to do any good. Spray all around the plants, the underside of leaves, stems, and the soil. Cover completely to get the full benefit.

■ Consider the conditions in the greenhouse for the best application. Moisture on the leaves will help a dust to cling and do its work. But that same moisture will dilute a water-based spray, perhaps too much. Never do any treatment during the heat of the day. Morning or evening coolness or a cloudy day are best.

■ Don't water plants right afterwards. Give the treatment a chance to do its work. You will wash away the effectiveness otherwise.

■ Keep the chemicals in original containers and under lock and key. Know where they are and what each is used for. Discard old and outdated substances.

■ Put your spraying and dusting equipment away clean and ready for the next time. Clean and safely store all measuring utensils. Fix or replace any problem equipment immediately. When it is needed it should be ready.

■ Some sprays are not safe on any plant that will be eaten; Always double check when treating food crops.

■ Safety first, last, and always for healthy plants and a healthy you.

Chapter 11

Extra Income Possibilities

Would you like your greenhouse to earn enough money to pay for itself? Would you like your hobby to become a source for extra income? Would you like to turn your part-time business into a full-time job when you retire or sooner? All these are possibilities if your hobby is a home greenhouse.   There are enumerable success stories of plant enthusiasts who turned their hobbies into very profitable businesses. Often these people had no intention of doing anything more than enjoying their plants. But soon friends and admirers were asking if they couldn't just sell one little "extra" plant that was such a nice healthy looking thing, so much better looking than those at the garden center. Before long, the garden center owner was asking if some sort of arrangement could be made and a new business venture was launched. It is certainly no secret that plants are enjoying enormous popularity and it looks like the trend will continue. It is also widely realized that any plant, even one that normally can be cultivated outside, will always look its best when raised in the optimum conditions provided by a greenhouse. Therefore, prospective purchasers will seek you out in order to buy desirable plants.

CASH CROPS

No matter what plants you want to raise, there will be people who will want to purchase them. Whether it's popular foliage plants like coleus or dieffenbachia, exotic bromeliads or practical Bibb lettuce, any plants you can spare will be snapped up by willing buyers. You can tailor your greenhouse production to suit yourself and be assured of having a salable commodity. You can plan to raise some or all of your plants according to what sells best for you.

One of the easiest ideas that is a sure money maker is simply to purchase starter plants in 2-inch pots and grow them to sell at maturity. A wide variety of plants can be raised in this fashion. Examples are geraniums, cyclamen, cineraria, and all manner of foliage plants. You can choose the plants you enjoy and keep turning your stock over.

For the specialist, the single-plant greenhouse is popular. Here, only one type or family of plants is raised. The most popular, by survey, is the orchid. Second place goes to the African violet. Other good plants for single culture include camillias, cacti, alpine, begonias, lilies, bromeliads, or amaryllis. The greenhouse will have a range of one type—all colors of blooms for the flowering ones— and you will become an expert in your chosen variety. With increasing knowledge, you can begin propagating from seeds, cuttings, or whatever and gain a reputation for the quality and quantity of plants you have available. If you have the space and the interest you could become a wholesaler in your specialty.

If more variety is the answer for you, you can arrange a growing schedule to change with the seasons and be assured of year-around buyers (see Chapter 12). Bedding plants that are purchased in the spring by homeowners for warm season color are the easiest to begin with. Then consider other seasonal specialties like chrysanthemums for fall, poinsettia, ornamental cherry, and pepper for the Christmas season and spring bulbs forced for late winter bloom.

SELLING METHODS

There are several ways to market the plants that you have available. The easiest way to start would be a small retail business. You would sell what you had currently available to local people. You can enjoy raising what you prefer in whatever quantity you like. Such a business is not as demanding as wholesaling with the deadlines to meet and the quantities promised that must be delivered. It is a less pressured way to convert your hobby into a money maker. There might be problem if customers' cars fill the street in front of your home. Local regulations might prohibit any type of retail selling in your area. Check first so you won't be disappointed after you have begun your business venture.

For the small retail greenhouse, there is not too much extra expense. Most of your advertising can be done by word of mouth from friends and previous customers. Maintain the standards of a clean and healthy culture discussed in this book and you will have a product that is ready to sell anytime. Be very careful that your plants are free of disease and pests. If a greenhouse is run properly, the conversion of it into a business should not be difficult one.

A second method is becoming a wholesale supplier. In that case, you would deal with a retailer and make an agreement to supply him with certain plants for his customers. Wholesaling provides a regular income and guaranteed sales, but it is also more demanding than retailing. You will have to agree to supply a certain number of plants on a specified date. No excuses will be acceptable if you cannot meet your obligations. Such an arrangement might turn your joy at working with plants into drudgery. Decide if you would be happy with such an obligation before trying to become a plant wholesaler.

If you do go into wholesaling, there are some advantages. You will not have to worry about customers' cars filling the street in front of your greenhouse. You will not have to deal with a steady stream of lookers wandering through your property. Sales will be assured in advance and so probably will be the selling price. It will be easier to please one buyer instead of dozens. You will be spared the aggravation of dealing with the public. Such a wholesale business might be the best for you.

It is also possible to raise plants for a mail-order business. Many plant magazines are filled with advertising from mail-order suppliers. It has become a popular way for many people to purchase plants. Such a business would bring in sales without people at your door. It might be exempt from zoning regulations that would not permit a retail business at your greenhouse. You can regulate the amount of orders somewhat by the amount of advertising you do. Mail-order houses often find a very high demand. Your business could outgrow your ability to raise plants. It will be necessary to learn postal regulations on the shipment of live plants and have the correct material for packing and shipping them. It will also be necessary to learn when you can ship plants and when the weather makes it impossible to do so. The postal service and private delivery companies will have to be tried in order to learn who handles your plants the best. There will be more paper work and bookkeeping in a mail-order business that someone will have to do for you if you don't like bookwork. Such a mail-order plant business can be very successful.

START RIGHT

If you do decide to begin to turn your home greenhouse into a business, there are several things you should do first. Contact local zoning officials to find out exactly what you will be allowed to do by law. You could easily begin a business without doing this, but if neighbors complain, you will be put out of business before long. It is possible that one type of business might be allowed where another type is not. Check for retail, wholesale, and mail-order regulations even if you are not really interested in all three. The official answers might change your mind. Don't try to operate outside the law because it is only a matter of time until you are stopped. It would be very painful to have to close, because you were forced to, when business was doing well.

With any type of business, you should contact an accountant and tax man first. Learn what sort of books you should keep and have them ready before ever making your first sale. It will be much more costly if an accountant must correct and change previous records that are wrong. Learn how your business will be taxed and how it will change your tax status. There are things that should be settled in advance so you won't get any nasty surprises later on. Any business must be handled efficiently to insure success and peace of mind.

Chapter 12

A Greenhouse Gardening Calendar

This chapter outlines some possible activities for the home greenhouseman during the year. It covers both plant culture and routine maintenance items during a normal calendar year. Many of the normal activities in a greenhouse are best carried on at certain times of the year. Some, like the propagation of spring flowering bulbs, can only be done at one time of the year. A year's schedule can be very helpful for planning your activities and using your time to the fullest (see Table 12-1). You will know what is coming up and you can purchase necessary supplies in advance of their being needed. You can order bulbs, seeds, and starter plants at the optimum time and have them on hand when you are ready to plant. You can buy the sprays and fertilizers you need before the bugs arrive. There are many greenhouse activities that need advance preparation before you can actually do them.

A schedule to refer to can make jobs a lot easier and more pleasant. You won't be left without an item you need on the morning you have set aside to do a certain job. Read the following plan for a greenhouse year and then write one of your own. Tailor it to fit your plants and your time table. Post it where you can check it at the start of every month and know what is coming up. Make notes when items must be ordered in advance and leave enough time for them to be shipped if necessary. Make your plan clear and workable and don't overload it with too many chores. It is not supposed to keep you hopping with an endless round of chores. It is supposed to make the necessary jobs easier by keeping you informed of what needs to be done and keeping you on schedule with the work.

JANUARY

This is likely to be one of the coldest months regardless where you live in this country. Start your January days by checking the greenhouse heating system. Consider installing an alarm to ring where people are likely to be in your home if the temperature dips to a specific low. Check your back-up heating system if you have one. If your heating fails and the greenhouse goes below freezing, follow this procedure to reheat it. Bring the temperature up slowly, about 5 degrees per hour, and keep misting the plants frequently during the warming process. This will help to save some plants that might be lost otherwise.

Remember to keep fresh air in your greenhouse during the cold months. Open your ventilators a little every day—even on the coldest days. Plants need air circulation to stay healthy. Fresh air also reduces the chances of disease and pests. Spray lightly for general pest control in January. Bugs like to come in from the cold if possible.

Use the quiet, post-holiday period to carefully check and groom your plants. Remove all old blossoms and withered leaves and do any necessary pruning. January is a glorious month for blooms. Bring your best plants into your home so everyone can enjoy them. Now is also the time to go through the new garden catalogs and order for the coming growing season. Plan for seeds to start and equipment needed for the busy months ahead. Few things are so refreshing as planning for a yard full of flowers and vegetables when there is snow on the ground.

The best project for January is the addition of flourescent lights to your greenhouse. During the short days of winter, the extra light is really needed. Consider placing lights beneath your benches or in the basement or spare room to greatly increase your growing space. Use these areas for starting seedlings and placing plants when their peak blooming period is past. This way your greenhouse benches and the favorite windows in your home will hold only your finest plants when they look their best.

January Blooms. Just about every popular greenhouse plant will bloom in January. These include the African Violet, begonia, gardenia, gloxinia, kalanchoe, and orchid. Among the seasonal favorites that look good now are chrysanthemum, amaryllis, poinsettia, and all the spring flowering bulbs that can be forced: crocus,

Table 12-1. Greenhouse Calendar.

Fall	Chrysanthemums through February Begonia-Tuberous Carnations	
Mid-Winter	Anenome Cineraria Daffodils Kalanchoe Poinsettias Tulip-Early	Azalea Christmas cactus Gardenia Marigold (sown Aug 1 to Sept 1) Sweet pea Wedgewood Iris
Late Winter/Early Spring	Alyssem Calendula Cyclamen Gladiolus Iris Pansy Snapdragon	Amaryllis Calla Forget-me-not Hyacinth Nasturtium Primula
All vegetables and bedding plants are started now for transplanting outdoors after the last frost.		
Spring/Early Summer	Aster Delphinium Hydranges	Coleus Geranium Larkspur
Summer	Aster Gloxinia Roses	Carnation Jasmine

daffodil, hyacinth, Dutch iris, narcissus, and tulip. It is also possible to have summer annuals blooming from seeds started in late fall. Impatiens, marigold, pansies, petunias and, snapdragons can fill flats and pots with a wealth of color and beauty. This is also a good month to start bulbs for amaryllis, calla lilies and gloxinia.

FEBRUARY

This is still a cold month, but the lengthening days hold the promise of spring. Now the many projects for the coming growing season are beginning. It is important to accomplish as much as possible in February. The next few months will be your very busiest in the greenhouse and in your yard as well.

Buy all the supplies you will need in February for the impending growing season. Place your catalog orders and visit your local suppliers. Get all the ordering finished before the first of March. You will need things like pots, labels, plant stakes, plant ties, fertilizer and pesticides, seeds for greenhouse and outdoor plants, and all the ingredients you use in your soil mixture. Make your lists, place your orders and do your buying in February. You will need all that you buy in the next several weeks.

This is also the month to sow the seeds that will be plants in your yard and garden in the summer. If you begin them in February, they will be at the bud stage when setting-out time arrives. All your neighbors will be envious of the lovely plants you have in your yard while they are still looking for the first seeds to sprout. Seeds can be started in flats under any extra lighting areas you have. Those that do not transplant well should be started in 2½-inch pots for setting out. Others are separated and transplanted as they mature.

Seeds can be started in various blends of vermiculite, peat-moss, Sphagnum moss, perlite and loam. Your growing medium must be sterile. Keep your mixture light and sow seeds with only a very thin covering. Fine seeds should not be covered at all. After sowing, water thoroughly, but use a trickle of water so the new seeds will not be displaced. Keep the growing medium evenly moist as the seeds sprout and grow.

With the lengthening days, increase the amount of fertilizer your greenhouse plants receive. Give a little more water to any dormant plants like cacti, other succulents, or those that die back over the winter. They will begin growing again now and need to get a little additional moisture as the daylight hours increase. Plants need to get an extra boost at the start of the growing season so they will do well for the coming year. Take cuttings now for any additional plants you will want this year. February is an excellent time to take and start cuttings. They will have the right combination of pleasant temperatures and good light in which to thrive and begin new growth.

Bring in the last pots and bulbs for spring forcing now. This month will mark the end of spring bulbs for the year. You will have blooms into April and you can then set the bulbs out.

February Blooms. This is an excellent month for a wide range of blooming plants. Standards like African violets and orchids, spring bulbs of every type, and summer annuals started last fall indoors. This month is also good for cacti, freesia, kalanchoe, and cineraria. Good bulbs to start now include amaryllis, tuberous begonia, caladium, and gloxinia.

MARCH

Outside, the month of March might come in like a lion and go out like a lamb, but in your greenhouse it will be wonderfully lamb-like for the whole month. This is a time of abundant bloom. March and April are the very best months for a greenhouse. Just about everything you can name will bloom in March. Traditional greenhouse plants, spring bulbs, summer annuals started in the fall, and Christmas favorites are all possible at this time. With so much to enjoy, it is a very rewarding time for the owner of a greenhouse.

166

All this blooming needs attention. Be sure to keep your plants groomed during March. Remove faded blossoms and dispose of them. Keep a watchful eye out for pests and spray accordingly. Extra water and fertilizer will be needed. As days grow warmer dormant plants will spurt new growth.

Warm weather will start in many parts of the country in March. The heat of summer is not far away. Now is the time to check your ventilation and cooling systems. Make sure all exhaust fans are in good working order. Test all aspects of your greenhouse cooling and make any repairs. Be sure the necessary equipment works before it is needed.

March Blooms. This is a superb month for every plant you enjoy. Take your prize examples into the house for the whole family to admire. Make elegant arrangements using orchids, dainty displays with African violets, and bowls of color with camellia, clematis, marigold, or pansy. The opportunities will be endless. This is a prime month for sowing seeds for your yard and garden. The following list offers some possibilities for a colorful summer:

Aster, China	Browwallia
Calendula	Carnation
Celosia	Coleus
Cosmos	Dahlia
Marigold	Nasturtium
Pansy	Periwinkle
Petunia	Phlox
Salvia	Snapdragon
Sweet Alyssum	Sweet Pea
Verbena	Zinnia

Remember your vegetable garden when sowing your seeds for the season and plan for them accordingly. With a staggered sowing schedule, you can be the first and last person in your area to harvest fresh garden produce. Those homegrown fruits and vegetables are always the best tasting ones around.

APRIL

This month brings spring outdoors to most of the country. Greenhouse plants will continue to do well. More water and fertilizer will be needed. Pests will be much more apparent now. Use whatever preventive treatments you prefer during April. Keep an eye out for any signs of infestation and treat them immediately. Bugs that get a firm hold are much more difficult to eliminate.

167

The hot summer weather is not far behind now. If you use any type of shading for your greenhouse, now is the time to have it ready for use. There are brush-on shading compounds, plastic film sheets for the outside of the lites and roller blinds for the inside among possible shading techniques. Your shading needs will depend on where you live and the kinds of plants you raise, but almost every greenhouse will need some shading during the hot, sunny months of summer. Have the necessary materials on hand by the end of April. You will be ready for the bright sun and you will not have any burnt plants to contend with.

Use the warmer weather to empty your greenhouse of those plants past their prime that will be spending the summer outdoors. All spring flowering bulbs that were forced into early bloom indoors should be planted outside in April and will give you outdoor blooms for the next several years. It is wasteful to just throw these bulbs out because most of them are good for many years. Any hardier plants that are through blooming can be set out now. If you live in the north, the danger of frost might not pass until May. Be careful with what you set out now.

Seedlings from earlier plantings will be growing well now. Transplant as necessary. Prepare your outdoor garden and bedding areas. Now is also a good time to divide and transplant indoor plants. Every plant has the best chance of doing well when the days are warm and bright and new growth is occurring naturally.

April Blooms. Just about everything you enjoy raising will be doing well now. Weather is really at a peak period for plant health and growth. Remember to keep them groomed and remove faded blossoms to the compost pile. Also keep a sharp eye out for pests and disease. They are much more likely to cause problems in the warmer weather.

MAY

The growing season is in full swing with the month of May. Now is the time to move all the started seedlings to their permanent locations outside. This final transplanting will occupy a good bit of your available plant time for May. Also, you can repot, divide and take cuttings from all the permanent houseplants you want in May. All types of plants will root readily now. It is the time of the natural growing season and all plants will respond to it.

By late May, the danger of frost has passed for all parts of the continental United States. Plan to move as many of your regular greenhouse plants as possible to the outside for summer at this time. They will enjoy a season outside and you will have room for greenhouse cleaning and repairs. Group your plants together outdoors as much as possible. When they need regular watering later on in the summer it will make the job much easier. Protect them from strong sun and wind as much as possible. Use a shade house or lath house, a sheltering wall or fence, or place them under larger shrubs or trees. Even delicate plants can spend the summer outdoors if their location is chosen with great care.

Shading might be necessary now in the southern states. Increased fertilizer and ventilation will also be part of the May routine. Occasional hot days will require extra watching of more delicate plants.

Your outdoor garden will need attention now. In most areas, there is still time to sow seeds outdoors. It is especially good to start melons, cucumbers, and squash at this time. Outdoor fruit trees will need feeding and pest control spraying.

May Blooms. This is a good month for most standard greenhouse favorites. Orchids and roses do well now. Indoor sown and raised annuals will be finishing up their blooming period. Summer favorites like fuchsia and hibiscus will put on a fine show of color in May. This is a good month for taking cuttings from the following: bougainvillea, cacti, chrysanthemum, geranium, hibiscus, passiflora, poinsettia and stephanotis. Also divide and repot African violets, begonia, cacti, and orchids.

JUNE

Summer has come to the greenhouse. The atmosphere is tropical. To keep things growing right, you will need to shade and ventilate and provide sufficient water and humidity. The tropical look will be provided by blooms from the hibiscus, orchid, and anthuriums plants you can have in flower now. Other plants will begin their summer resting period at this time. You should continue a regular schedule of fertilizing and pest control.

This is the month for a thorough cleaning of the greenhouse—inside and out. All the plants that can be moved outdoors are already there. The weather is good but not too hot yet. Refer to Chapter 10 for details on the kind of cleaning that you should do. Make it a really thorough cleaning inside and out. Dig into the corners to remove weeds and accumulated trash. Remember to clean and landscape the outside area around the greenhouse. Too often that is the place that is neglected. Don't become too involved with the plants inside to think of what the greenhouse looks like to those who see it from outside. Do not let it become the neighborhood eyesore. This happens all too often. Plan it so that it blends in with your house and yard and keep it looking right.

Clean the benches and scrub all the pots. Don't put anything back into the freshly cleaned greenhouse that is not clean. Now is the ideal time to fumigate if that is your preferred method for pest control. Any plants that are not staying outside for the rest of the summer should be carefully checked for pests and spot-sprayed or dipped before being returned to their home. This thorough cleaning will be your major project of the summer greenhouse season. With it behind, you will be able to relax a little and enjoy your outdoor garden for the very warm months of July and August that are coming up.

June Blooms. The tropics will be the theme for your June greenhouse. Among the lovely plants that bloom now are fuchsia, hibiscus, orchids of all kinds, and stephanotis. Regular greenhouse plants and summer annuals will provide a riot of color now. Cuttings can be taken now from such plants as clematis, hibiscus, and poinsettia. This is also a good month to start seeds for fall bloom. Good choices would be begonia, cineraria, cyclamen, impatiens, kalanchoe, pansy, petunia, primula and salvia.

JULY AND AUGUST

These are the hot months of the summer. They contain the "dog days" when you often can't be comfortable outside unless you are in a swimming pool. For your plants, growth will slow unless your greenhouse has a good cooling system. These are the months to take a vacation. Just be sure you have a responsible and reasonably knowledgeable plant sitter to keep everything healthy while you are away. Make a complete list of what needs to be done and go over it with your plant sitter in detail before you leave.

Regular programs of fertilizing and pest control will continue. Various insects are at their busiest now so special watchfulness is necessary. Remember to pay extra attention to those greenhouse plants that are spending their summer outside. They will be troubled by insects also. They will need good protection from the blazing summer sun now.

This is a good time for doing any building tasks that are necessary for your greenhouse. If new benches or flats are needed, build them. If you want a coldframe or hotbed, construct it. If your lath house needs repair, fix it. Summer is the best time for all those handyman tasks that are part of greenhouse management. Prepare for the coming winter with all your plant care areas in good condition.

Look through your catalogs and order some bulbs now for forcing this winter. Also, order the bulbs of freesias, calla lilies, and oxalis. For lovers of African violets, late summer is a good time to order new varieties you want to try. With so many violet hybridizers offering plants and leaves by mail, it is possible to raise a great many of the wonderful new types that are introduced each year. Consider the fantasy types with flowers of several colors in bright streaks. Every year, new varieties come increasingly closer to a true red. If you are pressed for space, grow miniature violets. They are very lovely and take up so little room.

Summer Blooms. Blooming will slow down a little as the weather heats up, but there should still be plenty of color. This is a good time to take cuttings of such plants as azaleas, camellias, geraniums, and poinsettia. Sow annual seeds for fall color in the greenhouse or outside until the first hard frost.

SEPTEMBER

This is my favorite month. The days are sunny and golden and the nights are cool and restful. This month marks the start of the greenhouse season again. Those plants that have spent the summer outside should all be returned to the greenhouse by the end of September or before the first frost for your area. Be sure to clean and check each one thoroughly before placing it in your spanking-clean greenhouse. Clean the pots all over and don't forget the bottoms. Use a chlordane drench in the soil to kill all pesky bugs looking for a warm home for the winter. Use a spray for the foliage of each as well. As you bring the plants in, it will be necessary to cull any of poor quality and those simply too large for the available space. Take a cutting of a favorite to start one of manageable size. There is only so much space in your greenhouse and you should try some new plants and varieties each growing season. It is necessary to harden your heart and discard those that have outgrown their usefulness.

The heating season will start soon so be sure all your automatic equipment is in tip-top shape. Test your thermostat and all other controls. Consider installing an alarm system if you don't already have one. Any shading used on your greenhouse is likely to need removal sometime this month or early October at the latest. It is possible to shade with a paint-on compound that simply wears off in the autumn rains. With the removal of shading, give the glass a good washing inside and out. The shorter daylight hours mean your plants will need all the light available. Dirty glass can reduce the light coming in by as much as 30 percent. Use the sunny September weather to remove any shading and clean the glass for the cloudy days ahead.

Pest control will have to be increased this month. More bugs will be trying to find a way in as the winter approaches. Use whatever method works for your situation. It is possible to fumigate with some very strong poisons if your greenhouse is free-standing and small children and pets are not a problem. Regular spraying with drenching of a severely infested plant is also possible. Those who want to maintain an organic greenhouse as much as they can use ladybugs, toads, or praying mantises for pest control. They will do a good job in eliminating unwanted insects. If you are careful, it is possible to use natural means for insect control to a great extent and only occasionally use spot spray when things get bad.

The first of the bulbs can be planted now and especially the paperwhite and Soleit D'Or narcissus. You could also start amaryllis, crocus, daffodil, hyacinth, Dutch iris, and ixia.

September Blooms. Most greenhouse favorites will be blooming now. Some summer plants such as celosia, fuchsia, geranium, impatiens, petunia and sweet alyssum will be adding their color. The earliest of your spectacular chrysanthemum display will be opening now. Plant seeds for winter display of China aster, cineraria, gloxinia, marigold, nasturtium, phlox, salvia, and snapdragon.

OCTOBER

Cooler days and chilly nights mark the October weather. Now both your heating and ventilating systems will come into use as the weather varies. Automatic controls are really appreciated when the weather changes often during a single day. Any problems in the systems will be noticed now and must be corrected immediately. If not, the cold days ahead could bring ruin to some of your plants as a system fails.

This is a time when orders of bulbs and starter plants will be arriving. Choose a wide range of bulbs for forcing. Plant at staggered intervals for color from January to April. Purchase starter plants, rooted clumps or leaves from favorite varieties or new plants you want to try. This is a good month for shipping plants and most suppliers prepare for a fall rush of orders. Do try a few plants that are new to you every growing season. There is such a remarkable range of plants to pick from that it isn't easy to narrow the field down too much. Make it a regular part of your fall orders to try at least two or three of those plants you always wanted to grow. You might find a new plant family to concentrate on in the coming year.

Clean the falling leaves off of your greenhouse glass now. Look to the outside of the greenhouse and make sure it is neat and attractive for the winter months. With new bulbs and plants expected, wash all the necessary pots and have them ready. You will also need labels, flats and soil mixture ingredients. Be ready for your new arrivals *before* they arrive.

Summer bulbs will be dying off now. Withhold water and place out of the light. Do a little inventory of your present and future flower display. Do you have all the bulbs and starter plants you want? Have you taken cuttings of all your favorites? Have you started enough seed flats? This is the last month for ordering and starting most plants for bloom during the coming greenhouse season. Look over your present plants and orders and make any additional ones now. Place rush orders as needed. Try to utilize your greenhouse to its fullest.

October Blooms. This is the month when a wonderful display of chrysanthemums fills the greenhouse with warm, autumn colors. Regular greenhouse bloomers and late annuals will also give color. Plant plenty of bulbs now. Consider amaryllis, crocus, daffodils, hyacinths, narcissus, and tulips. You might try one pot each of some of the less common bulbs like calochortus, winter aconite, muscari, snowdrops, and scillas. If you decide they are worth it, you can plan for several pots for the next year.

NOVEMBER

This is the grey month of cloudy skies and cold rains. If you live in the north, the first wet snows of winter might fall. Many plants are likely to become inactive now. Short, grey days are not conducive to much growth. Water sparingly and only in the morning so that moisture on the leaves will have time to evaporate before sunset. Withhold fertilizer from all but the most actively growing plants. I like to use November and December for resting months for all my regular indoor plants. This period has the shortest days of the year as well as the busy holiday season. It is a good one for both the plants and you to have a breather from fertilizing chores.

Keep the glass clean and polished so all available light can enter. Because all potting chores must be done inside now, keep that area neat and well organized. Have all the materials you need close at hand. Store bulk containers of soil ingredients elsewhere if your greenhouse is small.

This month is the last chance for potting spring flowering bulbs and those annuals you want this season. Dormant roses can be purchased and potted up for February blooms if you have space for them. Christmas favorites like poinsettias must be kept out of any artificial light so they will set buds for blooming at the proper time.

Early in this month, before the Thanksgiving rush, give the greenhouse a good cleaning and organize any materials you might need for plant giving at Christmas. Consider traditional (or unconventional) blooming plants trimmed in foil paper and bright ribbon. Or give bottle gardens and terrariums containing rooted cuttings and miniature plants. Scour the woods for natural material to decorate your tiny ecosystem. Give a container with one amaryllis bulb or several paper-whites that will brighten the home long after Christmas is over.

November Blooms. The show of chrysanthemums will continue in this month. Other bloomers include African violets, begonias, cyclamens, geraniums and orchids. Plant any remaining bulbs, annual seeds, and cuttings for spring growth and bloom.

DECEMBER

The very busy holiday season is here, so use your time wisely. Keep up with necessary plant chores, but don't plan for any extra greenhouse duty. You will be too busy with other activities now.

Give the bounty of your greenhouse for Christmas. Beautiful plants are enjoyed by everyone. Note what professional florists have for sale and see how you can duplicate, or improve, on their ideas. Favorites of the season that you can have blooming now include poinsettias, Christmas peppers and cactus, Jerusalem cherries, begonias, amaryllis and azaleas. All make fine plants for gift giving. Use a spray from your cymbidium orchid for holiday corsages for close family and friends. Gifts from your own greenhouse are so much more appreciated than something purchased from a store. The Christmas budget will stretch further when you can give what you have already raised. It helps convince family members your greenhouse pays for itself—at least a little!

Chapter 13

Other Homes Plants Enjoy

There are structures other than greenhouses which you can build that will help plants to thrive. They are not as costly as greenhouses and they do not give the same precise climate control, but they are effective. Often one of these structures is built first before thoughts of a home greenhouse begin. Their usefulness in relation to their cost makes them very attractive additions to a plant lover's yard. Consider them as a means of expanding the functions of a greenhouse or as a way of getting your feet wet before taking on a home greenhouse.

THE SHADE HOUSE

The shade house or lath house is a very inexpensive way of expanding the area you have available for delicate plants. It is a simple structure, usually of lath strips nailed to a wooden frame, that provides shade and wind protection. It can consist solely of a roof with open sides, but it is more effective if it has two or three sides. Plants growing in your home or a greenhouse can spend the summer in the shade house and be protected from the full heat of the summer sun. It is possible to cover the shade house with plastic film and use it as a sort of large coldframe during the winter months.

The easiest way to build a shade house is to cover the frame in lath snow fence as shown in Fig. 13-1. End and doorway construction of plywood, as shown in Fig. 13-2, is quite serviceable and very inexpensive. The frame can also be covered in netting to provide shade with minimum cost (see Fig. 13-3).

Fig. 13-1. This shade house is made of snow fence. It does the job and is very inexpensive.

If the shade house is an extention of the greenhouse, your home, or a backyard fence, one or two walls will already be there without added cost. If enough space is left in center of the shade

Fig. 13-2. Plywood is very practical for covering the short sides of a lath house.

Fig. 13-3. This shade house is made of netting secured over a Quonset-styled frame.

house for lawn furniture, it makes a very nice covered patio that can be enjoyed even in the hot afternoon. Side benches and hooks for hanging plants can be included to allow for the most plants in the allotted area. It is good planning to have a water faucet in or near the shade house to handle watering chores. An electrical hookup is advisable if you plan on using lights or a portable heater. A shade house of netting placed directly in front of the greenhouse is seen in Fig. 13-4.

Many plants, even those recommended for full sunlight, cannot be placed outside in the summer without some protection. The duration and intensity of the light they receive would cause wilting and burned leaves. Among those that would benefit from a shade house are fuchias, tuberous begonias, ferns, and many of the common foliage plants like the spider plant and the pothos vine.

When making use of the shade house in the winter months, cover it tightly in the film plastic recommended for one season's use. A small, portable heater also can be used. The idea is to protect the plants from killing frosts and not provide a tropical climate in winter as a true greenhouse might. If one wall of the shade house is a solid house wall, it can provide considerable frost protection. This type of structure is a good stepping stone for the houseplant enthusiast who is not quite ready to invest in a greenhouse yet. It does a nice job of expanding your growing area at minimal cost.

COLD FRAMES AND HOTBEDS

The coldframe and its artificially heated cousin, the hotbed, are simple greenhouses in miniature. They can do most of what an actual greenhouse can do, but on a smaller scale. They are not as convenient, but they are extremely useful. The many jobs they can do will free up space in your greenhouse for the more delicate plant culture.

The cold frame is a sash-covered pit in its simplest form. With low walls, it is easier to tend and not so likely to be damp. With glass walls, it will admit more light and be useful throughout the winter in all but the severest climates. It retains the heat of the sun for warmth and seals tightly to hold in moisture. During mid-winter it should be covered with straw or burlap bags full of leaves to protect against freezing. In the summer, the sash is left open for ventilation and some shade protection might also be provided. In site selection, construction materials and climate control it is handled in the same way as a greenhouse.

Fig. 13-4. The frame of this shade house is high enough for it to be built right at the entrance of the greenhouse.

179

The glass or plastic sash cover will be set on a slope to catch the sun's rays and allow for rain to run off. It should face south to make the most of the winter sun. A fence, a wall, or shrubs for protection from the north and northwest winds is a good idea. Choose a well-drained, easily accessible location. Drain tile can be used if it is in a wet, clay soil location. The basic pit cold frame is shown in Fig. 13-5. A more sophisticated design with glass walls and a ridge vent is shown in Fig. 13-6.

Most people think of the cold frame for starting annuals and vegetables outdoors before the last frost. It has many more uses than that. During the winter months, besides starting outdoor crops, it can be used for curing bulbs and flowering shrubs that will be brought indoors and forced for early color. It can also be used to protect perennials and semihardy plants. Azaleas, hydranges, and potted roses are just a few of the plants that benefit from winter storage in a cold frame. In the summer, perennials can be started for bloom the following year. Also, cuttings can be propagated and houseplants can be started in the protection offered by a cold frame. For fall, vegetables planted earlier can be harvested long after the outdoor garden has succumbed to frost. The seeds of annuals, started in a cold frame in the fall, can be brought indoors for mid-winter bloom.

The hotbed has one extra that the cold frame does not and that is artificial heat. The heat can be created by decomposing manure. light bulbs, or a soil-heating cable. With the addition of heat, the hotbed is truly useful the year around. By far, the best heating

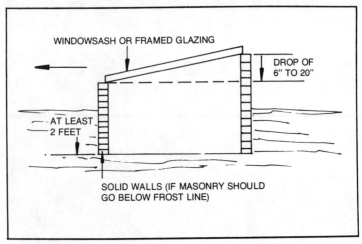

Fig. 13-5. The basic design for a pit cold frame.

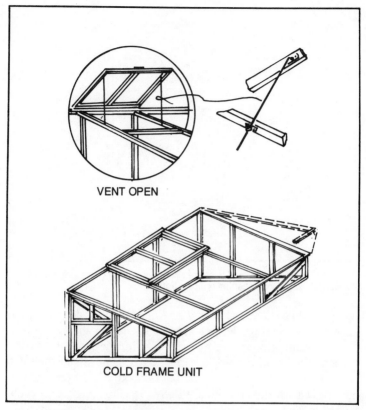

VENT OPEN

COLD FRAME UNIT

Fig. 13-6. This cold frame design has glass walls to permit more light to enter.

method is the electric cable that is thermostatically controlled and uses very little electricity.

The manure hotbed is dug out about 3 feet deep to hold the "hot" or fresh manure. It is placed in the pit several weeks before plants are added so the decomposition slows down and the temperature drops. In the beginning, the temperature will be over 100° but it will drop steadily. When it reaches 85°, about 4 inches of soil should be spread over the top and it is ready for plants. The manure will continue to supply heat for about four or five weeks. That is just enough time to give young plants a good start before moving them outdoors. Figure 13-7 shows the manure-heated hotbed.

Ordinary light bulbs can be set in a wooden tray and covered with metal covers (discarded cans can be used) and trays of seedings placed over the top will be sufficiently warmed. Care must be taken so that all electrical wiring is weatherproof. The warming

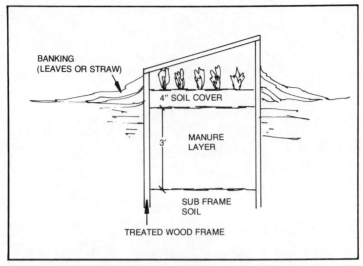

Fig. 13-7. This type of hotbed is heated with decomposing manure. For years, this was the standard construction for a hotbed.

lights should be thermostatically controlled and they do provide the necessary heat. However, a soil cable is a better idea.

Soil cables are covered in lead or plastic. They are set in a layer of sand beneath the hotbed. The cable can be hung around the sides of the hotbed rather than buried, but the bottom heat provided by burying is more effective. Figure 13-8 shows the design of the cable heated hotbed.

With a hotbed, spring crops can be started from seed around March 1st. When using a cold frame, the plants should be started about April 15th. One good way to "harden off" starter plants is to simply turn off the heat in the hotbed and use it as a cold frame as the season progresses and before setting the plants outdoors.

THE PROPAGATING BOX

Of the many structures that can be used to aid in plant culture, the propagating box is one of the best. It is very inexpensive to build and it is a great money saver. It can be constructed of scrap lumber and film plastic. A soil cable is used to supply the heat. It could be placed on a bench in the greenhouse or set up by itself under artificial light. A diagram of a propagating box is shown in Fig. 13-9.

What is the propagating box used for? It is used to start cuttings and to raise them into mature plants. When you locate a plant that is just what you have been looking for, but it is not for sale, you can

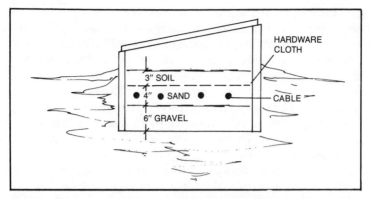

Fig. 13-8. This hotbed receives its heat from electric soil cables. It is simpler, cleaner, and easier to control than a manure heated hotbed.

raise a duplicate of it from a cutting. If seeds are taken and raised, they are often different from the parent plant. But a cutting—a small, healthy branch end—is exactly like the original plant. With plants like the African violet, only a single leaf cutting is needed to raise a new plant.

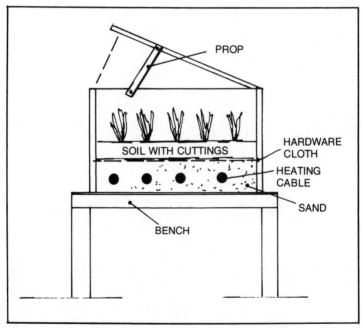

Fig. 13-9. The propagating box is used to start cuttings. It is the best way to increase the number and variety of plants you own at a minimum of cost.

183

Cuttings are the best way to acquire an extensive plant collection without the expense of purchasing started plants. Also, there are many occasions when a certain plant owned by an individual is simply not available when you check at the local commercial growers. Most plant enthusiasts will be willing to allow you to take a cutting or two and grow your own at no cost. That is a great way to get the plants you want. Always choose a healthy, mature cutting. One with new leaves at the tip is too young and one with an easily bent stem is too old. The best time to take softwood cuttings is late spring and summer. For hardwood plants take cuttings in the fall. Leaf cuttings can be taken just about anytime as long as the parent plant is healthy. It will not miss the loss of a couple of leaves if it is in good condition at the time.

Set up your propagating box out of direct sunlight and keep the temperature between 70° and 80°. The rooting medium and the air around the cuttings should be evenly moist. When cuttings have taken hold and developed a good root system, they can be transferred to small pots and placed in direct light. Be warned that it is easy to overdo when propagating plants from cuttings and your greenhouse could be filled with small pots very quickly.

Chapter 14

Using Available Space in Your Home

If you love plants, you are likely to have a houseful of plants even if there is a large greenhouse outside your back door. You will naturally want to display your finest plants inside where friends and family can see and enjoy them. A glance at any home-decorating magazine shows that plants and flowers are used to add elegance to every room and every style of decor. With your own greenhouse, you are way ahead of the game when it comes to decorating with plants. You can grow certain varieties that look good in your home and rotate them as needed so that your live decor is always looking its best.

Certain plants are fine for indoor display and at their peak of blooming belong inside for all to enjoy. This is what every greenhouse owner wants to do all along. Let the bounty that a greenhouse can provide become a real asset to your whole way of life. Regular houseplants are seldom as full and luxurious as those raised in a greenhouse. Delicate plants can be rotated between your home and greenhouse and kept healthy. Those with good flower display can be placed in the home for their best blooms to be admired and then returned to the greenhouse until buds are ready to open again. You can arrange for a constant and varied show all through the year. It is one of the most satisfying aspects of greenhouse culture.

Where to place plants in your home might seem like an easy decision at first thought. Smaller ones lining the windowsills and a large tub by the patio doors might appear to be all the thought needed, but it is possible to use plants in a wide range of very creative ways in the home. Confirm this by looking at decorator's articles in magazines and observing green plants used to enhance the decor of banks, restaurants and shops. Notice how the plants are grouped and displayed. Pay attention to what elevation they are at and in what type containers they are placed. Mentally pull apart the display and see what basic components make it up. Even the most elaborate-looking grouping will be simple when it is brought down to its basic components. Many of these displays will give you excellent ideas that can be adapted to a home interior. They will help to fire your imagination and you might realize those well-worn windowsills are not the only place for your plants.

In this chapter, I will cover basic locations in the home for plants and some effective display stands that can be built at a very reasonable cost. I will also discuss the "garden room" which can be just about any room converted to contain quite a few plants that create the atmosphere of the old-time conservatory.

All this is designed to launch you into the world that beautifully combines your hobby of raising plants with your desire to have as attractive a home as possible. The two can mesh into one in many areas. Your greenhouse will produce outstanding plants you couldn't raise on a windowsill. Your home can provide a showcase for them and can also increase your growing space. Plant lovers have a real problem when it comes to raising all they would like to. With a little planning, you can derive many benefits from your home and your home greenhouse at the same time.

THE PLANT LOVER'S HOME

If you collect and raise a certain type or group of plants, you will want the best ones "on show" in your home. Use the greenhouse for starters, ailing plants, and those in a non-flowering stage. Enjoy the best of your plants throughout your house.

First, consider the plants you like and the conditions under which they are raised. If you raise tropical orchids that require very high temperatures and humidity, it is obvious you will not be able to duplicate the conditions they need in your home. You have two choices. Rotate the plants frequently so that they will spend only short periods in the unsuitable house environment or add some different, more temperate orchids to your collection. These can spend more extended periods in your house. Plants that need high humidity such as ferns are good to place in the kitchen or bathroom where humidity is usually high. Cacti need a sunny location but low humidity. That is easy to find in most homes and especially in the winter.

Display your living treasures in groups for the best effect. Open cubes of glass or plastic can be stacked to give each plant a lovely, jewel-like setting. There is handsome furniture available that has built-in grow lights. This allows any location to be used for plants and not just those with natural light. Vining plants, like the many varieties of ivy, can be trained to encircle a window or a fireplace mantle. They are also excellent as room dividers. No matter what plants you raise and enjoy, it is possible to display them beautifully in your home if you invest a little time and imagination in finding the proper settings for them.

WINDOWS

The first place most people think of when considering where to put plants in any home is the windows. Because there is light and air there, it is usually a good location. Exposure for a window is similar to the proper exposure for a greenhouse; eastern and southern are the best. Western exposure gives a bit too much of the strong afternoon sun while northern exposure gives no direct sun. Absolutely every window in your home can have plants on it if you plan ahead.

Use your best windows, those with eastern and southern exposure, for the largest number of plants. Use shelves or a window greenhouse to increase the usable space. Figure 14-1 shows a good stanchion and bracket holder for shelves. The whole window area can be shelved to form a green curtain to the outside. This is especially nice when the view is better covered than seen. Use the sill to advantage with an extender shelf (see Fig. 14-2). This will increase the width of the average sill by at least two times and enable you to place regular 6-inch pots on the sill. For the upper portion of the same windows hanging plants in attractive containers will complete the picture. Plant hanging sets of colorful ceramic pots with matching beads and color-coordinated macrame cord are very pretty. Plant hangers can also be made of sea shells, woven fibers, and fine chain. There is a style that will suit the types of plants you have and the decor of the room.

When you place a row of plants together, as on a windowsill, use some imagination to make them attractive. Instead of a row of flower pots with saucers, try some alternatives. First of all, you can eliminate the saucers. They are unsightly and unnecessary. There

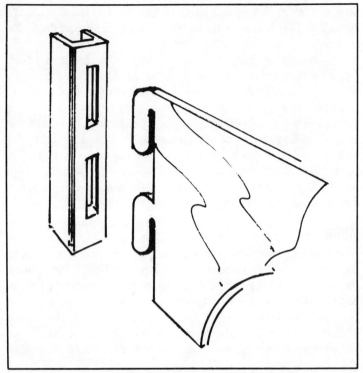

Fig. 14-1. This simple stanchion and shelf bracket will hold shelves across a window for plants.

are long, narrow trays on the market with very shallow sides that are excellent for a row of potted plants. These trays can be metal or plastic and they come in several colors and finishes. Fill them with a thin layer of pebbles. The pebbles will hold excess water drained from the pots and keep the plants above the water. The water will slowly evaporate from the tray to increase the humidity around the plants; this is always beneficial. With a single tray, plants can be moved or changed without the juggling of individual saucers.

Use attractive containers for plants that are inside your home. Regular pots can be slipped into slightly larger containers when they are on display. Plants can be rotated while using the same holders for them. There are attractive containers in woven plastic styles that are brightly colored and lightweight for window shelves. Baskets are very popular today. Many are available with plastic liners for plants. Ceramic containers come in all styles and sizes. As they are used, be sure to clean the buildup of mineral deposits that will occur along the edges of the holders. Deposits need to be removed regularily because they are quite unsightly.

There are several ways to hang plants effectively. A simple notched board will hold two or more pots. Such a notched board is shown in Fig. 14-3. The best way to hang several plants from the ceiling is to use a plant track as shown in Fig. 14-4. The tracks are often designed so that a second hanging track can be suspended from the first one. This allows for two tiers of hanging plants and that is a very effective arrangement. A plant track arrangement is especially useful for large windows and in front of the stationary half of sliding glass doors.

For large, specialty windows, like bay, bow, or corner windows, many plants can be grouped using a combination of techniques. The bay and bow windows are naturals for hanging plants and for riser shelving where two to four tiers of plants are grouped on the wide sill areas of such windows. Corner windows are especially attractive when filled with plants. Knock down shelves of painted or stained plywood can be made to customize a corner window area. Very large plants can be set on the floor in the center of the corner while smaller ones are grouped around on the shelves. Such an arrangement is shown in Fig. 14-5. Hanging plants also look quite nice in a corner area.

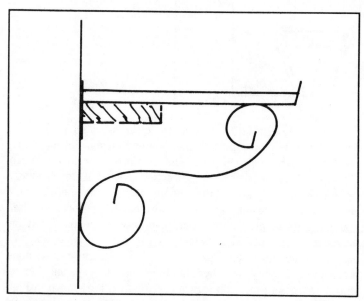

Fig. 14-2. Use an extendor like this to increase the space on a window sill.

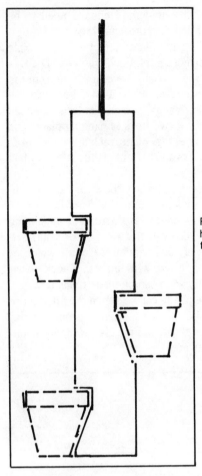

Fig. 14-3. Any board can become a hanging plant holder with the addition of notches to support the pots.

To create a beautiful, jewel-like setting for your plants, use sheets of glass or plastic to form open-end boxes. Set individual plants in each box you assemble. The clear material will allow each plant to be seen clearly from any direction. They will almost appear to be suspended in a sparkling bubble. This arrangement is very attractive and especially so with modern home interiors. Whether you use glass or plastic for the display boxes depends mainly on personal preference. Glass is more costly and breakable, but it is easy to keep clean and sparkling. Plastic is lightweight, non-breakable but easily scratched. In either case, use special clips to join the sheets to form the cubes. These clips are shown in Fig. 14-6. They are made to create triangles, squares, and even miniature greenhouses out of sections of glass or plastic sheeting. The clips allow you to easily build and change a delightful setting for your plants without any tools or special knowledge.

Any window in your home can be used for plants. This is true, but there are certain considerations to remember for successful cultivation. Use the best windows, those with eastern and southern exposure, for your flowering plants that need good light. For northern windows that give only cool light, choose plants that are suitable for such conditions. Alpine plants, ferns, and some succulents do well in low light. A Norfolk Island pine will tolerate low-intensity light quite well. It will merely grow at a slower rate. Windows facing west receive strong, afternoon sunlight. This light can damage and burn many plants. Cacti and others that can tolerate full sunlight can do well here. For other plants you want to place in a west window, hang a sheer curtain between the plants and the window. This will cut down on the strongest rays and allow a wider variety of plants to be placed there.

Keep a close watch on plants for the first several days in their new location. If they show signs of distress, move them quickly. Test different plants until you find some that are suitable. Remember that the changing seasons will affect the amount of light a

Fig. 14-4. A plant track will hold several hanging plants in one arrangement. Tracks come in various lengths with a choice of attachments.

Fig. 14-5. Corner windows can be used as the basis for a plant corner such as this one.

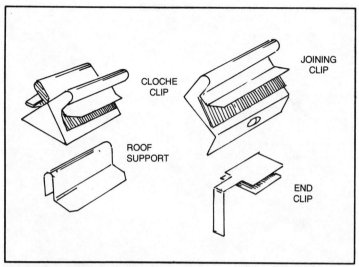

Fig. 14-6. Clips like these will hold glass or plastic panels to create plant display cubes and mini-greenhouses.

window receives. Learn to know which plants do well in each available window. You will increase your growing area and the amount of enjoyment your plants provide for the whole family.

GARDEN ROOMS

A garden room can be created from just about any room in your house that is not currently being used. The climate factors needed for a successful greenhouse will be needed here also, but on a modified scale. Any lack of a necessary climate factor can be made up artificially just as it is done in a greenhouse. But you would not keep a garden room as moist or as warm as a typical greenhouse. It is a room designed for both people and plants.

Humidity and temperature in the garden room should be as high as possible while still comfortable for people. Humidity ranging from 50 percent to 75 percent would be good for many plants. Temperatures in the 60s through low 70s would be comfortable. Plan the room to display plants attractively and provide seating for family and guests. It makes a very good reading room or quiet area for conversation. Don't put a television, stereo, or hobby equipment in your garden room. They will soon become the center of attention and the plants will go unnoticed. Leave them in the busy, and probably noisy, family room or den. Use the garden room for quiet pursuits while you are enjoying the beauty of your plants.

Fig. 14-7. An enclosed porch like this one can be converted into an excellent garden room.

A good choice for a garden room is an attached porch like the one shown in Fig. 14-7. Humidity, light, and ventilation are already present, to a useful degree, in this type of room. Some supplemental heating and winter humidity are all that is needed to make a good plant environment here. An interior room of a house with less window area and natural ventilation also can be used, but it will require more expense to supply plant needs artificially.

DECORATING WITH PLANTS

You can use your greenhouse to grow plants that enhance the decor of your house. Smart decorating books and magazines always show live plants and fresh flowers as part of the total decorating picture. With a home greenhouse you can have lush, rich-looking plants to decorate with. Those that have the professional look that interior decorator's use give you a real edge in making your home attractive.

No matter what style of furniture is in your home, it will always be enhanced with living plants. For instance, the ultra modern look of chrome, glass, and stark simplicity looks great with the bare beauty of cacti and succulents. For more traditional and antique pieces, lush ferns and foliage plants are nice. In warm, busy kitchens and frilly, colorful bedrooms, flowering plants are a natural. Notice the plant arrangements in offices and shopping malls where professional decorators are hired to make everything look just right. Consider the types and numbers of plants and how they are displayed. Notice changing seasonal decor in such places. They can provide some real inspiration for doing your own home with the professional touch.

Good lighting is essential for plant growth and health. Use artificial lighting to supplement natural light in dark areas where plants would be attractive. One good source for artificial light is the kind of track light shown in Fig. 14-8. This allows any number of separate lights to be set in the track and beamed in various directions. They can provide dramatic lighting for individual plants in any location. They are particularly effective along the hearth of a fireplace or beside a staircase.

Use plant containers that complement your decor and the beauty of the plants. Pretty, ceramic pots look good with flowering plants like African violets and with herbs in the kitchen and baby roses in the bedroom. Woven baskets are good in the family room or den with foliage plants or cacti. A large planter of metal or stone is nice in the foyer or on the patio. Choosing the right container for the

Fig. 14-8. Popular and versatile, track lighting can show off your plants in a dramatic way.

Fig. 14-9. Plants can hang against a wall with this metal rack.

plant and its location in the home is necessary to complete the picture and have the plants look "just right" wherever they are placed.

Use your imagination in finding locations for your plants. If you have a skylight, plants can be hung from it or set on the floor beneath it. Living curtains can be designed from a macrame curtain done in tiers with a hanging plant built right in. Pedestals of various materials can set one lovely plant off like a jewel in a setting. Vining plants can be trained to become a living room divider or curtain. Hanging plants on a wall is possible with an arrangement such as shown in Fig. 14-9. The hanger is similar to one used for kitchen tools. The pots are held by simple metal loops bent to the desired size. This hanger is unusual and very inexpensive to make. Any wall area that receives good lighting could accommodate such a hanger.

One especially nice place for plants is an unused fireplace. It is a natural focal point in any room. Close the damper and locate artificial lights in the base of the chimney. Fill the opening of the fireplace with plants. It becomes a year-around focal point.

When guests are coming, use the bounty of your greenhouse to make your home inviting. Plants can be table centerpieces, party favors and trim in the guest room, bathroom and bedroom. Tiny potted plants can hold placecards at a dinner. They also make good gifts for the hostess when you are the guest.

Use your plants in every way you can think of for your home, family, and friends. They add a warmth and a beauty that cannot be created any other way. Enjoy!

Chapter 15

Home Design with Plants in Mind

If you are fortunate enough to be building a new home or remodeling your present one, there are many innovations that will make your home easier to raise plants in as well as more attractive. This chapter highlights several ideas in home design that are especially suitable for raising plants. A number of simplified floor plans will give you ideas on what is available and how it can be incorporated into home design. Look at plan books for good ideas and sources of actual blueprints. Consult an architect for specifics that suit your needs. All ideas do not require huge expanses of glass that waste energy. Many current plans give plant-raising areas that actually reduce energy costs. Be sure to consider these factors when building for yourself. It is possible for the plant lover to have his cake and eat it too if designs are well thought out and the house is properly constructed. The following ideas and floor plans are to help you get started.

EXPOSURE

Gone are the days when every home on the street was built facing forward in a row like soldiers. Sound environmental planning means a house should be oriented to take advantage of the sun and wind to warm and cool a house naturally. Consider positioning your home much as you would a greenhouse. Southern and eastern exposures let in the sun in the mornings and on winter days. The short side of a house, preferably without windows, should face the harsh winds from the north. Covered porches and decks should face west to protect the house from the strong afternoon sun. Good orientation can add to the pleasure of living in any house and also reduce fuel costs.

Several floor plans are given here to offer some ideas on good orientation of a house. Figure 15-1 shows a home with a large terrace area that covers one entire end of the house. It provides for dining room and master bedroom access to the terrace. A portion of the terrace could easily be converted into a lath house or greenhouse. Letting the terrace face south, as shown, will protect it for optimum year-around use. Figures 15-2 and 15-3 show long terraces across the rear of the houses. Figure 15-2 also shows a sunken garden in the area. Facing these long sides to the east allows them to receive the morning sunlight which is best for plant growth. An open terrace is good for tubs of roses, patio tomatoes, or dwarf fruit trees.

The plan shown in Fig. 15-4 calls for a sheltered garden area and an open terrace. Because the garden has walls on three sides, it would be good for more delicate plants or bonsai trees. The orientation toward the south will give it maximum sunlight throughout the year. In Fig. 15-5, there are three large terraces with this house. Having them face east and south will provide the best light for plants. Covering one terrace for a lath house would be nice. Figure 15-6 shows two large bay areas on each end of a living/dining room combination. These are good for hanging plants and large indoor trees. Use the covered deck at the rear for a shade house. This area should face east for best use of the available light.

A smaller house with lots of outdoor living space is shown in Fig. 15-7. The long rear deck is fine for plants. The sheltered side deck could easily be enclosed further for garden room or greenhouse use. Angling the house so that a corner faces north allows for best use of the outdoor living area. The patio and corner garden in Fig. 15-8 are set at the rear of the house with access from the family room and conversation pit. This area will be seen and appreciated by family and guests to a great extent. Attractive potted plants on the patio and a very pretty garden area are a must here. Orientation to the east and south would be best.

PLANT PLACES

Many home plans include special areas set aside for plants. Certain standard building features are also excellent areas for raising plants. Among these, the bay window is most notable. Other

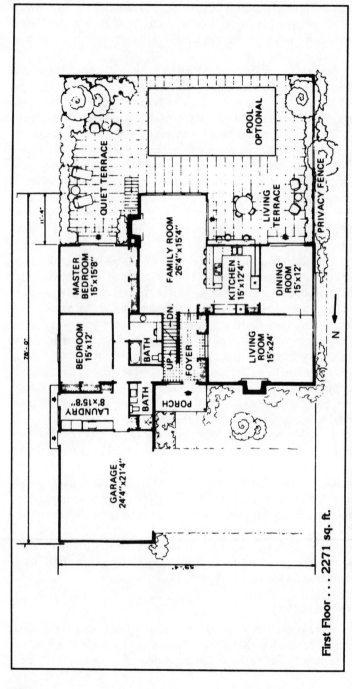

Fig. 15-1. This house should have the terrace and pool side facing south to get maximum sunlight throughout the year.

First Floor . . . 2271 sq. ft.

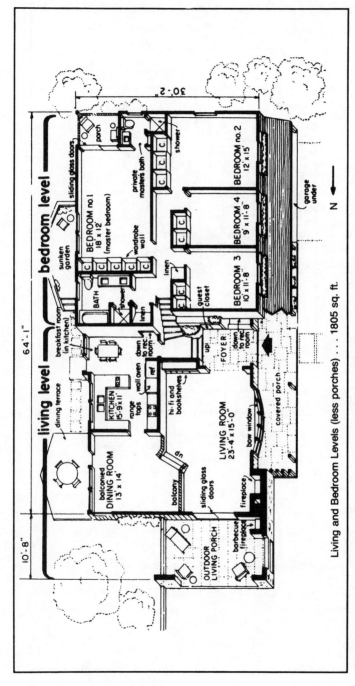

Living and Bedroom Levels (less porches) . . . 1805 sq. ft.

Fig. 15-2. Orient this house so that the long garden side at the rear faces east for best light for the plants.

201

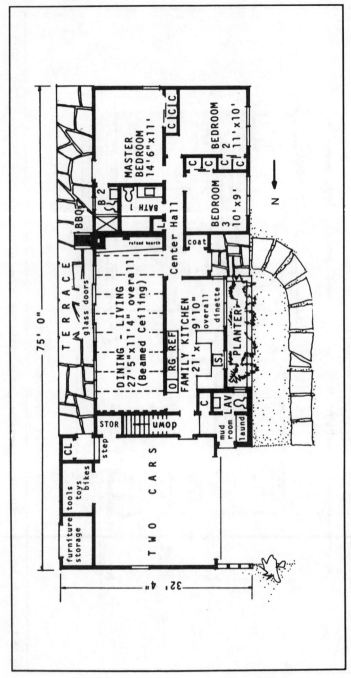

Fig. 15-3. The long terrace at the rear of this house should face east.

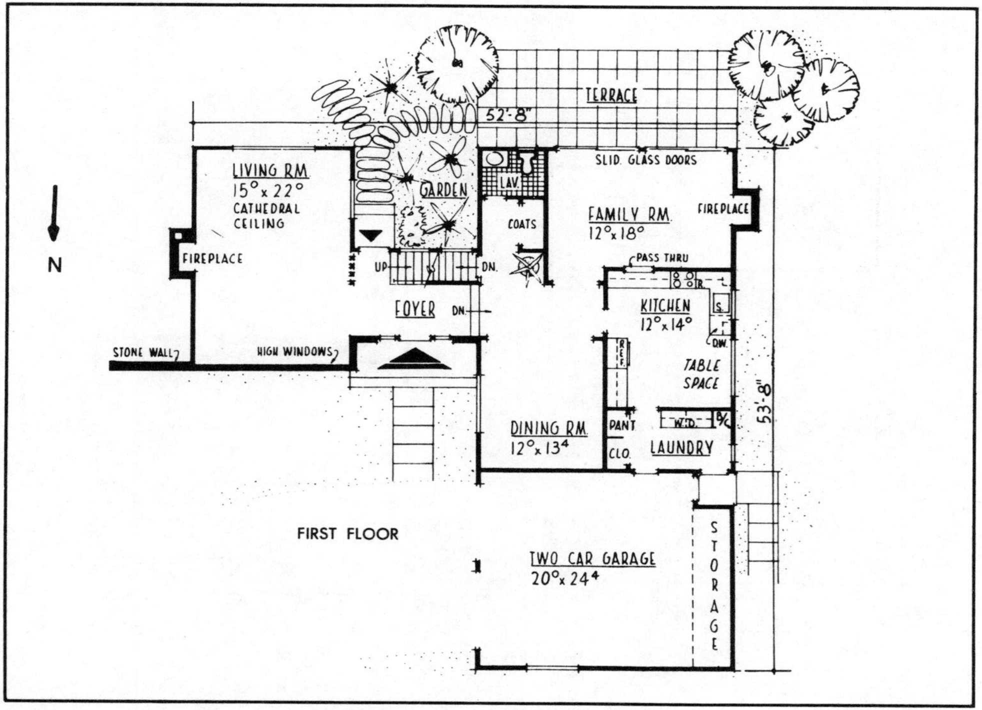

Fig. 15-4. The sheltered garden and terrace in this plan would be best if facing south.

FIRST FLOOR

LIVING RM.
15° x 22°
CATHEDRAL CEILING

FIREPLACE

STONE WALL?

HIGH WINDOWS?

FOYER

DN.

UP

DN.

GARDEN

LAV.

COATS

53'-8"

52'-8"

TERRACE

SLID GLASS DOORS

FIREPLACE

FAMILY RM.
12° x 18°

PASS THRU

KITCHEN
12° x 14°

TABLE SPACE

W/D

LAUNDRY

PANT.

CLO.

DINING RM.
12° x 13⁴

TWO CAR GARAGE
20° x 24⁴

STORAGE

N

203

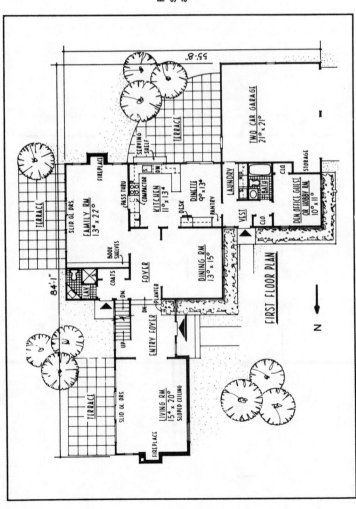

Fig. 15-5. This house should be built so that the three terraces face east and south.

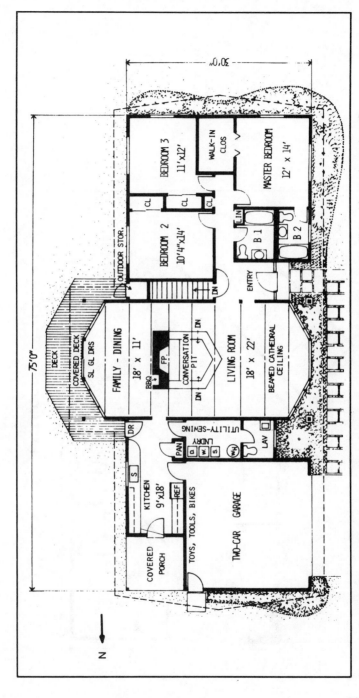

Fig. 15-6. Orienting the short side of this house, where the garage is located, to the north will provide maximum benefit.

205

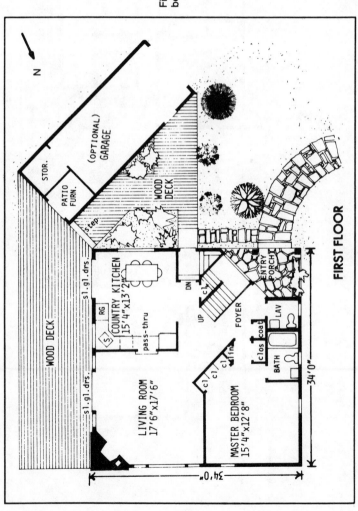

Fig. 15-7. This unusual house should be built with a corner facing north.

FIRST FLOOR

N

WOOD DECK

(OPTIONAL) GARAGE

STOR.

PATIO FURN.

step

WOOD DECK

sl. gl. drs.

COUNTRY KITCHEN
15'4"x13'2"

RG

S

pass-thru

DN

cl.

UP

FOYER

ENTRY PORCH

clos

coat

fin.

cl. cl. cl.

LAV

BATH

LIVING ROOM
17'6"x17'6"

MASTER BEDROOM
15'4"x12'8"

sl. gl. drs.

sl. gl. drs.

34'0"

34'0"

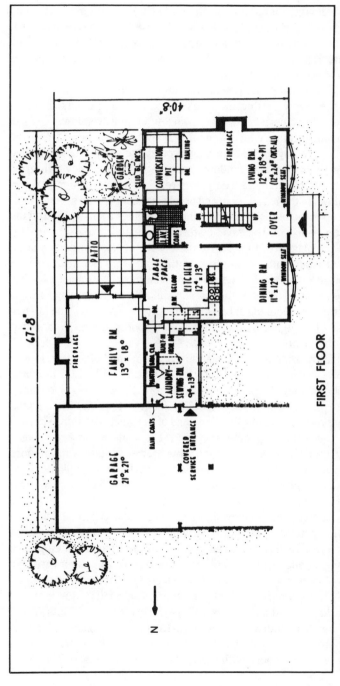

FIRST FLOOR

Fig. 15-8. Facing the garage end of this house to the north will provide extra protection in cold weather and give morning sun to the garden and patio plants.

207

good design elements for plants include skylights, screened porches, and sliding glass doors. All these items create areas that are beneficial for plants and areas that are easy to decorate with plants. Here are some floor plans that reflect the use of live plants as part of good house design.

Bay windows are one of my personal favorites for their beauty and the lovely setting they make for all sorts of plants. Hanging baskets look perfect in a bay window or bow window. Tiers of blooming plants are lovely on the window seat. Vines can frame the panels of a bay window in year around greenery. Plants receive better light in a bay window than a regular one. They will grow better and bloom more freely. Figure 15-9 shows a design with bay windows in the living room and breakfast nook. On the second floor, the top of the living room bay window becomes a small porch off the master bedroom. Here one feature has created two good areas for growing plants. In Fig. 15-10, the entire breakfast area is a large bay. It is also interesting to note the "garden windows" provided over the kitchen sink. Every homemaker knows how much time has to be spent standing at the kitchen sink. What better way to enjoy that time than looking at beautiful plants growing there. The kitchen usually has higher humidity than other rooms in a house and that aids the plants.

A low wall used as a planter is nice in any home. If it doesn't receive enough natural light, track lighting will add a dramatic touch and keep the plants healthy. Figure 15-11 shows an ordinary house plan with one special feature. Between the entry area and the dining room is a planter wall instead of a regular partition. This is a nice touch that separates the two areas while making the rooms seem bigger. It allows an open view between them. A much more intense use of planters is shown in Fig. 15-12. Built-in planters are located in the foyer, bathrooms, and staircase. Such a home will have a rich, tropical feeling throughout.

Skylights have enjoyed a renewed popularity lately. They can provide natural light where no windows can be built. They add a dramatic note in any room and look especially nice in contemporary settings. Hanging plants can surround a skylight, but, their care may be a problem for people who dislike ladders. Plants can be grouped on the floor where sunlight from the skylight falls. This arrangement looks good and allows you the chance to grow plants where you couldn't otherwise. Figure 15-13 shows the plans for a two-story house with a skylight otherwise. Figure 15-13 shows the plans for a two-story house with a skylight over the staircase. The stairs

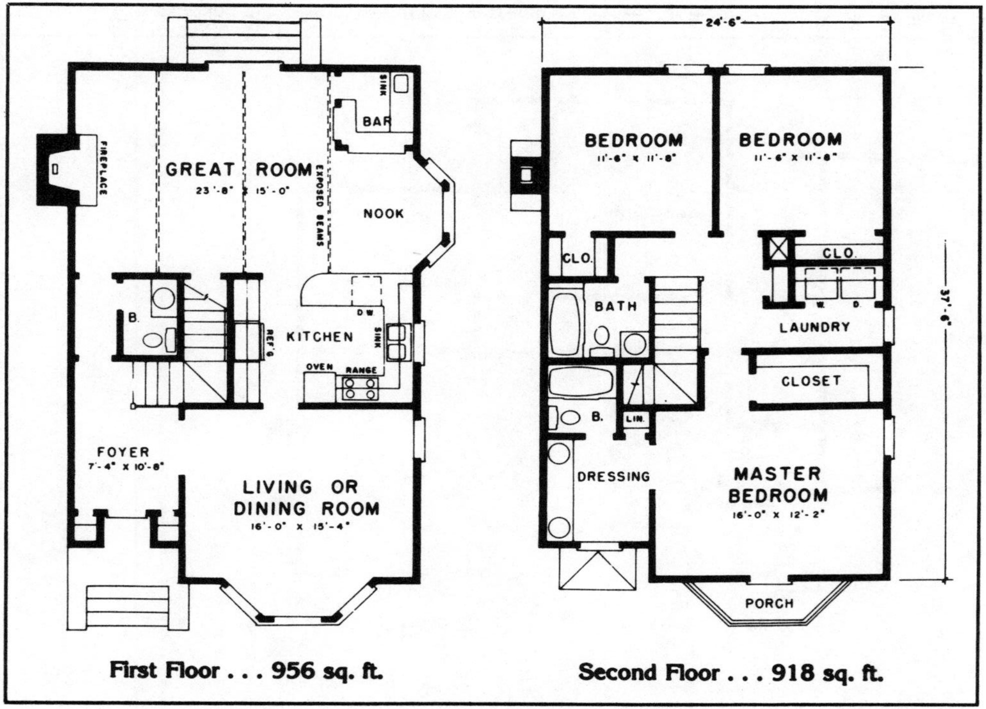

Fig. 15-9. The large bay windows in this plan are excellent spots for growing plants.

First Floor . . . 956 sq. ft.

Second Floor . . . 918 sq. ft.

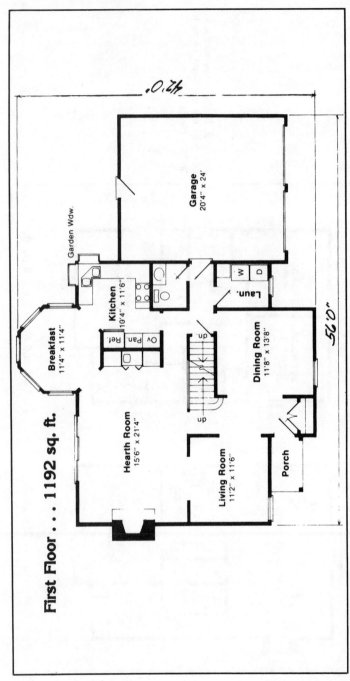

First Floor . . . 1192 sq. ft.

Hearth Room 15'6" x 21'4"

Living Room 11'2" x 11'6"

Breakfast 11'4" x 11'4"

Garden Wdw.

Kitchen 10'4" x 11'6"

Ref. | Pan.

Ov

up dn. dn.

Dining Room 11'8" x 13'8"

Laun.

W | D

Garage 20'4" x 24'

Porch

42'0"

51'0"

Fig. 15-10. The extra large breakfast bay in this plan would be great for plants.

210

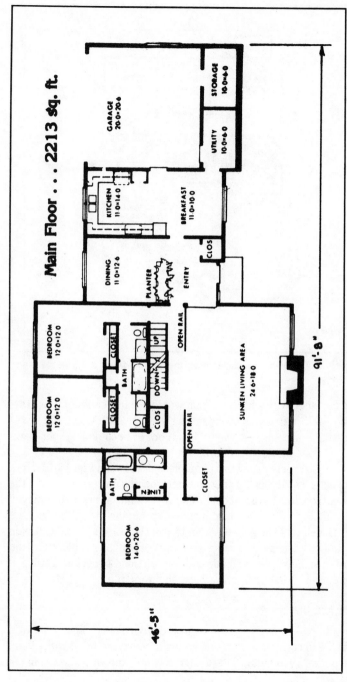

Fig. 15-11. A planter wall is used here to separate the entry from the dining room.

211

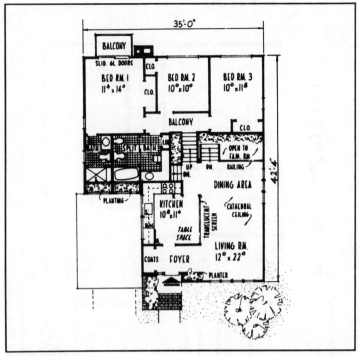

Fig. 15-12. This plan calls for planters in the bathrooms and along the stairs and balcony.

are designed with a landing. That would be an excellent place to set plants with the skylight above. The addition of this one item gives the stairs natural light and allows them to become a "green pathway" between the two floors.

A very nice plan with a plant place is shown in Fig. 15-14. Here a private garden is planned directly behind the garage with the garage roof used as a sun deck. This allows the garden to be enjoyed directly and also viewed from above by sun lovers. With this plan, the garden could be geometric and formal if desired. It could provide shade with trees or an arbor or lath roof. Anyone could enjoy the garden in the shade or sun themselves on the roof deck and still see the garden. This plan is practical and versatile.

THE ATRIUM

If you had lived in ancient Rome, your home might very well have been constructed around an inner courtyard filled with plants and perhaps a fountain. This design concept, known as the atrium, is being revived today. The home is designed so that all or most of the rooms open to this central courtyard. It might be left open to the sky or glass-covered in colder climates. Some plans call for the atrium to also function as a passive solar heating unit.

The atrium does increase construction costs and must be planned and built with care. It should not increase fuel use if it is designed properly. For passive solar heating use, the atrium needs one wall and a floor of heat-retaining concrete. Sliding doors can release this gathered heat into the main living areas. Shading and ceiling vents keep the atrium cool in hot weather.

In Fig. 15-15, the atrium opens onto the family room only. This idea keeps additional heating costs to a minimum while allowing the atrium to be enjoyed by people in the kitchen and family room. Those rooms are usually the two most active areas in a house. A "working" atrium, labeled a sun garden, is shown in Fig. 15-16. It is

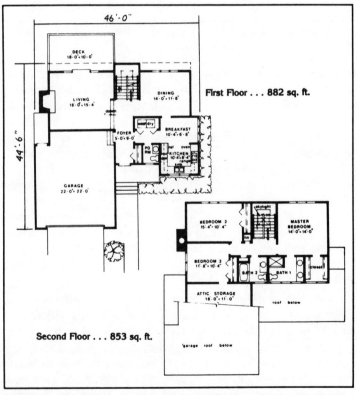

Fig. 15-13. The skylight over the stairway in this plan allows natural light for plants in a usually dark location.

Fig. 15-14A. This elegant home has a private garden with a sun deck overlooking it.

centrally located in the house and has sliding glass doors to separate it from the main living area. The floor and half of one wall are to be made of concrete or stone. This wall should face south. It is designed to be a passive solar collector. The sliding doors are opened when the heat collected is needed to warm the rest of the house. High vents in the atrium provide natural ventilation for cooling. Shades are used to keep out unwanted heat in the summer. They should be translucent to allow light to reach the plants in the atrium at all times.

Two other plans, with areas labeled atriums, are shown in Figs. 15-17 and 15-18. Actually, these are more like sheltered gardens enclosed on three sides rather than true atriums.

THE GARDEN COURT

To achieve the appearance of an atrium with less planning and cost, a garden court is the answer. It is generally constructed directly off the house with high walls for privacy and shelter. With a partial solid roof, it can be enjoyed by people in practically any weather. With a lattice roof it, easily serves as a shade house or lath house. Plants normally too delicate to be grown outdoors in your area, might thrive in a protected garden court. They should face east or south to receive maximum benefit from the sun.

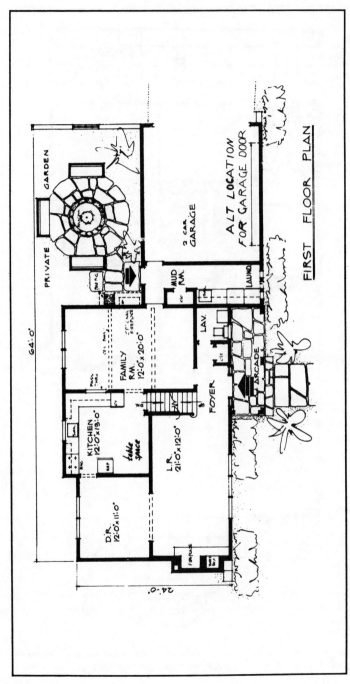

PRIVATE GARDEN

64'-0"

24'-0"

D.R.
12'-0"×11'-0"

KITCHEN
12'-0"×13'-0"

table space

FAMILY
RM.
12'-0"×20'-0"

OPTIONAL FIREPLACE

PASS-THRU

L.R.
21'-0"×12'-0"

FOYER

LAV.

MUD
RM.

LAUND.

2 CAR
GARAGE

ARCADE

FIREPLACE

ALT LOCATION
FOR GARAGE DOOR

FIRST FLOOR PLAN

Fig. 15-14B. Plans for the home shown in Fig. 15-14A.

215

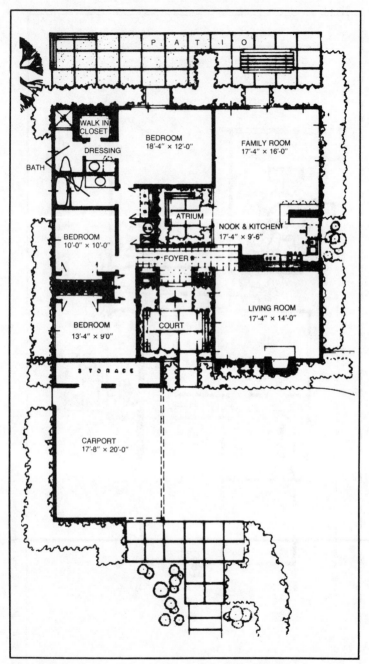

Fig. 15-15. This house has an atrium off the family room/kitchen.

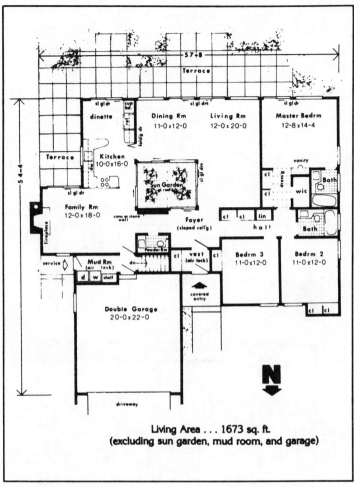

Fig. 15-16. The sun garden shown here is designed as a passive solar heater as well as a plant place.

One popular location for a garden court is next to the front entrance of a house. This allows guests to have a very attractive view up the front walk and while waiting at the door. It also gives more privacy because some of the front windows open onto the court rather than the street. Figures 15-19 and 15-20 show front garden courts adjacent to the main walkway and a front entrance to the house. This area can be planted with your favorite blooming plants, some shrubs, and a small tree or two. Good trees to plant in a garden court are Japanese maple, golden chain, Chinese cherry, or

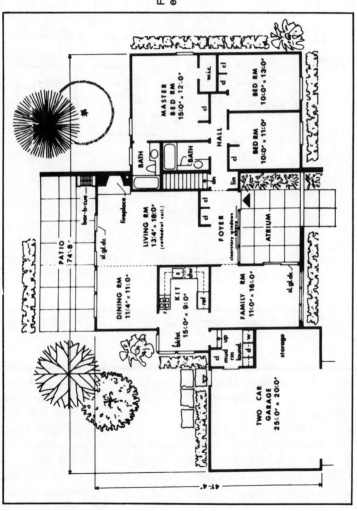

Fig. 15-17. This atrium is used as an entrance garden.

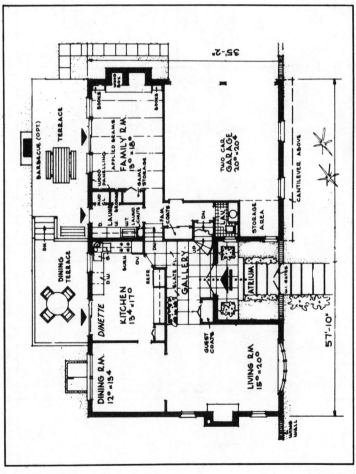

Fig. 15-18. This atrium is used as an entrance garden.

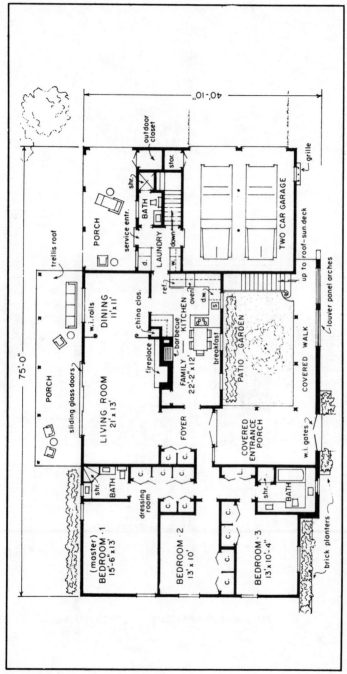

Fig. 15-19. The patio garden is adjacent to the entrance porch.

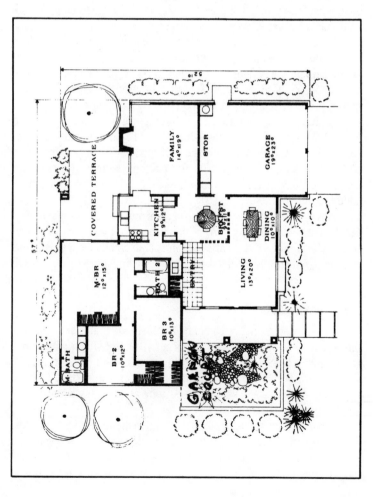

Fig. 15-20. This garden court can be seen through the living room.

smoke tree. Good blooming plants to try include gardenia, wisteria, hibiscus, all types of roses, and honeysuckle. Those flowers with a beautiful fragrance will fill your home with their perfume.

A garden court might have a focal point such as a fountain, a statue, or even a redwood hot tub. Two plans indicating a fountain are given in Figs. 15-21 and 15-22. Both of these garden courts are next to the front entry. In Fig. 15-23, the garden court is directly next to the entrance and an unusual circular foyer. This plan also shows an open porch, a screened porch, and a terrace. That gives plenty of plant places to use.

A front porch running the length of a garden court is shown in Fig. 15-24. This is a very attractive idea; the court can be enjoyed easily from the comfort of the covered porch. The surrounding brick wall and front gates screen the street view.

A very private garden court plan is shown in Fig. 15-25. Here the house, garage, and outdoor storage enclose the court on four sides. Sliding glass doors in the dining room and master bedroom provide a nice outdoor view. This plan is very workable with good use of the space and good planning for the garden court.

An interesting variation on the typical garden court is shown in Fig. 15-26. Here the first floor has a covered porch and a garage. Above this on the second floor is a roof garden with access from two bedrooms. A roof garden calls for potted plants and vines that require full sunlight. Some plant benches and a partial roof can be added as desired.

A way to double the pleasure of a garden court is shown in Fig. 15-27. This plan calls for two of them; one is at the front entrance and one is off the two regular bedrooms. One of these, especially the bedroom garden, would be very nice when converted into a greenhouse.

THE GARDEN ROOM

The garden room is a room inside the home that is set aside for the benefit of people and plants. It is set up as a plant-growing room and display room with good seating for people. In Chapter 14, I discuss garden rooms in general and give an example, (Fig. 14-7) of an attached porch used as one. Let's look at some floor plans with good rooms to use as garden rooms.

Figure 15-28 shows a plan with "old fashioned" names for the various rooms. There is a parlor, a morning room, and a conservatory. In Chapter 1, the conservatory is mentioned as the garden room of fine homes in the 19th century. Here the concept is being

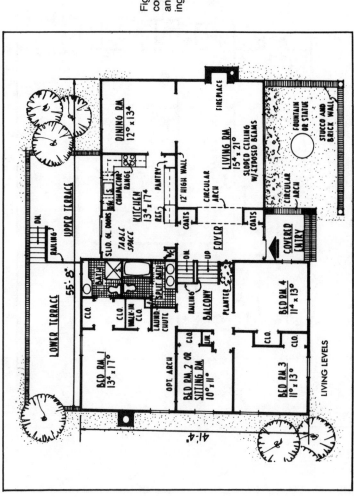

Fig. 15-21. This formal front garden court is surrounded by a privacy wall and can be enjoyed through the living room windows.

223

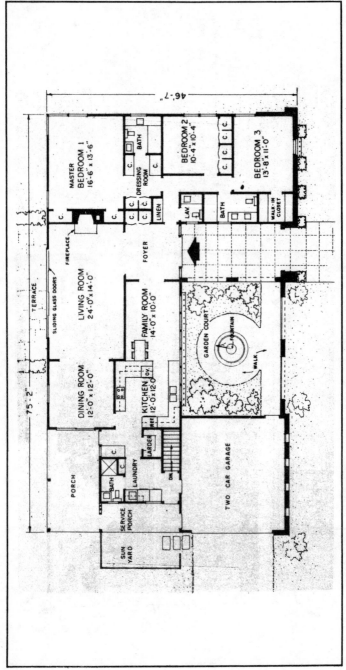

Fig. 15-22. The garden court is designed with a circular walk and fountain.

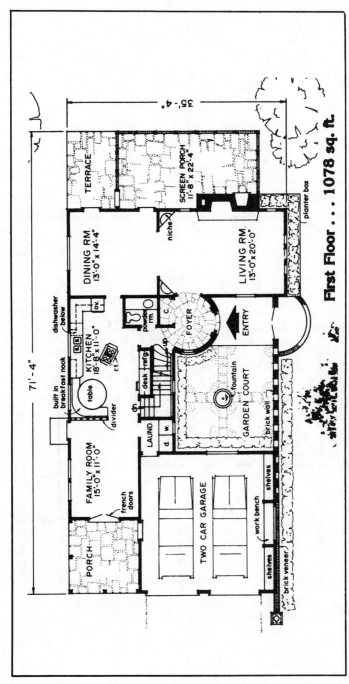

Fig. 15-23. This garden court is adjacent to an interesting circular foyer.

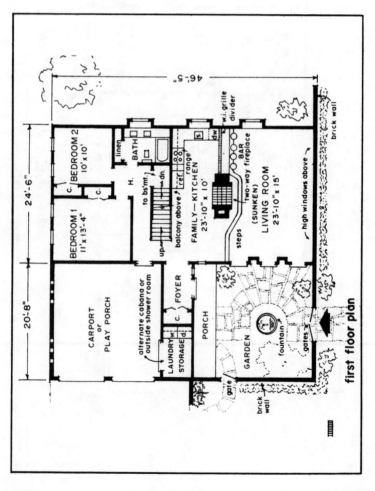

Fig. 15-24. Here the front porch overlooks a private garden.

first floor plan

BEDROOM 2
10' x 10'

BEDROOM 1
11' x 13'-4"

linen

BATH

H.

to bs'm't

dn.

up

balcony above

c.

c.

CARPORT
or
PLAY PORCH

alternate cabana or
outside shower room

LAUNDRY
STORAGE

w
d

FOYER

c.

PORCH

FAMILY—KITCHEN
23'-10" x 10'

range

ref.

dw

s.

w.i. grille
divider

BAR

"two-way fireplace"

steps

(SUNKEN)
LIVING ROOM
23'-10" x 15'

high windows above

brick wall

GARDEN

fountain

gate

gates

brick wall

46'-5"

24'-6"

20'-8"

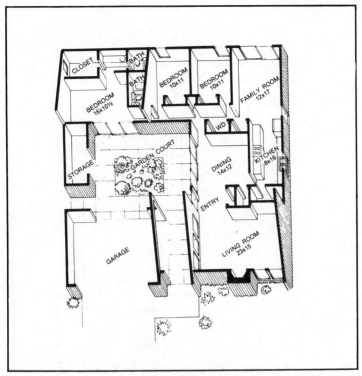

Fig. 15-25. This garden court is sheltered on four sides and located to be enjoyed from the dining room and master bedroom.

revived in a new house with old-fashion charm. This design calls for the parlor to step down to the conservatory that is flooded with light from the bay. This seems like it was designed to function just like the conservatory rooms of yesterday. The tiled floor is easy to care for when raising plants and the huge bay will emit plenty of natural light. This updating of an old home design concept is a most welcome one for plant lovers.

Modern home plans are shown in Figs. 15-29 and 15-30. In each case, the plan calls for a screened porch with a terrace off of it. Porches are excellent garden rooms with plenty of natural light and ventilation. With the adjacent terrace, plants can easily be moved outside during good weather. Storm windows can be added to the porch so that it can be used year around.

The use of a "spare room" that can be converted to a garden room is seen in Fig. 15-31. The spare room is off of the kitchen and the terrace. It has good access to the outside and garage for plant

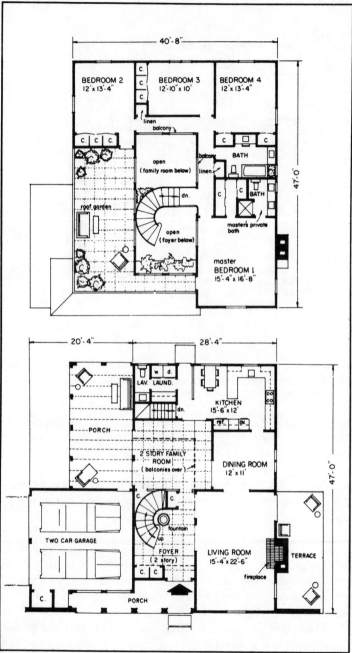

Fig. 15-26. This unusual plan calls for a roof garden.

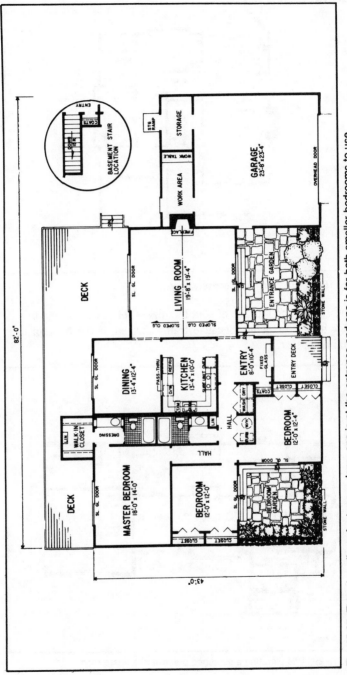

Fig. 15-27. This plan allows for two gardens; one is at the entrance and one is for both smaller bedrooms to use.

229

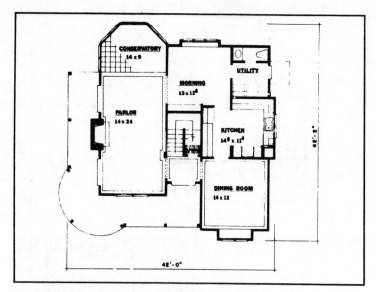

Fig. 15-28. This plan has a conservatory.

care duties and storage of soil, fertilizers, etc. A room like this is very handy for plants because traffic through it can be kept to a minimum.

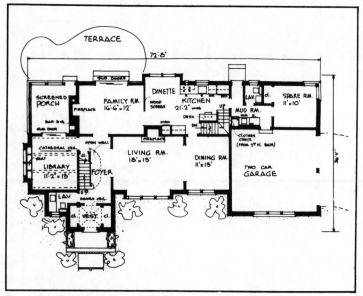

Fig. 15-29. This plan has a screened porch and a spare room.

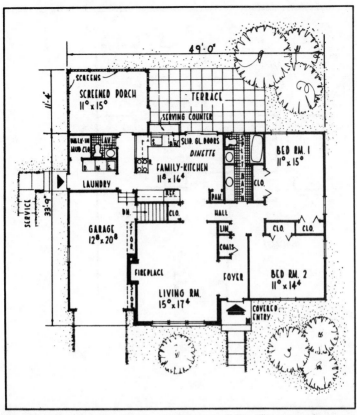

Fig. 15-30. This plan has a large screened porch off the utility area and terrace.

Another good spot for a garden room is shown in Fig. 15-32. It is a screened porch that connects the house to the garage. This was often called a breezeway and was open or enclosed as desired. It is well located with the garage for storage of plant care materials and the kitchen for water hook-up. It will be used as a walk-through, but plants can be concentrated on each end of the room. There will be an abundance of natural light and ventilation here.

A combination screened porch and arbor terrace is shown in Fig. 15-33. Both areas are excellent for plants. Sliding screen doors connect the porch and terrace and also the porch and the outside rear of the house. This is good for warm-weather cultivation of plants. The porch can be fully enclosed for year around use as desired.

Figure 15-34 calls for a different spare room arrangement. Here it is off the kitchen/utility area with no through access. Water

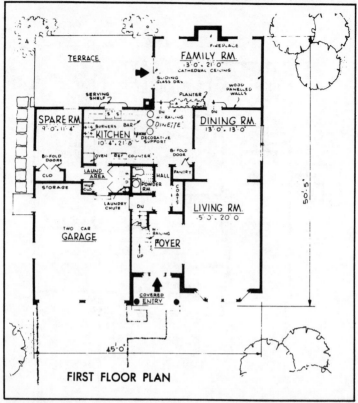

Fig. 15-31. The spare room in this plan has access from the utility area, terrace and directly from the outside. This would make raising plants and doing repotting chores easy.

hook-up and garage storage are very handy. The out-of-the way location makes this room especially nice for starting plants from seed or cuttings. It could be very much a work room for serious cultivation. Privacy would be available for the dedicated gardener.

A *lanai,* a Hawaiian term for a lounging porch, is shown off the master bedroom in Fig. 15-35. This would be easy to partially or fully enclose and create a very nice garden room. Watering chores can be done using the master bath for water. An outside entrance could be added to allow plants to be moved in and out without going through the house. In the master suite location, a garden room is private—yet accessible. It can double as a study, a reading room or relaxing room. Consider this location if you have an active, growing family and fear for the safety of your plants in a garden room with general access.

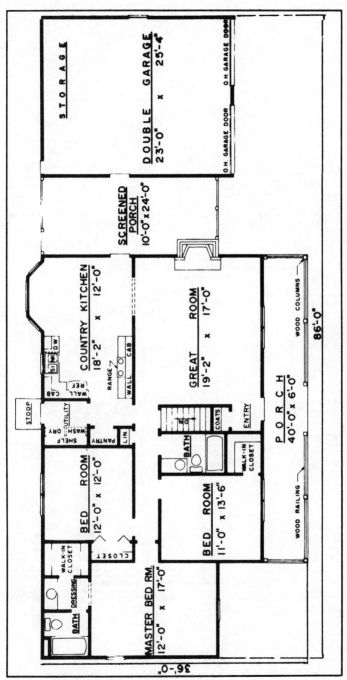

Fig. 15-32. The screened porch or breezeway between the house and garage is a great plant place.

233

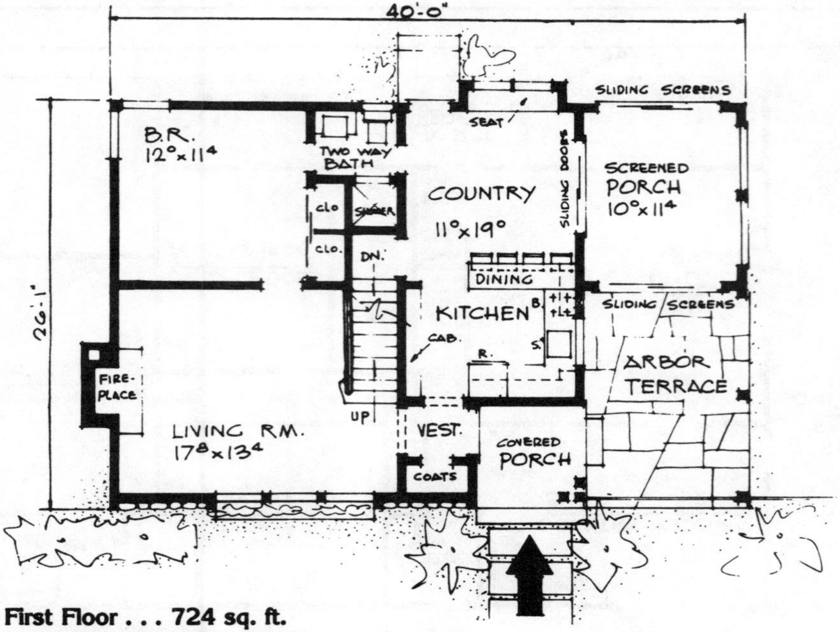

Fig. 15-33. The screened porch and arbor terrace in this plan are great plant places.

First Floor . . . 724 sq. ft.
(excluding screened porch)

SLIDING SCREENS

SCREENED PORCH 10' x 11'⁴

ARBOR TERRACE

SLIDING DOORS

SLIDING SCREENS

COUNTRY 11'⁰ x 19'⁰

DINING 8'

KITCHEN

CAB.

R.

SEAT

COVERED PORCH

VEST.

COATS

40'-0"

TWO WAY BATH

CLO.

CLO.

DN.

UP

B.R. 12' x 11'⁴

LIVING R.M. 17'⁸ x 13'⁴

FIRE-PLACE

26'-1"

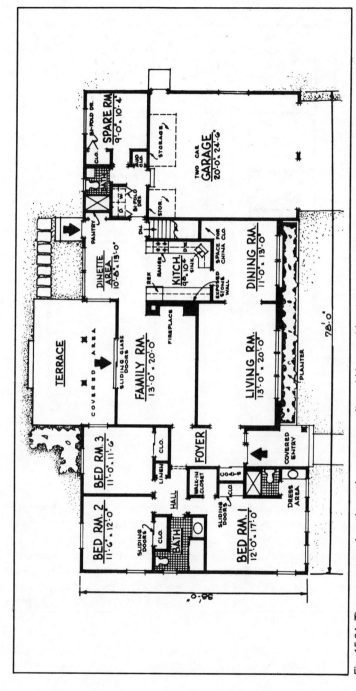

Fig. 15-34. The spare room here has only one access. It would be good for plant culture away from the family activities.

235

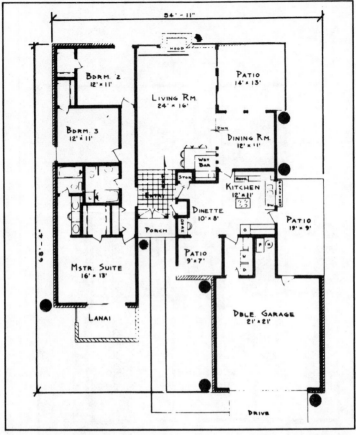

Fig. 15-35. The lanai, or lounging porch, off the master bedroom would make a good garden room with privacy.

A GREENHOUSE IN YOUR HOME

When building a new house, it is possible to use plans that call for a greenhouse as part of the home. It can be located just about anywhere in the house and can be a tiny corner or a large room. With this concept, your greenhouse will be where you want it and how you want it right from the start. It will fit in with the rest of the house and not have the added-on look of an addition. Design and style will be tailored to fit your preference. Anyone who loves plants should consider a greenhouse as part of their total home picture if they are building or remodeling.

Innovation is the key word to describe the plan shown in Fig. 15-36. The greenhouse is an L-shape and encircles two sides of the

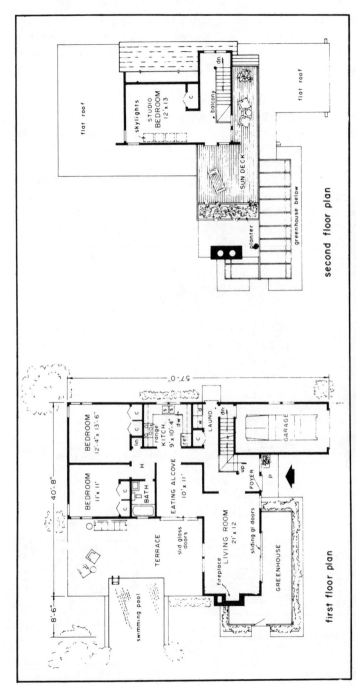

Fig. 15-36. This smartly styled house has an L-shaped greenhouse and a sun deck with large planter.

living room. It also has an outside entrance. One wall is the back of the living room fireplace and should be very attractive as a backdrop for plants. On the second floor, a sun deck with a large planter overlooks the greenhouse. This will provide a very different view of your plants.

Figure 15-37 shows a small, glassed-in greenhouse that overlooks the rear deck. It is accessible through the garage. That will allow the garage area to be used for potting and materials storage. Plants can be easily moved from the greenhouse to the deck for summers outdoors.

A house designed for the dedicated greenthumb is shown in Fig. 15-38. There is a greenhouse off the utility room and next to the terrace. The utility area will be used for some of the messier greenhouse chores. This plan also calls for a garden set in the

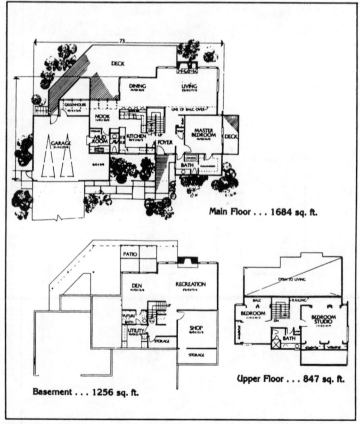

Fig. 15-37. This home greenhouse overlooks the large rear deck.

238

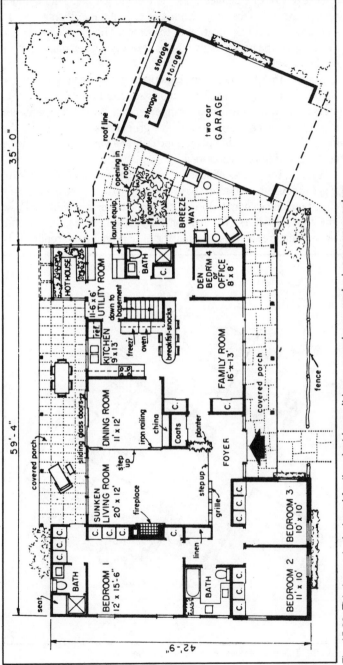

Fig. 15-38. This house is designed for the plant lover. It has a greenhouse and a breezeway garden.

The breezeway that connects the house and garage. This outdoor garden is readily accessible from the greenhouse. Plants can be easily moved from one location to the other. The garage is set at a 20° angle from the house to give the breezeway garden more privacy from the street.

Figure 15-39 shows a greenhouse off the master bedroom. Here one could enjoy the plants in privacy from the family activity centers. This would be a good arrangement for the serious gardener who prefers peace and quiet. If the greenhouse is used for the culture of rare or valuable plants, locating it away from the general household traffic is a good idea.

A large, home greenhouse is shown in the plans in Fig. 15-40. The greenhouse is a comfortable 10 feet by 16 feet in size and forms the front entrance room to the house. This means it will be on show to guests and visitors. Whether or not you want this kind of traffic through your greenhouse is a matter of personal preference. This

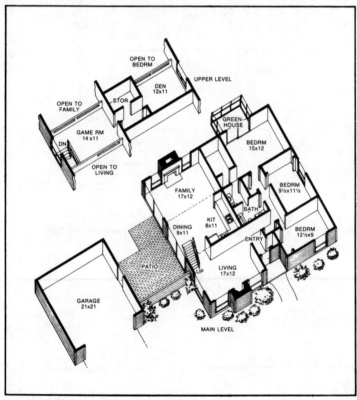

Fig. 15-39. This greenhouse is off the master bedroom.

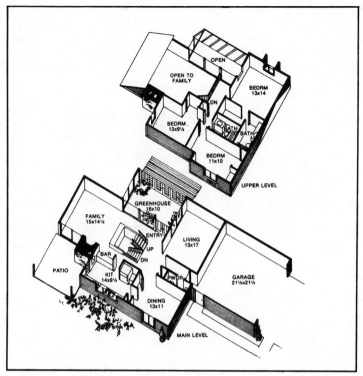

Fig. 15-40. This spacious greenhouse is designed as an entry into the home.

plan calls for the greenhouse to be two stories high so the master bedroom upstairs overlooks it—a nice touch.

These plans give you an idea of the many possibilities to building and enjoying a home greenhouse. It is possible to find a selection of stock plans that are designed to please the plant lover. You might want to work with an architect to draw up your personal combination of home and greenhouse.

Plans

Plan 1
Home Greenhouse

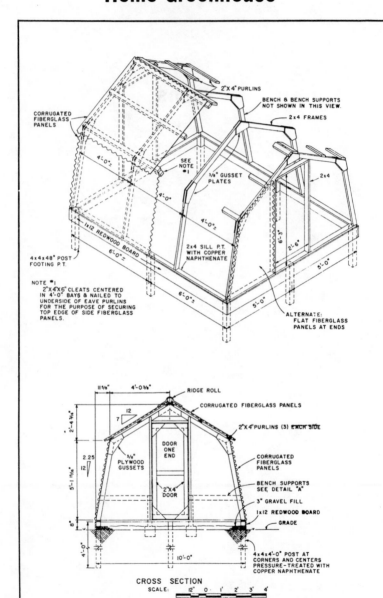

CORRUGATED FIBERGLASS PANELS

2" X 4" PURLINS

BENCH & BENCH SUPPORTS NOT SHOWN IN THIS VIEW.

2 x 4 FRAMES

SEE NOTE #1

3/8" GUSSET PLATES

2 x 4

4'-0"±

4'-0"

4'-0"±

6'-3"

2'-6"

5'-0"

1x12 REDWOOD BOARD

2x4 SILL P.T. WITH COPPER NAPHTHENATE

4 x 4 x 48" POST FOOTING P.T.

6'-0"±

6'-0"±

5'-0"

NOTE #1
2"X 4"X 6" CLEATS CENTERED IN 4'-0" BAYS & NAILED TO UNDERSIDE OF EAVE PURLINS FOR THE PURPOSE OF SECURING TOP EDGE OF SIDE FIBERGLASS PANELS.

ALTERNATE: FLAT FIBERGLASS PANELS AT ENDS

11 5/8"

4'-0 3/8"

RIDGE ROLL

CORRUGATED FIBERGLASS PANELS

2'-4 3/4"

12

7

2" X 4' PURLINS (3) EACH SIDE

2.25

12

3/8" PLYWOOD GUSSETS

5'-1 11/16"

DOOR ONE END

CORRUGATED FIBERGLASS PANELS

BENCH SUPPORTS SEE DETAIL "A"

2"X 4" DOOR

3" GRAVEL FILL

8"

1x12 REDWOOD BOARD

GRADE

4'-0"

10'-0"

4 x 4 x 4'-0" POST AT CORNERS AND CENTERS PRESSURE-TREATED WITH COPPER NAPHTHENATE

CROSS SECTION
SCALE: 12" 0 1' 2' 3' 4'

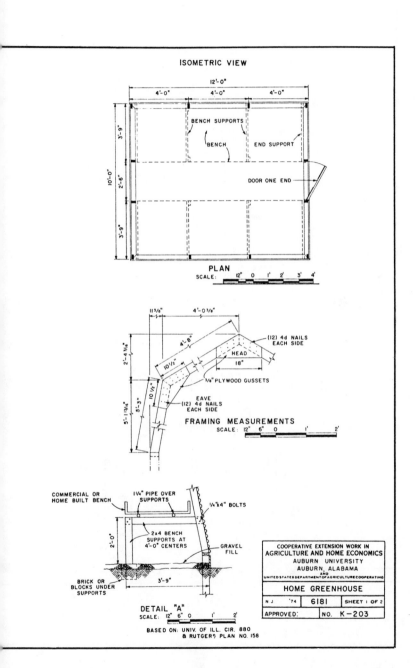

ISOMETRIC VIEW

12'-0"
4'-0" 4'-0" 4'-0"

BENCH SUPPORTS

BENCH   END SUPPORT

3'-9"

10'-0"

2'-6"

DOOR ONE END

3'-9"

PLAN
SCALE: 12" 0 1' 2' 3' 4'

11 ⅜"   4'-0 ⅜"

(12) 4d NAILS
EACH SIDE

4'-8"

2'-4 ¹⁵⁄₁₆"

HEAD

10 ½"   18"

⅜" PLYWOOD GUSSETS

5'-1 ¹³⁄₁₆"

5'-3"

10 ½"

EAVE
(12) 4d NAILS
EACH SIDE

FRAMING MEASUREMENTS
SCALE: 12" 6" 0 1' 2'

COMMERCIAL OR
HOME BUILT BENCH

1¼" PIPE OVER
SUPPORTS

¼"x4" BOLTS

2x4 BENCH
SUPPORTS AT
4'-0" CENTERS

2'-0"

GRAVEL
FILL

BRICK OR
BLOCKS UNDER
SUPPORTS

3'-9"

DETAIL "A"
SCALE: 12" 6" 0 1' 2'

BASED ON: UNIV. OF ILL. CIR. 880
& RUTGERS PLAN NO. 158

COOPERATIVE EXTENSION WORK IN
AGRICULTURE AND HOME ECONOMICS
AUBURN UNIVERSITY
AUBURN, ALABAMA
AND
UNITED STATES DEPARTMENT OF AGRICULTURE COOPERATING

HOME GREENHOUSE

| N J | '74 | 6181 | SHEET 1 OF 2 |
| APPROVED: | | NO. K-203 | |

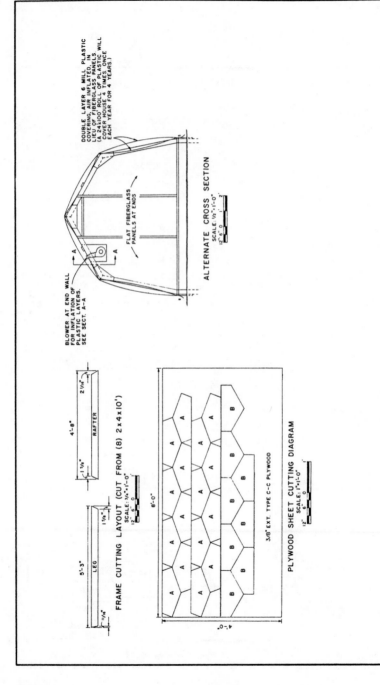

DOUBLE LAYER 6 MILL PLASTIC COVERING, AIR INFLATED, IN LIEU OF FIBERGLASS PANELS (A 24'x100' ROLL OF PLASTIC WILL COVER HOUSE 4 TIMES, ONCE EACH YEAR FOR 4 YEARS.)

ALTERNATE CROSS SECTION
SCALE: 1/2"=1'-0"

FLAT FIBERGLASS PANELS AT ENDS

BLOWER AT END WALL FOR INFLATION OF PLASTIC LAYERS. SEE SECT. A-A

FRAME CUTTING LAYOUT (CUT FROM (8) 2x4x10')
SCALE: 3/4"=1'-0"

RAFTER
4'-8"
2 1/4"
1 1/4"

LEG
5'-3"
1 1/4"
1 1/4"

PLYWOOD SHEET CUTTING DIAGRAM
SCALE: 1"=1'-0"

3/8" EXT. TYPE C-C PLYWOOD

8'-0"
4'-0"

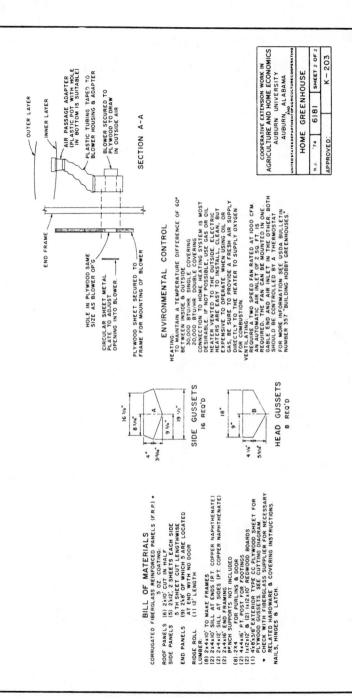

OUTER LAYER

INNER LAYER

AIR PASSAGE ADAPTER
(PLASTIC POT WITH HOLE
IN BOTTOM IS SUITABLE)

PLASTIC TUBING TAPE'D TO
BLOWER HOUSING & ADAPTER

BLOWER SECURED TO
PLYWOOD TO DRAW
IN OUTSIDE AIR

END FRAME

SECTION A-A

HOLE IN PLYWOOD SAME
SIZE AS BLOWER OP'G

CIRCULAR SHEET METAL
PLATE TO ADJUST
OPENING INTO BLOWER

PLYWOOD SHEET SECURED TO
FRAME FOR MOUNTING OF BLOWER

ENVIRONMENTAL CONTROL

HEATING:
TO MAINTAIN A TEMPERATURE DIFFERENCE OF 60°
BETWEEN INSIDE & OUTSIDE
30,000 BTU/HR SINGLE COVERING
20,000 BTU/HR DOUBLE COVERING
CONNECTION TO HOME HEATING SYSTEM IS MOST
DESIRABLE. IF NOT POSSIBLE, USE GAS OR OIL
HEATER VENTED TO THE OUTSIDE. ELECTRIC
HEATERS ARE EASY TO INSTALL, CLEAN, BUT
EXPENSIVE TO OPERATE. WHEN USING OIL OR
GAS, BE SURE TO PROVIDE A FRESH AIR SUPPLY
DIRECTLY TO THE HEATER TO SUPPLY OXYGEN
FOR COMBUSTION.
VENTILATING: TWO SPEED FAN RATED AT 1000 CFM.
REQUIRE A AUTOMATIC AIR INLET OF 2 SQ FT. IS
REQUIRED. THE FAN CAN BE MOUNTED IN ONE
GABLE END AND AIR INLET IN THE OTHER. BOTH
SHOULD BE CONTROLLED BY A THERMOSTAT
FOR MORE INFORMATION SEE USDA BULLETIN
NUMBER 357 "BUILDING HOBBY GREENHOUSES."

16 ⅓"

8 ¾"

9 ¾"

A

19 ½"

4"

3¾₆"

SIDE GUSSETS
16 REQ'D

18"

9"

B

4 ¼"

5⅛"

HEAD GUSSETS
8 REQ'D

BILL OF MATERIALS

CORRUGATED FIBERGLASS REINFORCED PANELS (F.R.P.) *
5 OZ. COATING.
ROOF PANELS (6) 2x10' CUT IN HALF
SIDE PANELS (5) 2x12', 2 SHEETS EACH SIDE
5 TH SHEET CUT LENGTHWISE
END PANELS (9) 2x8' OF WHICH 5 ARE LOCATED
AT END WITH NO DOOR
RIDGE ROLL (1) 12' LENGTH
LUMBER:
(8) 2x4x10' TO MAKE FRAMES
(2) 2x4x10' SILL AT ENDS (P.T. COPPER NAPHTHENATE)
(2) 2x4x12' SILL AT SIDES (P.T. COPPER NAPHTHENATE)
(2) 2x4x16' END FRAMING
BENCH SUPPORTS NOT INCLUDED
(8) 2x4 FOR PURLINS & DOOR
(2) 4x4x16' P.T. POST FOR FOOTINGS
(2) 1x12x12' & (2) 1x12x10' REDWOOD BOARDS
(1) 4'x8'x3/8" EXTERIOR TYPE CC PLYWOOD SHEET FOR
PLYWOOD GUSSETS. SEE CUTTING DIAGRAM.
* CHECK WITH FIBERGLASS SUPPLIER FOR NECESSARY
RELATED HARDWARE & COVERING INSTRUCTIONS.
NAILS, HINGES & LATCH.

COOPERATIVE EXTENSION WORK IN
AGRICULTURE AND HOME ECONOMICS
AUBURN UNIVERSITY
AUBURN, ALABAMA
AND
UNITEDSTATESDEPARTMENTOFAGRICULTURECOOPERATING

HOME GREENHOUSE

| N.J. | '74 | 6181 | SHEET 2 OF 2 |

| APPROVED: | | | K - 203 |

Plan 2
Plastic-Covered Greenhouse

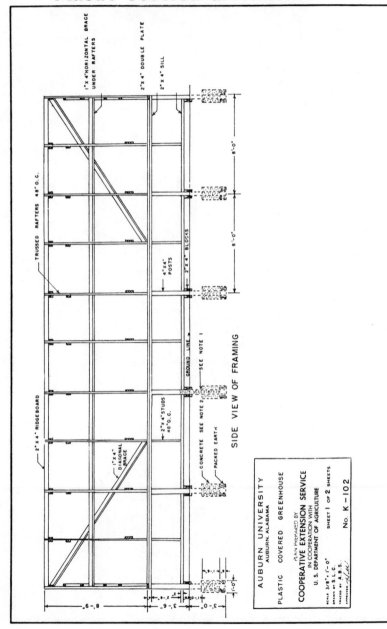

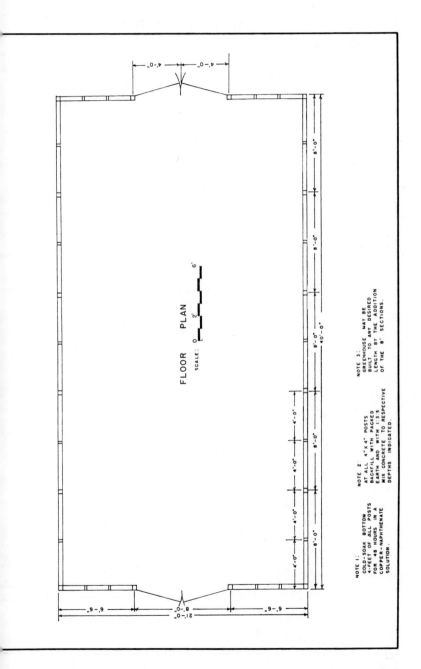

FLOOR PLAN

SCALE: 0   2'   6'

NOTE 1:
COLD-SOAK BOTTOM
4-FEET OF ALL POSTS
FOR 48 HOURS IN A
COPPER-NAPHTHENATE
SOLUTION.

NOTE 2:
AT ALL 4"x 4" POSTS
BACKFILL WITH PACKED
EARTH AND WITH 1:3:5
MIX CONCRETE TO RESPECTIVE
DEPTHS INDICATED.

NOTE 3:
GREENHOUSE MAY BE
BUILT TO ANY DESIRED
LENGTH BY THE ADDITION
OF THE 8' SECTIONS.

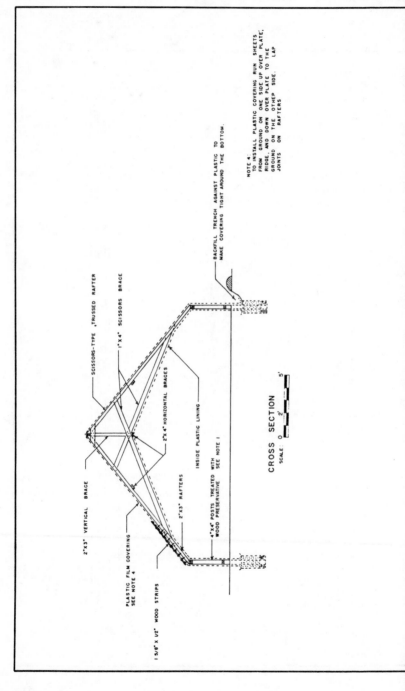

2"x3" VERTICAL BRACE

SCISSORS-TYPE TRUSSED RAFTER

1"x4" SCISSORS BRACE

2"x4" HORIZONTAL BRACES

PLASTIC FILM COVERING SEE NOTE 4

INSIDE PLASTIC LINING

2"x3" RAFTERS

1 5/8" X 1/2" WOOD STRIPS

4"x4" POSTS TREATED WITH WOOD PRESERVATIVE SEE NOTE 1

BACKFILL TRENCH AGAINST PLASTIC TO MAKE COVERING TIGHT AROUND THE BOTTOM.

NOTE 4:
TO INSTALL PLASTIC COVERING RUN SHEETS FROM GROUND ON ONE SIDE UP OVER PLATE, RIDGE, AND DOWN OVER PLATE TO THE GROUND ON THE OTHER SIDE. LAP JOINTS ON RAFTERS

CROSS SECTION

SCALE: 0   2'   5'

250

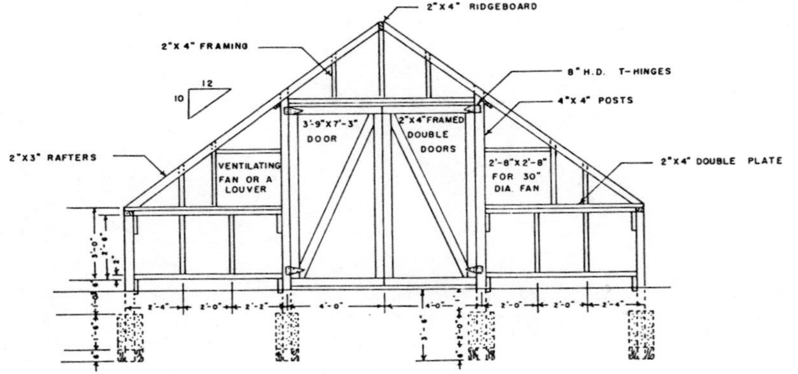

END VIEW OF FRAMING

SCALE: 0   2'   6'

NOTE:
THIS PLAN WAS ADAPTED FOR USE IN
ALABAMA   FROM V.P.I. PLAN NO. N-315 B

Labels on drawing:
2"×4" RIDGEBOARD
8" H.D. T-HINGES
4"×4" POSTS
2"×4" DOUBLE PLATE
2"-6"×2'-8" FOR 30" DIA FAN
2"×4" FRAMED DOUBLE DOORS
3'-9"×7'-3" DOOR
2"×4" FRAMING
VENTILATING FAN OR A LOUVER
2"×3" RAFTERS
12
10

AUBURN UNIVERSITY
AUBURN ALABAMA

PLASTIC COVERED GREENHOUSE

PLAN PREPARED BY
COOPERATIVE EXTENSION SERVICE.
IN COOPERATION WITH
U. S. DEPARTMENT OF AGRICULTURE

SCALE SHOWN
DRAWN BY S L.C.
TRACED BY A.B.S.
APPROVED

SHEET 2 OF 2 SHEETS

No. K—102

Plan 3
Tri-penta Greenhouse

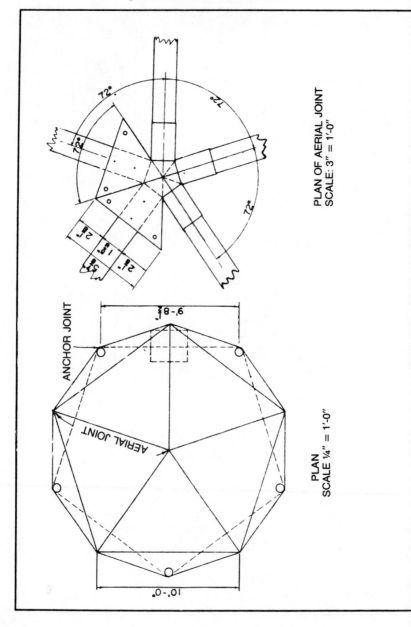

PLAN OF AERIAL JOINT
SCALE: 3" = 1'-0"

PLAN
SCALE 1/4" = 1'-0"

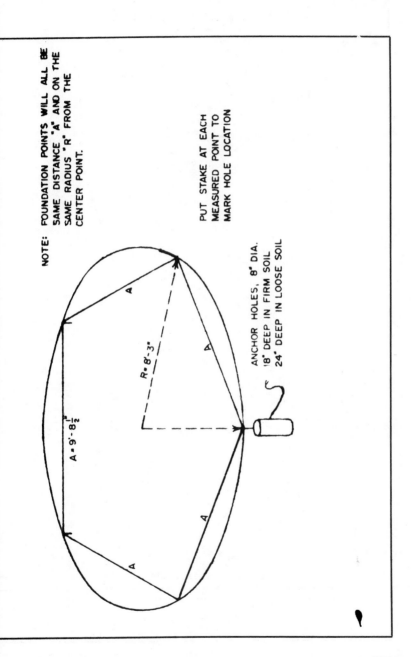

NOTE: FOUNDATION POINTS WILL ALL BE SAME DISTANCE "A" AND ON THE SAME RADIUS "R" FROM THE CENTER POINT.

PUT STAKE AT EACH MEASURED POINT TO MARK HOLE LOCATION

ANCHOR HOLES, 8" DIA.
18" DEEP IN FIRM SOIL
24" DEEP IN LOOSE SOIL

R = 8'-3"

A = 9'-8½"

A

A

A

A

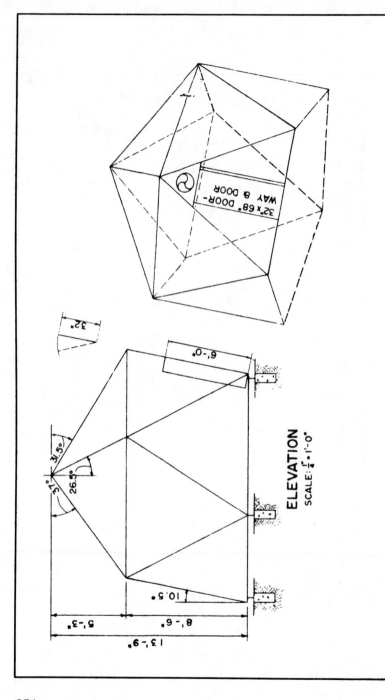

ELEVATION
SCALE: $\frac{3}{4}'' = 1'\text{-}0''$

32" x 68" DOOR-
WAY B DOOR

9'-0"

32°

3.5°
37°
26.5°

10.5°

5'-3"
8'-6"
13'-9"

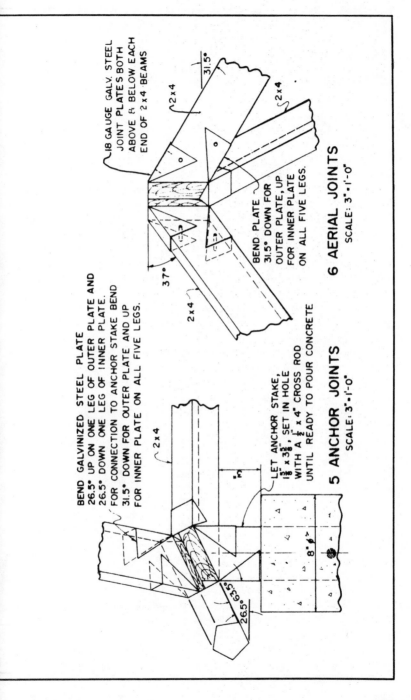

BEND GALVINIZED STEEL PLATE
26.5° UP ON ONE LEG OF OUTER PLATE AND
26.5° DOWN ONE LEG OF INNER PLATE.
31.5° DOWN FOR OUTER PLATE AND UP
FOR INNER PLATE ON ALL FIVE LEGS.

2×4

LET ANCHOR STAKE,
1⅝" × 3⅝", SET IN HOLE
WITH A ½" × 4" CROSS ROD
UNTIL READY TO POUR CONCRETE

26.5°

8"Ø

5 ANCHOR JOINTS
SCALE: 3" = 1'-0"

18 GAUGE GALV. STEEL
JOINT PLATES BOTH
ABOVE & BELOW EACH
END OF 2×4 BEAMS

31.5°

2×4

2×4

37°

2×4

BEND PLATE
31.5° DOWN FOR
OUTER PLATE, UP
FOR INNER PLATE
ON ALL FIVE LEGS.

6 AERIAL JOINTS
SCALE: 3" = 1'-0"

255

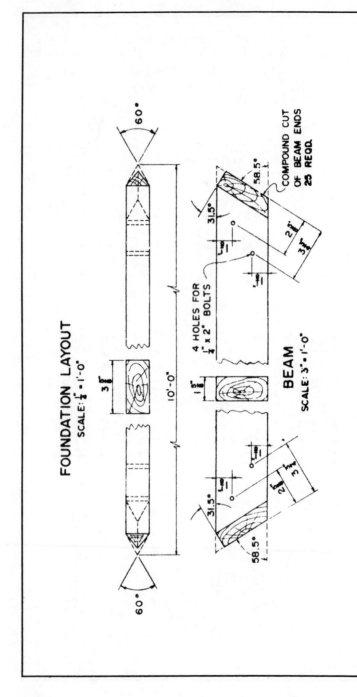

FOUNDATION LAYOUT
SCALE: 1½" = 1'-0"

BEAM
SCALE: 3" = 1'-0"

COMPOUND CUT
OF BEAM ENDS
25 REQD.

4 HOLES FOR
1¼" x 2" BOLTS

256

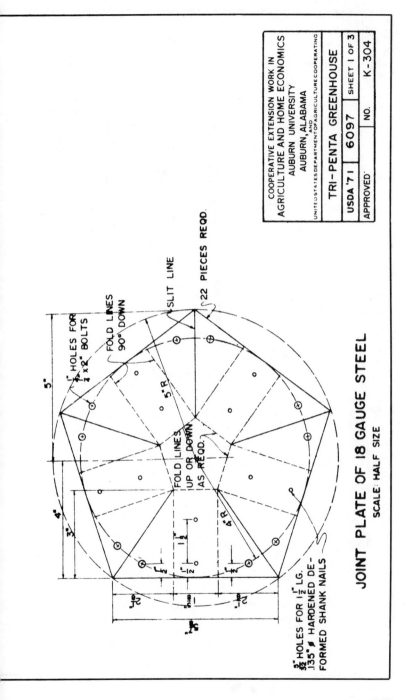

JOINT PLATE OF 18 GAUGE STEEL

SCALE: HALF SIZE

5" HOLES FOR 1½" LG.
.135" ∅ HARDENED DE-
FORMED SHANK NAILS

¼" HOLES FOR
¼ x 2" BOLTS

FOLD LINES
90° DOWN

SLIT LINE

22 PIECES REQD.

5" R

4" R

FOLD LINES
UP OR DOWN
AS REQD.

COOPERATIVE EXTENSION WORK IN
AGRICULTURE AND HOME ECONOMICS
AUBURN UNIVERSITY
AUBURN, ALABAMA
AND
UNITED STATES DEPARTMENT OF AGRICULTURE COOPERATING

TRI-PENTA GREENHOUSE

| USDA '71 | 6097 | SHEET 1 OF 3 |
| APPROVED | NO. | K-304 |

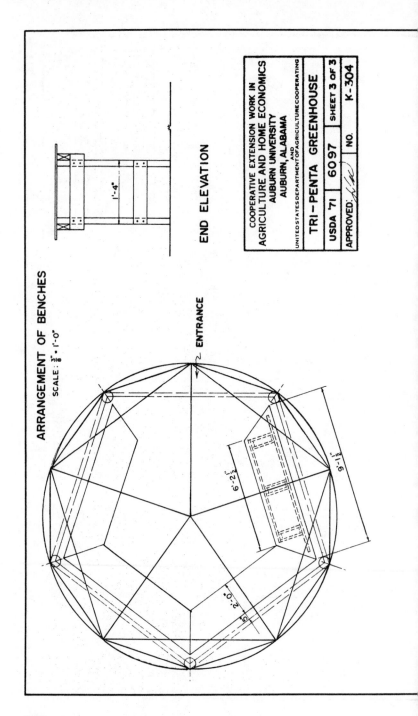

ARRANGEMENT OF BENCHES

SCALE: $\frac{3}{8}$" = 1'-0"

ENTRANCE

END ELEVATION

1'-4"

6'-2 1/2"

9'-1 1/2"

5'-2'-0"

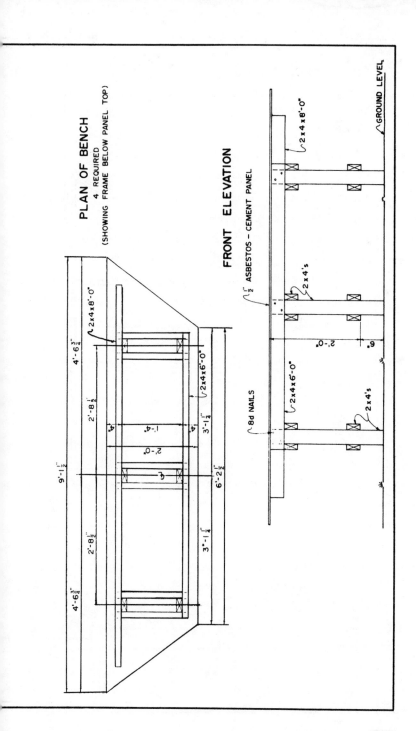

PLAN OF BENCH
4 REQUIRED
(SHOWING FRAME BELOW PANEL TOP)

FRONT ELEVATION

259

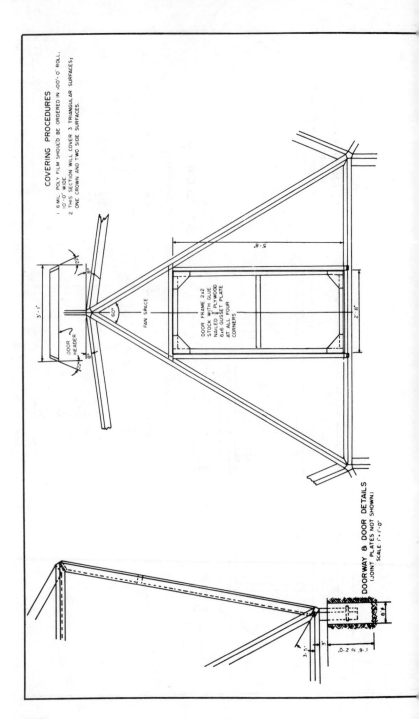

COVERING PROCEDURES

1. 6 MIL. POLY FILM SHOULD BE ORDERED IN 100'-0" ROLL, 10'-0" WIDE
2. THIS SECTION WILL COVER 3 TRIANGULAR SURFACES; ONE CROWN AND TWO SIDE SURFACES.

FAN SPACE

3'-1"

20°

8"

60°

DOOR HEADER

½x2"

8"

5'-8"

DOOR FRAME 2x2 STOCK WITH GLUE NAILED ¾" PLYWOOD 6x6 GUSSET PLATE AT ALL FOUR CORNERS

2'-8"

DOORWAY & DOOR DETAILS
(JOINT PLATES NOT SHOWN)
SCALE 1"=1'-0"

3'-5"

3'

6"

1'-6" to 2'-0"

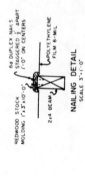

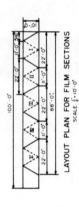

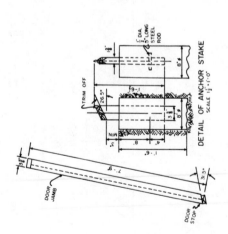

Plan 4
Plastic Greenhouse

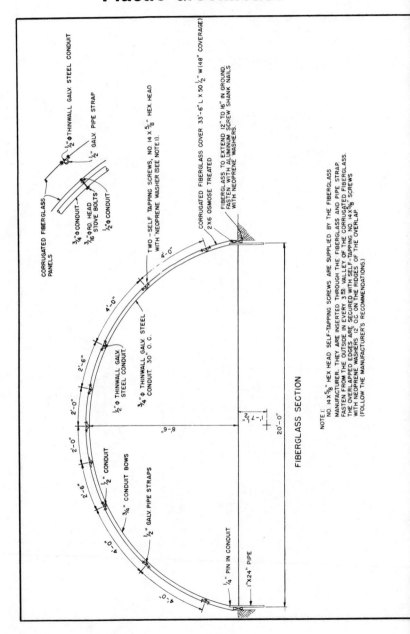

FIBERGLASS SECTION

CORRUGATED FIBERGLASS PANELS

1/2"Φ THINWALL GALV. STEEL CONDUIT

1/2" GALV. PIPE STRAP

3/4" Φ CONDUIT

3/8"Φ RD. HEAD STOVE BOLTS

1/2"Φ CONDUIT

TWO-SELF TAPPING SCREWS, NO. 14 X 5/8" HEX HEAD WITH NEOPRENE WASHER (SEE NOTE 1).

CORRUGATED FIBERGLASS COVER 33'-6" L X 50 1/2" W (48" COVERAGE)

2"X 6" OSMOSE TREATED

FIBERGLASS TO EXTEND 12" TO 16" IN GROUND. FASTEN WITH ALUMINUM SCREW SHANK NAILS WITH NEOPRENE WASHERS.

4'-0"

1/2" Φ THINWALL GALV. STEEL CONDUIT

3/4" Φ THINWALL GALV. STEEL CONDUIT. 30" O.C.

4'-0"

2'-6"

2'-0"

2'-0"

8'-6"

1/2" CONDUIT

3/4" CONDUIT BOWS

1/2" GALV. PIPE STRAPS

2'-6"

3/4" GALV. PIPE STRAPS

1/2" CONDUIT

4'-0"

1/4" PIN IN CONDUIT

1"X 24" PIPE

4'-0"

20'-0"

1'-7 1/2"

NOTE 1:
NO. 14 X 5/8" HEX HEAD SELF-TAPPING SCREWS ARE SUPPLIED BY THE FIBERGLASS MANUFACTURER. THEY ARE INSERTED THROUGH THE FIBERGLASS AND PIPE STRAP FASTEN FROM THE OUTSIDE IN EVERY 3 RD VALLEY OF THE CORRUGATED FIBERGLASS. THE OVERLAPPED EDGES ARE SECURED WITH SELF-TAPPING NO. 14 X 5/8" SCREWS WITH NEOPRENE WASHERS 12" O.C. ON THE RIDGES OF THE OVERLAP (FOLLOW THE MANUFACTURER'S RECOMMENDATIONS.)

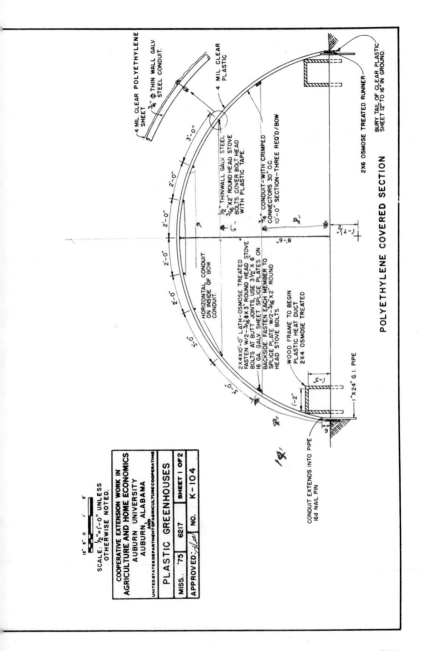

POLYETHYLENE COVERED SECTION

4 MIL CLEAR POLYETHYLENE SHEET

3/4" Ø THIN WALL GALV. STEEL CONDUIT.

4 MIL CLEAR PLASTIC

1/2" THINWALL GALV. STEEL 3/16"x2" ROUND HEAD STOVE BOLTS. COVER BOLT HEAD WITH PLASTIC TAPE.

3/4" CONDUIT-WITH CRIMPED CONNECTORS 30" O.C. 10'-0" SECTION—THREE REQ'D/BOW

2x6 OSMOSE TREATED RUNNER

BURY TAIL OF CLEAR PLASTIC SHEET 12" TO 16" IN GROUND.

HORIZONTAL CONDUIT ON INSIDE OF BOW CONDUIT.

2x4x10'-0' LATH-OSMOSE TREATED FASTEN W/2-3/16 Ø x3" ROUND HEAD STOVE BOLTS AT BUTT JOINTS, USE 3/2" x 6" BOLTS. BACKSIDE FASTEN EACH MEMBER TO SPLICE PLATE W/2-3/16"x2" ROUND HEAD STOVE BOLTS.

16 GA. GALV. SHEET SPLICE PLATES ON BACKSIDE.

WOOD FRAME TO BEGIN PLASTIC HEAT DUCT 2x4 OSMOSE TREATED

1"x24" G.I. PIPE

CONDUIT EXTENDS INTO PIPE 16d NAIL PIN

3'-0"   3'-0"   2'-0"   2'-0"   2'-0"   2'-0"   3'-0"   3'-0"

8'-6"

1'-7½"

1'-2"

1-2½"

6"

11'-2"

SCALE: 1/2"=1'-0" UNLESS OTHERWISE NOTED.

12" 6" 0   1'   2'

COOPERATIVE EXTENSION WORK IN
AGRICULTURE AND HOME ECONOMICS
AUBURN UNIVERSITY
AUBURN, ALABAMA
UNITED STATES DEPARTMENT OF AGRICULTURE COOPERATING

PLASTIC GREENHOUSES

| MISS. | '75 | 6217 | SHEET 1 OF 2 |
| APPROVED: | | NO. | K-104 |

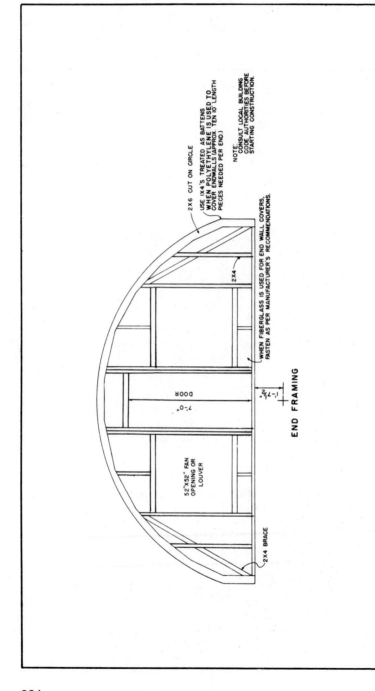

END FRAMING

2X6 CUT ON CIRCLE

USE 1X4'S TREATED AS BATTENS
WHEN POLYETHYLENE IS USED TO
COVER ENDWALLS (APPROX. TEN 10' LENGTH
PIECES NEEDED PER END.)

NOTE:
CONSULT LOCAL BUILDING
CODE AUTHORITIES BEFORE
STARTING CONSTRUCTION.

2X4

WHEN FIBERGLASS IS USED FOR END WALL COVERS,
FASTEN AS PER MANUFACTURER'S RECOMMENDATIONS.

DOOR

7'-0"

1'-7 1/2"

52"X52" FAN
OPENING OR
LOUVER

2X4 BRACE

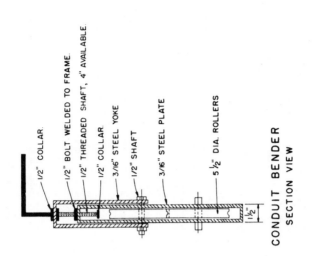

CONDUIT BENDER
SECTION VIEW

1/2" COLLAR.
1/2" BOLT WELDED TO FRAME.
1/2" THREADED SHAFT, 4" AVAILABLE.
1/2" COLLAR.
3/16" STEEL YOKE
1/2" SHAFT
3/16" STEEL PLATE
5 1/2" DIA. ROLLERS
1 1/2"

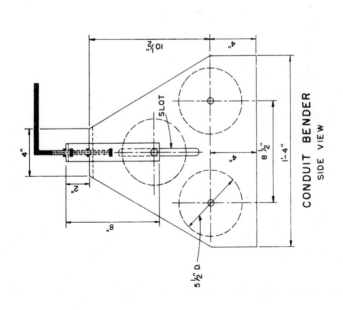

CONDUIT BENDER
SIDE VIEW

10 1/2"
4"
SLOT
4"
8 1/2"
1'-4"
2"
8"
5 1/2" D.
4"

265

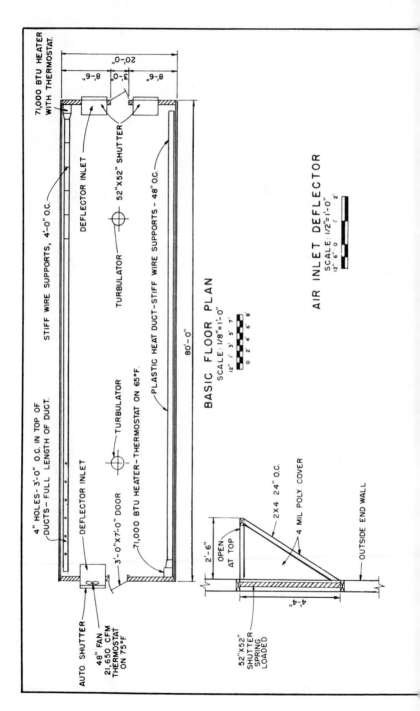

BASIC FLOOR PLAN
SCALE: 1/8" = 1'-0"

AIR INLET DEFLECTOR
SCALE: 1/2" = 1'-0"

71,000 BTU HEATER WITH THERMOSTAT.

20'-0"

8'-6"   3'-0"   8'-6"

STIFF WIRE SUPPORTS, 4'-0" O.C.

DEFLECTOR INLET

52"x52" SHUTTER

TURBULATOR

80'-0"

PLASTIC HEAT DUCT-STIFF WIRE SUPPORTS - 48" O.C.

4" HOLES- 3'-0" O.C. IN TOP OF DUCTS- FULL LENGTH OF DUCT.

DEFLECTOR INLET

TURBULATOR

3'-0"x7'-0" DOOR

71,000 BTU HEATER-THERMOSTAT ON 65°F.

AUTO SHUTTER

48" FAN 21,650 CFM THERMOSTAT ON 75°F

OPEN AT TOP

2'-6"

2 x 4 24" O.C.

4 MIL POLY COVER

4'-4"

52"x52" SHUTTER SPRING LOADED

OUTSIDE END WALL

266

BILL OF MATERIALS

NO. REQ'D	DESCRIPTION
GRP I	
16	FRAMING - 2 ENDS AND SIDES 2X6X10' OSMOSE TRTD. NO. 2 PINE
6	2X6X8' " " " " "
18	2X4X12' " " " " "
8	2X4X8' " " " " "
5 LBS.	6d COMMON NAILS
12 LBS.	10d " "
2	3'X7' SCREEN DOORS WITH HINGES AND LATCHES
GRP II	
	FIBERGLASS-TYPE FRAMING
72	10' LENGTHS 1/2" DIA. STEEL CONDUIT
99	10' LENGTHS 3/4" DIA.
63	1/2" CRIMPED TYPE COUPLING
66	3/4" " " "
300	3/16"X2" STEEL STOVE BOLTS-ROUND HEAD
132	1" BLACK PIPE (USED PIPE SATISFACTORY)
GRP III	
	POLYETHYLENE-TYPE FRAMING SAME AS FIBERGLASS WITH THE FOLLOWING ADDITIONAL ITEMS AND ONE ITEM CHANGED.
16	2X4X10' OSMOSE TRTD. NO. 2 PINE (ADDITIONAL)
56	10' LENGTHS 1/2" DIA. STEEL CONDUIT (CHANGED)
20	1X4X10' OSMOSE TRTD. NO. 2 PINE (BATTEN)
GRP IV	
	FIBERGLASS PANELS AND SUPPLIES
20	PANELS 33 1/2"-6"X50 1/2" WIDTH (48" COVERAGE)
4	PANELS 8'-9"
7	PANELS 6'-0"
4	PANELS 9'-4"
1200	1/2" PIPE STRAPS-EVERY 3RD. VALLEY ON ALL HORIZONTAL MEMBERS
2400	1/2" PIPE STRAP FASTENERS (NO. 14X5/8" HEX.HEAD SELF-TAPPING SCREWS)
300	ALUMINUM SCREW NAILS
700	SIDELAP FASTENERS (NO. 14X5/8" HEX.HEAD SELF-TAPPING SCREWS)

NO. REQ'D	DESCRIPTION
25	PLASTIC CORRUGATED CLOSURE STRIPS
24	VERTICAL " "
GRP V	
	POLYETHYLENE FOR POLY-TYPE
1	ROLL 100'X32', 4 MIL. CLEAR
GRP VI	
	EQUIPMENT AND SUPPLIES-COMMON TO BOTH
1	48" SINGLE-SPEED FAN W/IHP MOTOR AND SHUTTER
2	52"X52" SPRING LOAD SHUTTERS
2	TURBULATORS-1/6 HP MOTOR
2	21 KW-71,000 BTU INPUT HEATERS
160 FT.	6" WIDTH 2 MIL. POLY. FOR HEAT DUCTS

POLYETHYLENE —— USE GRPS. I, II, III, V, & VI

FIBERGLASS —— USE GRPS. I, II, IV, V, & VI

SCALE: 3"=1'-0" UNLESS OTHERWISE NOTED.

COOPERATIVE EXTENSION WORK IN
AGRICULTURE AND HOME ECONOMICS
AUBURN UNIVERSITY
AUBURN, ALABAMA
UNITED STATES DEPARTMENT OF AGRICULTURE COOPERATING

PLASTIC GREENHOUSES

MISS. '75	6217	SHEET 2 OF 2
APPROVED: _[signature]_		NO. K-104

Plan 5
Portable Plastic Greenhouse

Plan No. K-201
Sheet 1 of 1

BILL OF MATERIALS
FARM BUILDING PLAN NO. K-201
PORTABLE PLASTIC GREENHOUSE

I. LUMBER

QUANTITY	SIZE OR DESCRIPTION	WHERE USED
2 pcs - 20 bf	1" x 10" x 12'-0"	Ridge Board
4 pcs - 26.4 bf	1" x 8" x 10'-0"	Boards on ends
4 pcs - 32 bf	1" x 8" x 12'-0"	Side boards
7 pcs - 14 bf	2" x 2" x 6'-0"	Door Frame
2 pcs - 2 bf	1" x 2" x 6'-0"	Door stops
6 pcs - 24 bf	2" x 4" x 6'-0"	Door bucks
2 pcs - 13.3 bf	2" x 4" x 10'-0" (treated)	Stakes
3 sheets	1/4" x 4' x 8' Plywood (Ext.)	Bands & Gussets
1 pc - 1.33bf	1" x 4" x 4'-0"	Cleat

II. MISCELLANEOUS ITEMS AND HARDWARE

QUANTITY	SIZE OR DESCRIPTION	WHERE USED
4 pcs	2 1/2" x 2 1/2" Loose Joint Butt Hinge	Vent door
6 pcs	3" x 3" Loose Pin Butt Hinge	Doors
370	1 3/4" No. 10 Wood Screws (countersunk, galvanized)	Throughout
300 sq. feet	Plastic cover	Top & Ends

HW/bl

1-76

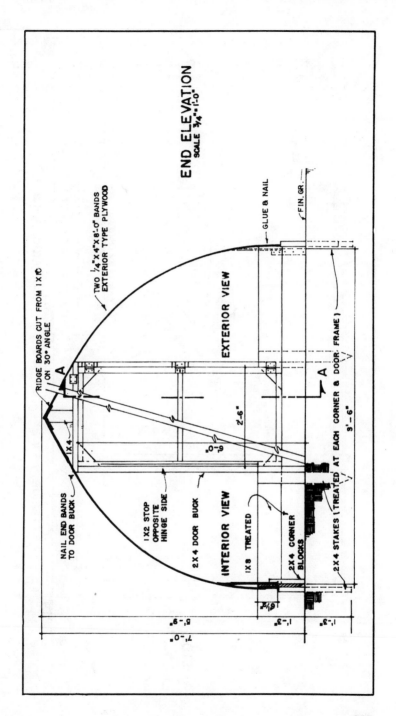

END ELEVATION
SCALE 3/4" = 1'-0"

TWO 1/4" X 4" X 8'-0" BANDS
EXTERIOR TYPE PLYWOOD

RIDGE BOARDS CUT FROM 1 X 10
ON 30° ANGLE

GLUE & NAIL

FIN. GR.

EXTERIOR VIEW

1 X 4

2'-6"

9'-0"

A

A

NAIL END BANDS
TO DOOR BUCK

1 X 2 STOP
OPPOSITE
HINGE SIDE

3'-6"

2 X 4 DOOR BUCK

INTERIOR VIEW

1 X 8

2 X 4 STAKES (TREATED AT EACH CORNER & DOOR FRAME)

1 X 8 TREATED

2 X 4 CORNER
BLOCKS

9 1/2"

5'-9"

1'-3"

1'-3"

7'-0"

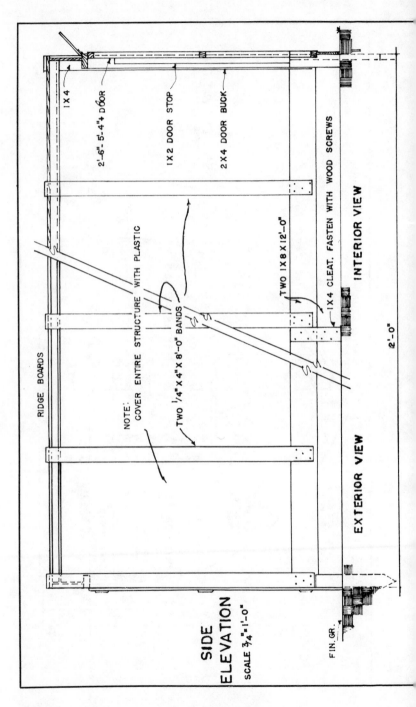

RIDGE BOARDS

1 X 4

2'-6"-5'-4"+ DOOR

1 X 2 DOOR STOP

2 X 4 DOOR BUCK

NOTE:
COVER ENTIRE STRUCTURE WITH PLASTIC

Two 1/4" X 4" X 8'-0" BANDS

TWO 1 X 8 X 12'-0"

1 X 4 CLEAT. FASTEN WITH WOOD SCREWS

INTERIOR VIEW

EXTERIOR VIEW

12'-0"

FIN. GR.

**SIDE
ELEVATION**
SCALE 3/4" = 1'-0"

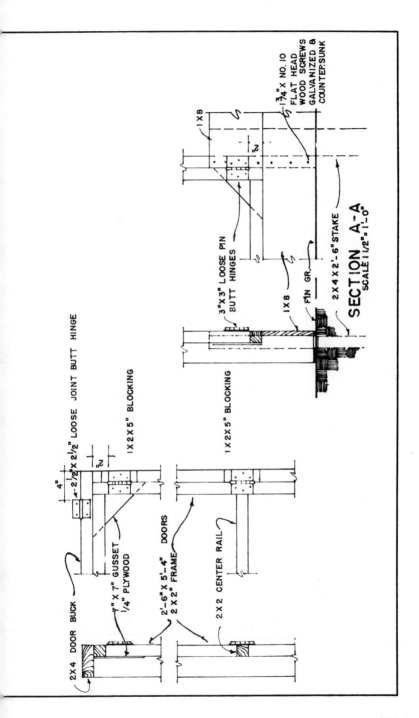

2X4 DOOR BUCK

2½"X 2½" LOOSE JOINT BUTT HINGE

4"

1X2X5" BLOCKING

7"X 7" GUSSET ¼" PLYWOOD

2'-6"X 5'-4" DOORS 2 X 2" FRAME

1X2X5" BLOCKING

2 X 2 CENTER RAIL

1X8

3"X3" LOOSE PIN BUTT HINGES

1X8

FIN. GR.

1¾"X NO. 10 FLAT HEAD WOOD SCREWS GALVANIZED & COUNTERSUNK

2X4 X 2'-6" STAKE

SECTION A-A
SCALE 1 ½"=1'-0"

271

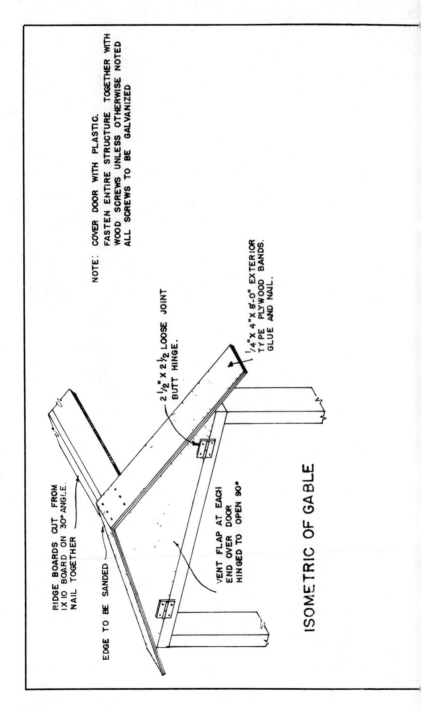

NOTE: COVER DOOR WITH PLASTIC.
FASTEN ENTIRE STRUCTURE TOGETHER WITH
WOOD SCREWS UNLESS OTHERWISE NOTED
ALL SCREWS TO BE GALVANIZED

2 1/2" x 2 1/2 LOOSE JOINT
BUTT HINGE.

1/4"x 4"x 8'-0" EXTERIOR
TYPE PLYWOOD BANDS.
GLUE AND NAIL.

RIDGE BOARDS CUT FROM
IX IO BOARD ON 30° ANGLE.
NAIL TOGETHER

EDGE TO BE SANDED

VENT FLAP AT EACH
END OVER DOOR
HINGED TO OPEN 90°

ISOMETRIC OF GABLE

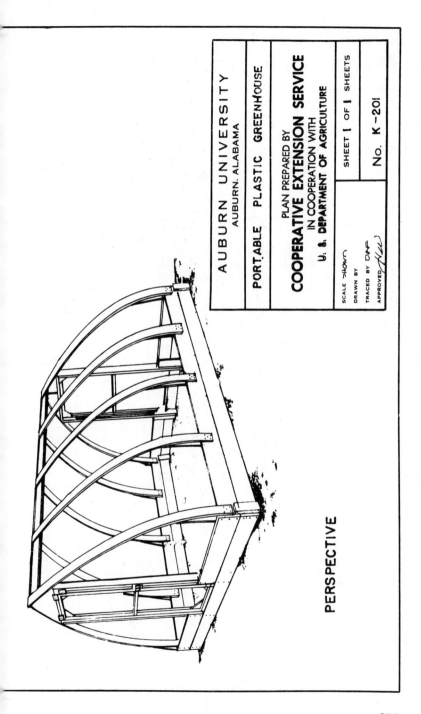

PERSPECTIVE

AUBURN UNIVERSITY
AUBURN, ALABAMA

PORTABLE PLASTIC GREENHOUSE

PLAN PREPARED BY
COOPERATIVE EXTENSION SERVICE
IN COOPERATION WITH
U. S. DEPARTMENT OF AGRICULTURE

SHEET 1 OF 1 SHEETS

No. K-201

SCALE SHOWN
DRAWN BY
TRACED BY DAF
APPROVED

273

Plan 6
Mini-hotbed and Propagating Frame

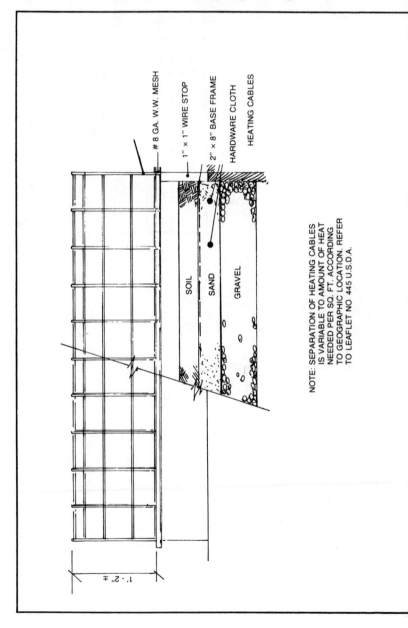

8 GA. W.W. MESH

1" × 1" WIRE STOP

2" × 8" BASE FRAME

HARDWARE CLOTH

HEATING CABLES

SOIL

SAND

GRAVEL

1' - 2" ±

NOTE: SEPARATION OF HEATING CABLES
IS VARIABLE TO AMOUNT OF HEAT
NEEDED PER SQ. FT. ACCORDING
TO GEOGRAPHIC LOCATION. REFER
TO LEAFLET NO 445 U.S.D.A.

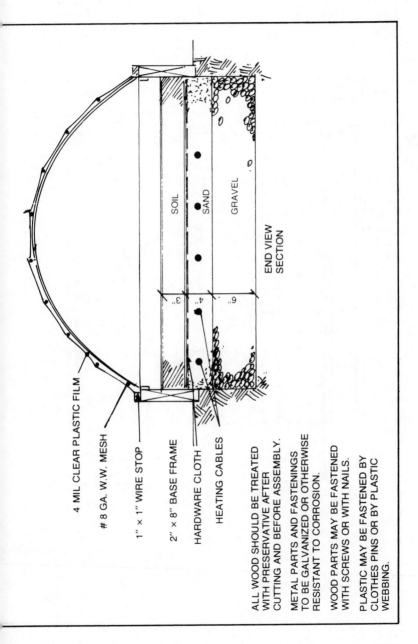

4 MIL CLEAR PLASTIC FILM

8 GA. W.W. MESH

1" × 1" WIRE STOP

2" × 8" BASE FRAME

HARDWARE CLOTH

HEATING CABLES

SOIL

SAND

GRAVEL

3"

4"

6"

END VIEW
SECTION

ALL WOOD SHOULD BE TREATED
WITH PRESERVATIVE AFTER
CUTTING AND BEFORE ASSEMBLY.

METAL PARTS AND FASTENINGS
TO BE GALVANIZED OR OTHERWISE
RESISTANT TO CORROSION.

WOOD PARTS MAY BE FASTENED
WITH SCREWS OR WITH NAILS.

PLASTIC MAY BE FASTENED BY
CLOTHES PINS OR BY PLASTIC
WEBBING.

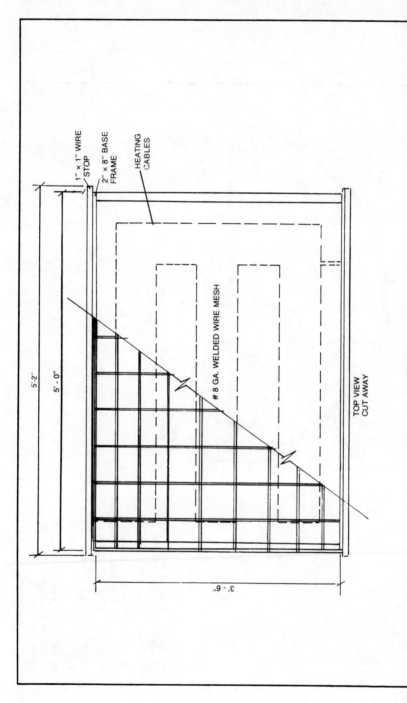

1" × 1" WIRE STOP

2" × 8" BASE FRAME

HEATING CABLES

8 GA. WELDED WIRE MESH

TOP VIEW
CUT AWAY

5'-2"

5'-0"

3'-6"

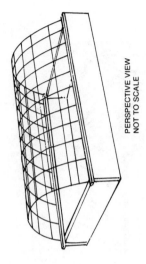

PERSPECTIVE VIEW
NOT TO SCALE

MATERIAL LIST
2 PCS. 2" × 8" 5' LONG FOR SIDES

2 PCS. 2" × – 5' LONG FOR SIDES
2 PCS. 2" × 8" – 3' – 6" LONG FOR ENDS
2 PCS. 1" × 1" WIRE STOP – 1" WIRE STOP – 5' – 2" LONG FOR SIDES
1 PC. NO. 8 GAUGE 6" × 6" WELDED WIRE, 5' LONG
        4' – 6" WIDE FOR TOP OF WOOD FRAME TO
        SUPPORT PLASTIC FILM.
3 PCS. PLASTIC WEBBING 2" WIDE – 5' LONG
2 PCS. PLASTIC FILM, 4 MIL, CLEAR 3' WIDE
        7' LONG.
1   360-WATT SOIL HEATING CABLE, THERMO-
        STATICALLY CONTROLLED TO SHUT OFF
        AT 70°F.
1 PC.   WHITE PLASTIC FILM, 4 MIL, 5' × 8' FOR
        COVERING FRAME, DURING WINTER.
2 PCS. CHEESECLOTH, 3' × 7'
4 IN.   SAND – 2" ABOVE, 2" BELOW HEATING CABLE
1 PC.   1/2" HARDWARE CLOTH, 5' × 3 1/2'

DESIGNED IN COOPERATION WITH:
CROPS RESEARCH DIVISION

SCALE 1½":1'-0" UNLESS
OTHERWISE NOTED

COOPERATIVE EXTENSION WORK IN
AGRICULTURE AND HOME ECONOMICS
AUBURN UNIVERSITY
AUBURN, ALABAMA
AND
UNITED STATES DEPARTMENT OF AGRICULTURE COOPERATING

MINI-HOTBED AND PROPAGATING
FRAME

| U.S.D.A. '69 | 6080 | SHEET 1 OF 1 |
| APPROVED: | | NO. K-303 |

Plan 7
Plastic Greenhouse

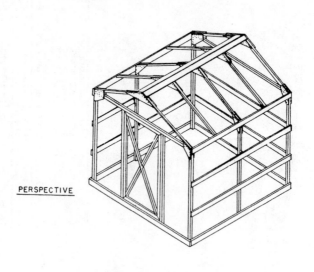

PERSPECTIVE

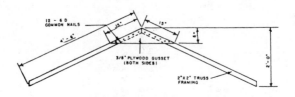

12 - 6 D
COMMON NAILS

4' - 6"

3/8" PLYWOOD GUSSET
(BOTH SIDES)

2"X2" TRUSS
FRAMING

2'-0"

TRUSS - DETAIL "A" (2 REQUIRED)

SCALE: 12" 6" 0   1'   2'

AUBURN UNIVERSITY
AUBURN, ALABAMA

PLASTIC GREENHOUSE

PLAN PREPARED BY
COOPERATIVE EXTENSION SERVICE
IN COOPERATION WITH
U. S. DEPARTMENT OF AGRICULTURE

SCALE SHOWN
DRAWN BY D. W.
TRACED BY A. B. S.
APPROVED

SHEET 1 OF 2 SHEETS

No. K-202

NOTE:
GREENHOUSE MAY BE CONSTRUCTED IN
UNITS OF 4'-0" LENGTH OR 8'-0" LENGTH

278

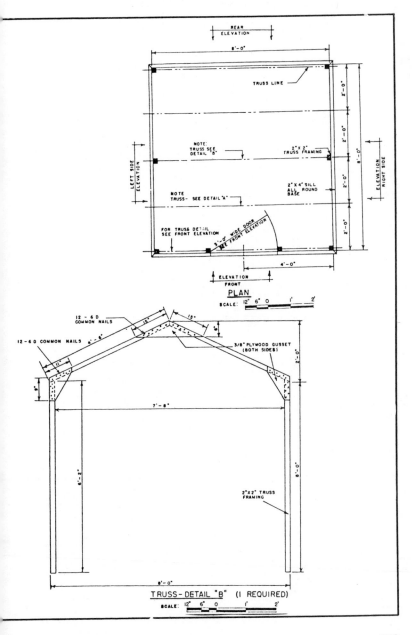

REAR
ELEVATION

8'-0"

TRUSS LINE

2'-0"

LEFT SIDE
ELEVATION

NOTE:
TRUSS SEE
DETAIL "B"

2"X 2"
TRUSS FRAMING

2'-0"

ELEVATION RIGHT SIDE

8'-0"

NOTE
TRUSS- SEE DETAIL "A"

2"X 4" SILL
ALL ROUND
BASE

2'-0"

FOR TRUSS DETAIL
SEE FRONT ELEVATION

3'-0" WIDE DOOR
SEE FRONT ELEVATION

2'-0"

ELEVATION
FRONT

4'-0"

PLAN
SCALE: 12" 6" 0   1'   2'

12 - 6 D
COMMON NAILS

15°

15°

6°

12 - 6 D COMMON NAILS

4'-8"

11

3/8" PLYWOOD GUSSET
(BOTH SIDES)

2'-0"

6"

7'-8"

6'-2"

8'-0"

2"X 2" TRUSS
FRAMING

8'-0"

TRUSS-DETAIL "B" (I REQUIRED)
SCALE: 12" 6" 0   1'   2'

279

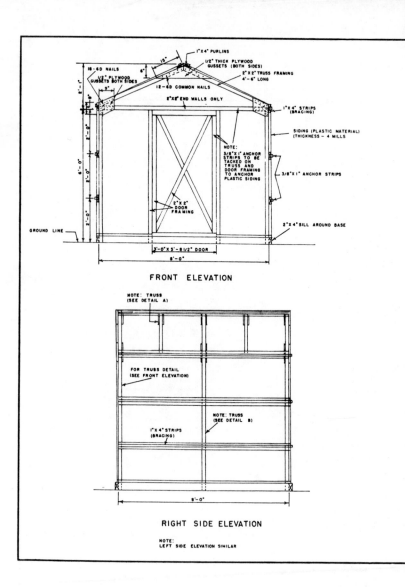

FRONT ELEVATION

RIGHT SIDE ELEVATION

NOTE:
LEFT SIDE ELEVATION SIMILAR

280

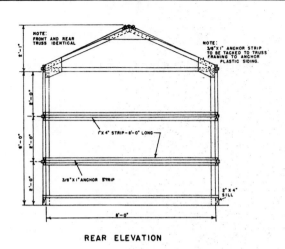

NOTE:
FRONT AND REAR
TRUSS IDENTICAL

NOTE:
3/8"X1" ANCHOR STRIP
TO BE TACKED TO TRUSS
FRAMING TO ANCHOR
PLASTIC SIDING.

1"X 4" STRIP-8'-0" LONG

3/8"X1"ANCHOR STRIP

2" X 4"
SILL

8'-0"

REAR ELEVATION

12" 6" 0   1'   2'

AUBURN UNIVERSITY	
AUBURN. ALABAMA	
PLASTIC GREENHOUSE	
PLAN PREPARED BY	
COOPERATIVE EXTENSION SERVICE	
IN COOPERATION WITH	
U. S. DEPARTMENT OF AGRICULTURE	
SCALE 3/4" = 1'-0"	SHEET 2 OF 2 SHEETS
DRAWN BY D.W.	
TRACED BY A.B.S.	No. K-202
APPROVED	

Plan 8
Plastic Greenhouse:
Rigid-frame Construction

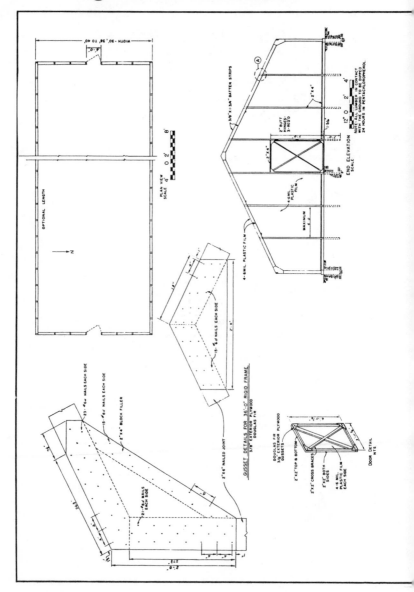

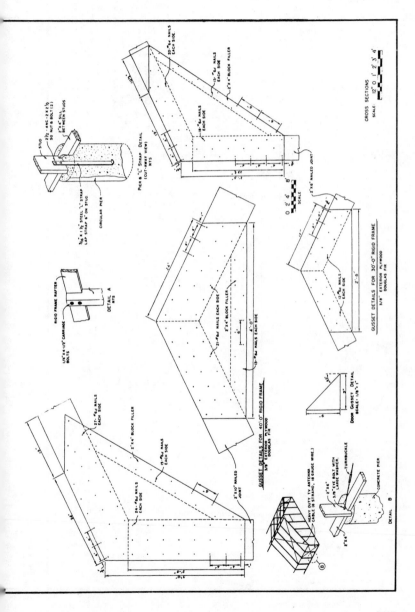

STUD

2½"-4NC-2 x 2½"
SQ NUT & BOLT(2)

2"x 4" SILL
BETWEEN STUDS

³⁄₁₆" x 1½ STEEL "L" STRAP
LAP STRAP 4" ON STUD

CIRCULAR PIER

Pier & "L" Strap Detail
(CUT-AWAY VIEW)
NTS

RIGID FRAME RAFTER

DETAIL A
NTS

¼"x4-½" CARRIAGE
BOLTS

20-°6d NAILS
EACH SIDE

19-°6d NAILS
2"x 4" BLOCK FILLER

19-°6d NAILS
EACH SIDE

2"x4" NAILED JOINT

CROSS SECTIONS
SCALE: 12" 0 1' 2' 3' 4'

0 2' 4'   8'
SCALE

12-°6d NAILS
EACH SIDE

GUSSET DETAILS FOR 30'-0" RIGID FRAME
³⁄₈" EXTERIOR PLYWOOD
DOUGLAS FIR

21-°6d NAILS EACH SIDE

2"x 4" BLOCK FILLER

19-°6d NAILS EACH SIDE

Door Gusset Detail
SCALE: 1/8"=1'

27-°6d NAILS
EACH SIDE

2"x4" BLOCK FILLER

19-°6d NAILS
EACH SIDE

24-°6d NAILS
EACH SIDE

2"x10" NAILED
JOINT

GUSSET DETAILS FOR 40'-0" RIGID FRAME
³⁄₈" EXTERIOR PLYWOOD
DOUGLAS FIR

HEAVY DUTY TV ANTENNA
GUIDE (6 STRAND, 18 GAUGE WIRE.)

³⁄₈" "EYE BOLT WITH
LARGE WASHER.

TURNBUCKLE

CONCRETE PIER

2"x4"

DETAIL B

283

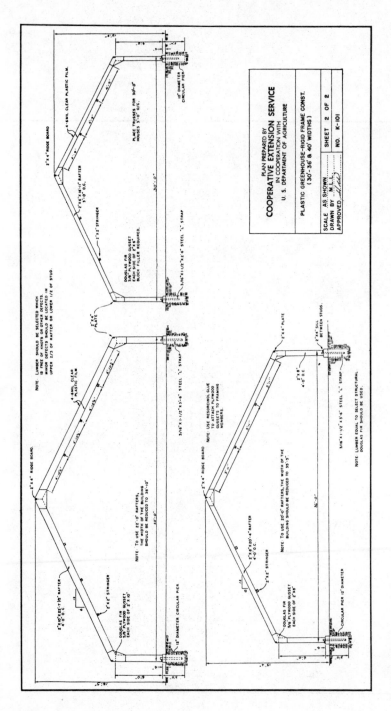

NOTE: LUMBER SHOULD BE SELECTED WHICH IS FREE OF KNOTS OR OTHER DEFECTS. MINOR DEFECTS SHOULD BE LOCATED IN UPPER 2/3 OF RAFTER OR LOWER 1/2 OF STUD.

2"x 4" RIDGE BOARD

4-6MIL. CLEAR PLASTIC FILM.

2"x16"x14'-11" RAFTER 3'-0" O.C.

2"x2" STRINGER

DOUGLAS FIR 3/8" PLYWOOD GUSSET EACH SIDE OF 2"x 6" BLOCK FILLER REQUIRED.

PLACE TRUSSES FOR 30'-0" HOUSES 3'-0" O.C.

10" DIAMETER CIRCULAR PIER

3/16"x 1-1/2"x2'-6" STEEL "L" STRAP

2"x 4" PLATE

30'-0"

2"x 4" RIDGE BOARD

4-6MIL. CLEAR PLASTIC FILM

NOTE: USE REGONCIN/OL GLUE TO ATTACH PLYWOOD GUSSETS TO FRAMING MEMBERS.

2"x16"x22'-7 7/8" RAFTER 4'-0" O.C.

2"x2" STRINGER

DOUGLAS FIR 3/8" PLYWOOD GUSSET EACH SIDE OF 2"x6"

10" DIAMETER CIRCULAR PIER

3/16"x1-1/2"x3'-6" STEEL "L" STRAP

NOTE: TO USE 22'-0" RAFTERS, THE WIDTH OF THE BUILDING SHOULD BE REDUCED TO 38'-10"

40'-0"

2"x 4" RIDGE BOARD

NOTE: TO USE 20'-0" RAFTERS, THE WIDTH OF THE BUILDING SHOULD BE REDUCED TO 35'-5"

2"x16"x20'-4" RAFTER 4'-0" O.C.

2"x2" STRINGER

DOUGLAS FIR 3/8" PLYWOOD GUSSET EACH SIDE OF 2"x6"

2"x4" PLATE

2"x4" SILL BETWEEN STUDS.

2"x6" 4'-0" O.C.

3/16"x1-1/2"x3'-6" STEEL "L" STRAP

CIRCULAR PIER 12" DIAMETER

36'-0"

NOTE: LUMBER EQUAL TO SELECT STRUCTURAL DOUGLAS FIR SHOULD BE USED.

PLAN PREPARED BY
COOPERATIVE EXTENSION SERVICE
IN COOPERATION WITH
U. S. DEPARTMENT OF AGRICULTURE

PLASTIC GREENHOUSE-RIGID FRAME CONST.
(30'-36' & 40' WIDTHS)

SCALE: AS SHOWN
DRAWN BY: M.L.L.
APPROVED:

SHEET 2 OF 2
NO. K-101

Suppliers

The following suppliers offer greenhouse kits and equipment. In addition, check your local telephone book under "Greenhouses" and "Garden Equipment."

Aluminum Greenhouses, Inc.
14615 Lorain Ave.
Cleveland, OH 44111

American Leisure Industries Inc.
Box 63
Deep River, CT 06417

BACO Leisure Products Inc.
19 East 47th St.
New York, NY 10017

W. Atlee Burpee Co.
5556 Burpee Building
Warminster, PA 18974

Cap-N-Nail Mfg. Co.
625 Poinsettia St.
Santa Ana, CA 92701

Casaplanta
9489 Dayton Way
Beverly Hills, CA 90210

Columbia Gorge Rehabilitation Center
Route 1, Box 705
Hook River, OR 97031

Continental Greenhouse Distributors
3471 Peachtree Road, NE
Atlanta, GA 30326

Creative Living
Dept. 102-AZ
2627 Hillegass
Berkeley, CA 94704

Dome East
325 Duffy Ave.
Hicksville, NY 11801

Fremont Greenhouses
P.O. Box 2397
Dublin, CA 94566

Gardendome Greenhouses
P.O. Box 1239
Corvallis, OR 97330

Geodesic Domes
RR1
Bloomington, IL 61701

Gothic Arch Greenhouses
P.O. Box 1564
Mobile, AL 36601

The Greenery
P.O. Box 489
Soquel, CA 95073

Peter Reimuller
The Greenhouseman
980 Seventeenth Ave.
Santa Cruz, CA 95063

Janco Greenhouses
Box 348
Beltsville, MD 20705

Ickes-Braun Greenhouse Manufacturing Co.
Box 147
Deerfield, IL 60015

Lord & Burnham
2 Main St.
Irvington, NY 10533

McGregor Greenhouses
Box 36
Santa Cruz, CA 95063

Monterey Greenhouses
P.O. Box 806
Freedom, CA 95019

National Greenhouse Co.
Box 100
Pana, IL 62557

J. A. Nearing Co., Inc.
10788 Tucker St.
Beltsville, MD 20705

Pacific Coast Greenhouse Mfg. Co.
430 Hurlingame Ave.
Redwood City, CA 94063

Redfern Greenhouses
57 Mount Hermon Rd.
Scotts Valley, CA 95066

Redwood Domes
P.O. Box 666
Aptos, CA 95003

Santa Barbara Greenhouses
2675½ Daily Drive
Camarillo, CA 93010

Sturdi-Built Manufacturing Co.
11304 SW Boones Ferry Rd.
Portland, OR 97219

Sun World Gardens Inc.
10250 E. McDowell
Scottsdale, AZ 85251

Terra-Phernalia
Earth Oriented Imports
P.O. Box 504
Millbrae, CA 94030

Texas Greenhouse Co. Inc.
2723 St. Louis Ave.
Ft. Worth, TX 76110

Turner Greenhouses
P.O. Box 1260
Goldsboro, NC 27530

Vis Vita Solarium
P.O. Box 9020
Seattle, WA 98109

H. Wolff Manufacturing Co.
955 Celia Way
Palo Alto, CA 94303

Index

Index

Edited By Steven Bolt